Black migration to South Africa

BLACK MIGRA- TION to SOUTH AFRICA

A SELECTION OF POLICY-ORIENTED RESEARCH

EDITED BY W. R. BÖHNING

Published with the financial support
of the United Nations Fund
for Population Activities

International Labour Office   Geneva

ISBN 92-2-102759-7 (limp cover)
ISBN 92-2-102758-9 (hard cover)

First published 1981

Photocomposed in India
Printed in Switzerland

CONTENTS

"It is from numberless diverse acts of courage and belief that human history is shaped. Each time a man strikes out against injustice, he sends forth a ripple of hope, and crossing each other from a million different centres of energy and daring, those ripples build a current than can sweep down the mightiest walls of oppression and resistance."

Robert Kennedy
South Africa, 1966

INTRODUCTION

W. R. Böhning

1

Late in 1976 the International Labour Office initiated a range of research activities on the migration of Black workers to South Africa. A generous grant from the United Nations Fund for Population Activities (UNFPA) supported the work to a considerable extent. Research teams were formed at the National University of Lesotho, the University College of Swaziland and the Institute of Political Studies at the University of Copenhagen, Denmark; Duncan Clarke and Charles Stahl joined me for a while in Geneva.

Lesotho and Swaziland were thus directly covered by on-the-spot researchers. Botswana was at that time preparing its National Migration Survey with greater financial resources than the ILO and the UNFPA could muster, but it was nevertheless covered in one particular respect by the Copenhagen team (Woods, 1978).[1] Pre-independence Zimbabwe was examined by Clarke (1978). Post-independence Mozambique began an investigation of its own at the Centro de Estudos Africanos of the Universidade Eduardo Mondlane, Maputo (as yet unpublished). Malawi, the only other major labour supplier of the region, had voluntarily stopped the flow of its labour in 1974 and would have been an attractive country to study because of its short-run and long-run adjustment problems; but recruitment started again in 1977, and in any case it proved impossible to carry out any significant research into these questions in the country.

The improvement of what was at that time an insufficient knowledge base was naturally one of our objectives. However, policy orientation determined the work from the start—not in that vague way in which researchers often wrap up predictable findings in some half-baked moral principles of questionable relevance, but directly, comprehensively and forcefully, as the selection in this book will demonstrate.

Two key policy objectives dominated the research. First, *how can one improve the working and living conditions of both the migrants and their dependants as long as migration continues?* This question, as applied to South Africa, was by no means uncontroversial, since in some people's minds it conjured up a vision of unintended accommodation to the apartheid regime. It goes without saying that this was not our aim. Change can arise either way: through deprivation or through unfulfilled rising expectations. It usually comes by the latter way. Only the anarchic fringe of revolutionary philosophy did not share our concern with this first policy objective.

Second, *what ways and means are there for reducing the migrant-sending countries' dependence on employment opportunities in South Africa under the migrant labour system as it has been constituted by the ruling White minority?* In this context, buck-passing was not indulged in. The question was not whether domestic employment creation, international trade (between the countries concerned or with others) or some external miracle would be the answer. The question was how the migration link could be used in such a way as to rid the countries of their need to send workers to South Africa. It was presumed from the beginning that this would require some form of co-operation between the migrant-sending countries. This was expected to be made easier by the fact that the bulk of the migrants were miners, almost all of whom were employed in the gold-mines—which, in turn, were for all practical purposes synonymous with the Chamber of Mines of South Africa.[2]

Several broad and wide-ranging studies (Bardill et al., 1977; Böhning, 1977; Clarke, 1977b; Stahl, 1979) added to our store of knowledge. Stahl's contribution is published here as Chapter 2. A number of country-specific studies made general evaluations or examined particular issues relating to Lesotho (Rugege, 1979; Sebatane, 1979; Wallis, 1977), Swaziland (Doran, 1977; Low, 1977; Rosen-Prinz and Prinz, 1978; de Vletter, 1978) and Zimbabwe (Clarke, 1978). Fion de Vletter has completed a new case study on Swaziland especially for this book (Chapter 3).

The first key objective (the improvement of migrants' and dependants' working and living conditions) was reflected in work done on Swazi miners (de Vletter, 1980), on Basotho migrants' attitudes and perceptions (Sebatane, 1979), and on the wives of Basotho migrants (Gordon, 1978) who have to stay behind when their husbands cross into the Republic. Chapters on Swazi miners (Chapter 4) and Basotho women (Chapter 5) are included in this book. The work on migrants' conditions has already borne fruit, albeit only to a very small extent: Union Corporation, one of the companies on whose mines Fion de Vletter had placed students, publicly acknowledged that the research had shown that there was room for improvement and that the recommendations made by de Vletter were being "taken into consideration" (Union Corporation, 1979, p. 57). As regards the women left behind, Elizabeth Gordon's contribution takes the findings of her Lesotho survey (Gordon, 1978) as a starting point to develop here a combination of short-run and long-run policy proposals which are, in some respects, far reaching and would tax any labour-supplying country's administrative and political organisation. That does not mean that they are unrealistic. Realism means different things to different people. Politics is the art of the possible in trying circumstances.

Politics and realism were the constant companions of those working on the second key objective (reducing migration dependence). After some initial exploratory work (Böhning, 1977, pp. 52–59; Stahl, 1977), a holistic "think-piece" was issued in working paper form (Stahl and Böhning, 1979—see Chapter 7 here). Several supporting pieces of research covered crucial questions such as the projection of labour demand in South Africa's mines up to the year 2000 (Bromberger, 1979); the compatibility of certain measures with and their feasibility under the types of agreement that labour-supplying countries had previously drawn up with South Africa (Rugege, 1979); the likely reaction of the people most directly concerned, i.e. the migrants (Sebatane, 1979); and the families' scope for or problems of adjusting to a future without migration (Woods, 1978; also Doran, 1977, and Low, 1977—see Chapter 6 in this book for a condensed presentation of the various research techniques and results).

Our "think-piece" takes as its starting point "the desirability of eliminating the migratory labour system and of hastening the withdrawal of migrant labourers from South Africa"[3] expressed by, inter alia, Botswana, Lesotho and Swaziland as far back as 1978.[4] Chapter 7 attempts to work out and submit for discussion what might be a practicable approach. It is designed to stimulate fresh ideas and innovative approaches and to open up new vistas rather than to provide definite solutions. It is worth while summarising its content briefly here. It first recalls the factors that gave rise to the dependence of countries in the vicinity of South Africa on labour migration. It indicates how migration widens the gap between the booming White core economy and the Black periphery.[5] It then argues that, as long as apartheid persists, the migrant-sending countries could rid themselves of this dependence by reducing progressively and in a planned manner the number of workers South African employers may engage. The elimination of migration dependence appears to be feasible only under two conditions. First, there must be a mutually agreed formula on the modalities of withdrawal, preferably in the framework of what we call an Association of Home Countries of Migrants (AHCM). Two possible formulae are illustrated which determine the number of migrant workers to be made available on a decreasing scale over a hypothetical 15-year period. Second, today's migrant workers who find it necessary or attractive to take up jobs in South Africa would have to be provided with decent alternative employment opportunities in their own countries. Jobs at home are bound to remain a pious wish as long as the countries are not in a position to amass the requisite finance. We find that the AHCM could successfully put pressure on South Africa to pay for the creation of alternative employment opportunities within the AHCM economies. The economic and other pressure that the AHCM could bring to bear would be sufficient to persuade a rational employer or government to accept a comparatively small addition to current operating costs, an addition which would be less than the cost of more disruptive courses of action. However, as one cannot be sure that South Africa would react in a rational economic manner, it would be prudent for the countries of the AHCM to put their case to the United Nations and to solicit voluntary contributions for a special fund large enough to make possible an immediate and total withdrawal from South Africa, if such a step proved necessary.

Nothing has happened in southern Africa since Chapter 7 was first drafted to invalidate its basic ideas. If the slowly continuing replacement of migrants from abroad by South Africans points to the major weakness of the scheme, the upward trend in the price of gold demonstrably makes it easier to pay for it.[6] In fact, the Chamber of Mines will probably never want to replace all labourers from other countries by South Africans. As one astute observer put it: "It is in the [Chamber of Mines'] interest to keep as many potential labour sources on tap as possible as a hedge against the sudden loss of any one source. Although, with wages what they are and Black unemployment in South Africa as high as it is, there seems to be no short-term obstacle in South Africa to increased internalisation of supply, there is always the possibility that the internalisation of supply could backfire. There is certainly no guarantee that the mines will find it easier to control increasingly militant and better-educated South African Blacks than foreign Blacks. Further, there will always be the temptation—especially if the gold price starts dipping—to allow real mine wages to fall and to use the foreign sources once again as a reserve army of cheap labour to break internal resistance to wage losses" (Massey, 1980, p. 14). In this perspective, therefore, our "think-piece" retains its topicality; indeed, it actually gains in urgency. As a first attempt to work through some of the implications of co-operation between the supplier States, it will be of interest even to scholars concerned with other areas and subjects. Of course, an Association of Home Countries of Migrants could, and should, also undertake a wide variety of mundane but no less topical or urgent measures of co-ordination and collaboration on matters of contract conditions, working and living conditions, and so on. Several of these will be touched upon in the following contributions; and some are under active consideration by the recently constituted Southern Africa Labour Commission set up by Botswana, Lesotho and Swaziland. It is for this reason that our original "think-piece" is published here unfudged, for scholarly scrutiny. The first big swing with the axe usually provides the best idea of the strength of the tree and the sharpness of the blade.

Notes

[1] The bibliographical details for all chapters appear at the end of the book. Only authors' surnames and the year of publication are given in the text.

[2] *Note on the terminology adopted in this book.*With very few exceptions, Black people born in South Africa are treated by the White minority Government as though they were migrants in their own country. However, in this book, "migrant", "migration" and related terms refer to citizens of countries other than South Africa. South African migrants will be identified as such and not considered as international migrants, irrespective of the status that South Africa may have accorded to a particular "homeland".

The recruiting arm of the Chamber of Mines used to be called the Mine Labour Organisation (MLO). Between 1912 and 1977 the Native Recruitment Corporation (NRC) was responsible for South Africa, Botswana, Lesotho and Swaziland; the Witwatersrand Native Labour Association (WNLA or WENELA) operated in other countries between 1901 and 1977. The two were amalgamated under the acronym TEBA (The Employment Bureau of Africa) in March 1977; but as the name WNLA is so well known, it has been retained in the countries where WNLA still operates.

[3] "Resolution on the creation of a labour committee for southern Africa", in United Nations, Economic Commission for Africa: *Report of the Conference on Migratory Labour in Southern Africa (Lusaka, 4–8 April 1978)* (doc. E/CN.14/ECO/142, ECA/MULPOC/LUSAKA/109, 19 Apr. 1978; mimeographed), p. 11.

[4] Since this book was written, the International Tripartite Meeting on Action against Apartheid, held in Livingstone (Zambia) from 4 to 8 May 1981, has proposed that the ILO should co-operate with "the governments of the States in the immediate neighbourhood of South Africa in devising and implementing policies which will enable them to reduce their dependence on South Africa, and in particular the supply of migrant labour to South Africa". This proposal was taken up and adopted by the International Labour Conference in June 1981 as part of the updated Declaration concerning the Policy of Apartheid in South Africa (see ILO: *Provisional Record* No. 19, International Labour Conference, 67th Session, Geneva, 1981, p. 19/16).

[5] The question might be asked: "Why did you not concern yourself with White migration to South Africa? It is just as much a cause of the widening gap between the Republic and its neighbours as is Black migration, and it deprives the Black people of the region of jobs!" Irrespective of the debatable merits of this position, it was simply not our brief to inquire into White migration movements at all.

[6] The average price of gold in 1979 was $285. The impact on the Republic's export earnings (43 per cent in 1979) and public finances (R 1,800 million) is enormous. "Sources in the Johannesburg stock exchange suggest that gold prices, coupled with record diamond sales in recent years, could have given Anglo [i.e. the major mining company, Anglo American Corporation] cash and near cash reserves of R 3,000 million" (*The Times* (London), 24 Jan. 1980). In the autumn of 1980 South Africa's Central Bank suspended gold sales because foreign currency reserves were flowing over.

MIGRANT LABOUR SUPPLIES, PAST, PRESENT AND FUTURE; WITH SPECIAL REFERENCE TO THE GOLD-MINING INDUSTRY

2

C. W. Stahl

THE FORMATION OF AFRICAN LABOUR SUPPLIES AND THE ROLE OF LABOUR FROM ABROAD

The history of labour migration in southern Africa begins with the discovery of the vast mineral wealth of South Africa in the second half of the nineteenth century. The exploitation of that mineral wealth required enormous supplies of labour, and the need to sustain a rapidly growing urban population made heavy demands on agriculture too. The development of commercial agriculture likewise required large amounts of labour.

The demand for labour by a rapidly expanding economy in a relatively underpopulated southern Africa led to growing labour shortages. In this first section we investigate how South Africa in general, and the gold-mining industry in particular, responded to shortages of African labour, how labour supplies were formed and what changes occurred in the African labour market over the years. We concentrate on the gold-mining industry because this has been the largest single employer of international African labour.

South Africa before the mineral revolution

In the 1860s, on the eve of the discovery of the tremendous mineral wealth of South Africa, the territories comprising the country were almost totally dependent upon agricultural production. The poorest of the four White-dominated territories were the Afrikaner republics of the Orange Free State and the Transvaal. In the latter territory, subsistence agriculture was the main economic base for the great majority of Europeans and Africans. The Orange Free State, with its extensive pasture land, was suitable for sheep-raising; and its inhabitants maintained some contact with the exchange economy of the coast by selling or bartering wool with itinerant or resident traders. The British colonies of Natal and Cape Province were at the time somewhat better off than the Afrikaner republics, although they were still poor. Natal, with its generous rainfall, had experimented with various export crops and had finally settled on sugar. Since the employment of Africans on the sugar plantations proved unsuccessful, indentured Indian labourers were imported from 1860 onwards. Along the coastal belt of Cape Province the climate was particularly suited to the production of wheat, fruit, butter and maize; these were marketed internally, along with hides, wine and ostrich feathers for export. As this farming area was near the sea, produce could be transported by ship at reasonable cost, whereas transport from the interior of South Africa was prohibitively expensive. Transport between the coast and the interior was of the most rudimentary form, and hence expensive, as is shown by the fact that it took three months for goods to reach Bloemfontein, in the heart of the Orange Free State, from Port Elizabeth, only 400 miles away (Wilson, 1971, p. 108).

During the preceding 200 years there had been a slow expansion of the eastern frontier about the Cape settlement. Few immigrants came to reinforce the European population, and in this South Africa differed from North America, Australia and New Zealand. Indeed, the great nine-teenth-century wave of immigration from the British Isles and Europe simply passed South Africa by. By the middle of that century the estimated European population of South Africa was approximately 200,000. In 1854 the White population of Cape Province was 140,000 and that of the Orange Free State 15,000. In 1872 the Transvaal had 30,000 White inhabitants and in 1856 Natal had 8,500 (Houghton, 1967, p. 7). No figures are available for Africans.

The Afrikaners, as the predominantly Dutch and French settlers came to be known, never willingly accepted the controls to which the colonial governing authorities attempted to subject them. Their resentment of colonial authority became even more pronounced when the British assumed control of Cape Province in the early nineteenth century. The comparatively liberal social attitude that the British brought to the Cape conflicted with a basic philosophical tenet of the Afrikaner race: that of White supremacy. Their use of Hottentots, imported slaves and Bantu to perform manual labour on their farms imbued the Afrikaners with the attitude that menial physical labour on the part of Whites was degrading. No White was to perform physical labour for another. These attitudes were to have a considerable impact on the political economy of resource allocation throughout South Africa's development. It was these doctrines that were to be most fundamental to the Afrikaner political ideology, which was eventually to prevail against the integrating tendencies of competitive market forces. When the British emancipated slaves in Cape Province in 1834 the reaction of the Afrikaners was predictable. Herding their cattle and transporting their few household effects by ox-wagon, the "voortrekkers" moved out of Cape Province in great numbers.

As a result of their comparative isolation from the economic and social influences of a changing Europe, the Afrikaner frontiersmen, or "trekboers", as they were called, underwent a process of economic and social retrogression that coincided with their penetration into the vast interior plains of South Africa. Pushing into the Cape interior, they became, for all practical purposes, subsistence farmers and graziers having minimal contact with the exchange economy of the coast. Their right to settle these new lands was hotly contested by the many indigenous African tribes (Thompson, 1971), but by the 1860s they had secured this area, carving out huge farms on which to graze their cattle and to grow the crops they required for subsistence. Many Africans, dispossessed of their land, went into the service of Whites or squatted on White farms. Since land was plentiful for the Whites, whereas capital and labour were scarce, the majority of Afrikaner farmers did not discourage such squatting. Indeed, they charged the African squatters rent that was payable in the form of labour services, crops or both. Thus, in the Orange Free State and to a considerable extent in the Transvaal, the relationship between African and Afrikaner had all the economic markings of feudalism.

In the African territories (the most important of which, measured in terms of population density, were Zululand, Basutoland (now Lesotho), Swaziland and the Transkei) the trekboers had little social or economic impact at first, except that they increased the population density by containing African movement and pushing Africans off White land. Agricultural production was still subsistence-oriented.

On the eve of the mineral discoveries which were to transform South Africa, the economy was entirely based on agriculture. Farming was extensive and largely for subsistence, and in no way was it ready to meet the demands of the mining-town markets that were to mushroom in the next few decades.

Mineral developments and the formation of labour supplies

In 1867 an event occurred which was to transform the economy of South Africa and move it along the road toward industrialisation: diamonds were discovered along what was to become the eastern frontier of Cape Province after the British had annexed the diamond-producing area. By 1869 the first diamond rush was on, with diggers pouring into the area along the Orange and Vaal rivers to work alluvial deposits. Several years later diamonds were discovered where the mining city of Kimberley now stands. These diamonds were found in four large volcanic pipes. Such deposits were unique in the history of diamond-mining; previously, diamonds all over the world had been found in alluvial deposits. At Kimberley deep-level mining became necessary, and thus was established the basis for an urban mining complex.

By 1877 the population of Kimberley was estimated at 45,000, comprised of 15,000 Whites, 10,000 Coloureds and 20,000 Africans (Knowles, 1936, p. 206). This was second only to the population of Cape Town. Of the Africans employed on the digging, a large proportion were brought in by recruiters and supplied to the companies for a capitation fee. Once the level of demand for labour stabilised, this practice became unnecessary as a sufficient number of workers came to the diggings of their own accord.

The deep-level mining of diamonds ran into technical difficulties during the first years at Kimberley. Thousands of individual claims within the small area of the pipes made excavation exceedingly difficult as the diggings went deeper and deeper. However, by 1888 the financial and administrative counsel of Cecil Rhodes had prevailed and the consolidation of the many diamond-mining companies was completed (van der Horst, 1942). The consolidation made it possible to use machinery that was uneconomical on smaller holdings. From then on, De Beers Consolidated Mines Ltd. dominated the South African diamond-mining industry. Output was reduced (as was the demand for labour) and was henceforth adjusted to world demand so as to stabilise world diamond prices: a classic case of market strategy by a monopolist. However, the Kimberley diamond-mining industry was to be completely overshadowed by the discovery, in 1886, and the subsequent development of the Witwatersrand gold-fields.

Located where Johannesburg now stands, the Witwatersrand lay deep in the Transvaal, at that time the poorest and most backward of the four White South African territories. Foreigners poured into the Transvaal, bringing the skills needed by the many gold-mining companies. The period between 1890 and 1913 saw an average annual White immigration of 24,000 (Hobart Houghton, 1967b, p. 13). The demand for labour by the rapidly expanding industry was insatiable. From the beginning, production was based on a relatively small number of skilled workers, in combination with large numbers of unskilled Africans. The latter were recruited from all over southern Africa, both inside and outside South Africa itself, at considerable expense to the mines. In 1889 only about 6,000 Africans were employed in the Witwatersrand mines; a decade later they numbered approximately 97,000 (Transvaal Chamber of Mines: *Annual reports*, 1889 and 1899). The growth in the employment of White workers was equally great. Table 1 indicates the average number of European and African workers employed by the gold-mines in selected years.[1]

Wages for the skilled workers were necessarily high, in order to attract experienced miners from overseas. But skilled labour has always represented but a small fraction of the total labour force employed in the

Table 1. Number of European and African workers employed in gold-mines, selected years between 1889 and 1979

Year	Europeans ('000s)	Africans ('000s)	Africans from abroad as % of all Africans[1]
1889	–	6	–
1894	6	43	–
1899	12	97	–
1906	11	81	77
1911	25	190	60
1916	22	204	56
1921	21	173	61
1926	20	182	62
1931	23	210	50
1936	35	297	48
1941	41	368	52
1946	40	305	59
1951	44	299	64
1956	49	336	65
1961	49	399	64
1966	43	370	66
1970	39	401	76
1971	38	386	78
1972	37	414	79
1973	37	422	80
1974	37	364	75
1975	37	365	67
1976	38	361	56
1977	38	422	49
1978	40	456	45
1979	41	479	43

[1] End-of-year Africans from abroad in total number employed at end of year.

Sources: Mine Labour Organisation (WNLA): *Annual reports,* various issues; Mine Labour Organisation (NRC): *Annual reports,* various issues; TEBA: *Annual reports,* various issues.

mines. Given the distribution of the various grades of ore and the desire to maximise profits over the years, the gold-mining industry has always relied heavily on African labour and hence has always been concerned with the terms on which it could secure their services. In its infancy the industry experienced rapidly rising costs, as competition among the mining companies for the limited number of African workers resulted in rising wages for Black labour. To prevent further increases in this significant cost component, many of the companies recommended the elimination of wage competition for African labour. It appears that this was a fundamental reason behind the creation of the Chamber of Mines in 1889, as shown by the following quotation from its sixth annual report, published in 1895:

Since formation of the Chamber continuous attention has been given to the subject of devising means by which the supply of labour could be made to meet the constantly growing requirements of the mining industry, and by which also wages could be reduced to a reasonable level.

With regard to the recruitment of labour, the Chamber recognised that the outlay of considerable sums for labour recruitment would not be justified unless the individual firms were assured that recruited workers could not legally break their contract by moving on to another mine or, perhaps, to another industry. To ensure the firms an adequate return for their recruitment expenditures, the Chamber formulated a "pass law" that was adopted and enforced by the Transvaal Volksraad in 1894. Reference to this law was made at the sixth annual meeting, held in 1895:

. . . the Chamber drafted a set of pass regulations, which provided means for the proper registration and identification of natives, and for compelling them to fulfil contracts voluntarily entered into. With these regulations in force the companies would be warranted in incurring the very considerable expense of bringing "boys" from a distance; as, though the initial cost would be heavy, full compensation would be found in the reduced rate of wages (Transvaal Chamber of Mines: *Annual report*, 1895).

During the 1890s the Chamber was not completely successful in achieving its objectives. When the demand for African workers was greater than the supply, competition for the limited supply forced up wage rates. It was not until after the South African War (1899–1902) that the Chamber was successful in reducing the cost of Black labour while, at the same time, increasing its supply. This was achieved mainly by centralising the recruitment of African labour. In 1901 the Chamber established the Witwatersrand Native Labour Association (WNLA) for this purpose, hoping thereby to reduce the cost of recruitment. The WNLA's regulations stipulated that:

No company, whilst a member of the Witwatersrand Native Labour Association, will be allowed under any circumstances to engage any but White labour, except through the agency of the Association. This will apply: (1) to all natives who, from having previously worked on your mine, or who from any cause may come forward and seek such work voluntarily; (2) to those who have been recruited within or without the Transvaal—in fact to all natives or coloured men employed either above or below ground on your property (Transvaal Chamber of Mines: *Annual report*, 1900–01, p. 112).

This move was to have significant repercussions in the market for African labour. Clearly, by acting in concert with respect to the recruitment and distribution of labour the industry would be able to derive the profits associated with being a perfectly discriminating monopsonist.[2]

In addition to centralising the recruitment and distribution of Black labour on a non-profit basis, the Chamber also attempted to reduce wages. In this it was not successful. Social dislocations caused by the South African War, together with alternative wage-employment oppor- tunities for Africans (on infrastructural projects at higher rates of pay), caused the number of Africans recruited to work in the mines to fall far below pre-war levels. In general, there were many complaints that there was not enough Black labour in southern Africa to meet the labour requirements of South African industry and agriculture—an opinion which was confirmed by the 1904 report of the Transvaal Labour Commission. The Commission was especially influenced by testimony from the Chamber to the effect that it had explored every avenue in its search for African labour. Every avenue, that is, except for wages. Two members of the Commission dissented from the majority report, noting their belief that the shortfall in the mining sector's labour requirement was largely a result of the Chamber's abortive attempt to reduce wages. None the less, the result was that the mines were allowed to import indentured Chinese labour. However, humanitarian opposition in the United Kingdom soon put an end to this importation, and in 1907 the legislation permitting it was repealed. The mines were able, however, to maintain their supplies of labour as a result of intensified recruitment and a fall-off in the postwar boom which reduced the demand for labour in other sectors.

Thus, little more than a decade after the opening up of the gold-fields, the many firms comprising the industry were acting in concert in the market for African labour. Recruitment had been completely centralised, and the firms' wage rates were being dictated by the Chamber, using the system of fixing a maximum average wage. Fixing a maximum average rather than a simple maximum rate was designed to achieve a dual purpose: to prevent individual mines from bidding up average rates of pay while allowing individual mines some degree of flexibility with regard to the organisation of their workforce through the adjustment of wages to reflect differing degrees of productivity among individual workers (van der Horst, 1942, pp. 165–166).

Over the years the Chamber of Mines has displayed keen awareness of the importance of the size of the recruitment area as a choice variable in its efforts to meet the labour requirements of its members. The geographical area over which it has spread its recruitment of African labour increased considerably as the years went by. Table 2 provides information about the proportion and country of origin of the African workers coming from various countries within southern Africa to work on the gold-mines.

Legislated labour supplies in the first decades of the twentieth century

Legislation and African agriculture

The Chamber of Mines was set up principally to prevent wage competition among individual mines by centralising labour recruitment. Although at first it was not successful in achieving the desired reduction in

Table 2. Sources of African labour by country of origin, employed by affiliates of Chamber of Mines (expressed as a percentage of the total number employed at 31 December)

Country of origin	1906	1911	1916	1921	1926	1931	1936	1941	1946	1951	1956	1961	1966	1971	1976	1979
South Africa	22.80	40.32	44.32	38.69	38.23	49.80	52.18	48.17	41.26	35.29	34.71	36.46	34.04	22.40	43.88	57.30
Botswana	0.40	0.49	1.68	1.11	1.01	1.49	2.25	2.51	2.30	2.69	3.10	3.19	4.95	4.14	4.28	3.91
Lesotho	2.60	3.82	7.63	10.56	10.93	13.62	14.46	13.10	12.49	11.67	11.93	13.02	16.77	17.78	26.67	22.81
Swaziland	0.70	2.07	2.05	2.28	2.12	2.24	2.21	1.93	1.81	1.84	1.61	1.57	1.13	1.25	2.38	2.09
Mozambique	70.79	51.59	43.73	47.08	47.54	32.71	27.83	27.00	31.54	34.45	30.78	24.22	28.43	26.52	13.44	7.87
Tropicals[1]	2.47	1.66	0.58	0.27	0.17	0.14	1.07	7.29	10.60	13.45	17.87	21.54	14.68	27.91	9.35	5.69
Total no. employed ('000)	81	174	191	188	203	226	318	372	305	306	334	414	383	379	361	479

[1] Africans recruited from north of latitude 22° S, chiefly from Malawi (in 1976 and 1979 there were respectively 17,300 and 8,014 recruits from Zimbabwe).

Note: Discrepancies between total numbers employed in tables 1, 2 and 3 reflect different times during the year of enumeration; and figures in this table also include Africans employed in coalmines affiliated to the Chamber of Mines.

Sources: As for table 1.

Table 3. Average annual cash wage, current and real, and number of Africans employed in the gold-mining industry (1881–1966 = base year 1938 = 100; 1969–80 = base April 1970 = 100)[1]

Year	Current rands	Real wage (rands)	No. employed ('000s)
1885	72		6
1889	72	84	51
1906	68	80	81
1911	60	72	190
1916	65	70	204
1921	69	58	173
1926	71	67	182
1931	69	69	210
1936	71	75	297
1941	71	67	368
1946	88	67	305
1951	110	64	299
1956	133	64	336
1961	146	64	399
1966	183	70	370
1969	199	209	371
1970	208	208	401
1971	221	209	386
1972	257	227	414
1973	350	282	422
1974	565	408	364
1975	948	602	365
1976	1 103	631	361
1977	1 235	634	422
1978	1 420	656	456
1979	1 669	675	479
1980[2]	1 813	682	.

[1] Cash wages only, not including payment in kind, which forms a considerable proportion of Black labour costs. In 1972 it was estimated that the value of payments in kind to Black workers was R 589, of which food accounted for R 328. [2] First quarter grossed up to annual data.

Sources: As for table 1; Bureau of Census and Statistics: Statistical year book, various issues; idem: Monthly Bulletin of Statistics (for consumer price index).

wage rates, it did succeed in preventing further wage increases. As indicated in table 3, wages did not increase in spite of a significant growth in labour demand. In the early part of the twentieth century the agricultural sector of South Africa also exhibited an insatiable growth in demand for African labour without forcing up wage rates.

Some scholars have argued that the lack of growth of wages derives from a division and specialisation of labour in the African subsistence-agricultural sector which results in redundant male labour, i.e. "surplus labour". If surplus labour exists, redundant workers can seek temporary

15

employment outside the subsistence sector without reducing output on (family) agricultural holdings. However, if the withdrawal of a worker reduces farm output, i.e. if surplus labour is exhausted, additional wages will have to be offered to compensate the worker and his family for such a loss. Thus, so long as there is surplus labour, the modern sector can continue to expand, withdrawing labour from the subsistence sector at a non-increasing wage rate.

According to Barber (1961), it was the existence of redundant male African labour in the subsistence sector that explained the non-increasing wage trend in the modern sector in Southern Rhodesia (now Zimbabwe) from 1929 to 1945. However, Arrighi (1970) has cast serious doubt on the validity of Barber's analysis and, consequently, on the whole notion of endemic surplus labour. According to Arrighi, the explanation of the non-increasing wage trend in Rhodesia lay in previous changes in the African subsistence sector which made it more and more necessary for Africans to undertake wage employment. Basically, these changes were a rising conventional subsistence level, which increasingly included non-traditional goods requiring cash for their purchase; and a lower capacity of Africans to obtain these goods through the sale of agricultural commodities. The latter was in turn traceable to the displacement of African agriculture by state-subsidised White agriculture and the voluntary and involuntary removal of Africans from White agricultural areas, near transport routes, to the comparatively inaccessible "reserved" areas where over-stocking and crowding led to a deterioration of African agricultural productivity. In a nutshell, the ever more uncompetitive position in which African agriculture found itself increased the "effort price" of securing cash through the sale of agricultural commodities relative to the "effort price" of securing cash through entering wage employment.

For South Africa, Clarke (1977b) sees a similarity between Rhodesian and South African experience in the proletarianisation of African labour supplies. He lays great stress on the role of the colonial administration in undertaking or backing measures which virtually force African workers into wage employment. These measures essentially are asset confiscation of both land and cattle, and the taxing of Africans. Also important to the proletarianisation process is the subsidised development of White agriculture and the neglect of African agriculture. By these actions, Clarke argues, the "natural economy" of the traditional African people is subordinated to the imperatives of the dominant sector(s) of the economic system, with the result that its self-reproductive capacity is impaired and oriented to a new set of requirements. The transformation of the "natural economy" creates a surplus of labour, given that adequate means of subsistence necessary to "reproduce the labour supply" can no longer be guaranteed after land and cattle assets have been expropriated. Thus, surplus labour finds it necessary to migrate to wage employment to obtain part of its subsistence. However, since part of the migrant's subsistence is drawn from traditional agriculture, the capitalist employer only has to pay a wage equal to the difference between total subsistence requirements and that portion of subsistence requirements derived from traditional agriculture in the so-called Labour Reserve. Through this "primitive accumulation", the capitalist sector reaps large profits: "accumulation comes to assume the form of a labour transfer below cost of reproduction. So it is the *indirect use* made of the social means of subsistence, continuously reproduced within the Labour Reserve, which forms the foundation for the accumulation of a large element of stock [of capital]" (Clarke, 1977b, p. 18). Not only are short-run labour supplies secured, but capitalist penetration results in a process of "disinvestment" and a "restructuring of the asset base" of the Labour Reserve which leads to their agricultural deterioration. "Asset appropriation and erosion in asset values, combined with primitive accumulation based on migrant labour . . . , work to reduce productive capacity in the Reserve economy" (Clarke, 1977b, p. 24). This, in turn, ensures continued and increased supplies in the long run. Eventually this process can lead to a "structural labour surplus" in the Labour Reserve.

Thus, Clarke would attribute the increase in labour supplies mainly to political manipulations of the labour supply through the appropriation of African rural assets and the concomitant erosion of African agricultural productivity. Unlike Arrighi (1970), whose analysis he draws heavily upon, Clarke neglects the importance of the rising *conventional* subsistence requirements of Africans, which required more and more cash to fulfil, on the supply of African wage labour. Instead, he holds to the thesis advanced by Wolpe (1972) that wages paid by capitalists will tend to adjust to the partial subsistence derived from agriculture in the Labour Reserve in such a way that the sum of the two sources of income fulfil *basic* subsistence requirements. Yet there is abundant evidence that *conventional* subsistence income levels of South African Blacks have risen considerably over the years, mainly through participation in wage employment. Further, Clarke fails to recognise that, in part, declining agricultural production in the Labour Reserve is a response to rising wages in the industrial sector, which results in a greater level and intensity of migration. In short, the deterioration of African agricultural productivity is both a cause and an effect of migration.

This is not to argue that the use of political measures to generate labour supplies was not an important feature in the early political economy of South Africa. It was. It is, however, to argue that the history of the formation of African labour supplies is more complex than

Clarke's interpretation would suggest. However, let us continue by reviewing the evidence on the political manipulation of labour supplies. Later we shall analyse the effects of the "colour bar" in holding down the wages of administratively induced labour supplies.

The northward and eastward expansion of the Cape Province frontier and the voortrekker occupation of the Transvaal and the Orange Free State left the indigenous African peoples in those areas dispossessed of their land. Many stayed in the newly White-owned areas, others remained in what are now Natal and eastern Cape Province; there they were able to maintain control of the land (as a combined result of tribal military strength, treaties and British intervention). At the time of union in 1910, African areas comprised about 7 per cent of territorial South Africa and 60 per cent of the African population resided in those areas. The remainder were living on European-owned land, both occupied and unoccupied (Native Land Commission, 1916). Of those living on White-owned land, a considerable proportion were sharecroppers. This type of arrangement was especially characteristic of the Orange Free State, where only 244 square miles out of 50,000 were reserved for Africans, who numbered something over 440,000. Another type of relationship between Africans and White farmers was that of "squatting". If an African was a squatter he was required to provide, each year, some quantity of labour services to the owner of the property. In return, the tenant was allowed to raise enough crops for his family's subsistence and perhaps to run a few head of stock. These arrangements were severely criticised by many. The basis of their objections was that such arrangements served to diminish the supply of African labour. Complaints were also registered against "free traffic" in land, which permitted Africans to purchase land from Whites. What was happening was that Africans were using the money they had acquired by selling agricultural surpluses and working in wage employment to buy up White-owned land.

In 1903, just after the British defeat of the Boers, the British High Commissioner, Lord Milner, set up the Native Affairs Commission for the purpose of adopting a common policy on the relationship of Africans and Whites throughout colonial southern Africa. Labour utilisation on White farms and free traffic in land occupied much of the Commission's attention; and their conclusions and recommendations were to provide the basis for legislation that was, in time, to have a substantial impact on the productivity of African agriculture and, hence, on the supply of African labour to the industrial and the White agricultural sectors. The Commission's opinion with regard to the continuation of free traffic in land is illustrated by the following excerpt from its report:

If this process goes on, while at the same time restrictions exclude Europeans from purchasing within Native areas, it is inevitable that at no very distant date the amount of land in Native occupation will be undesirably extended. Native wages and earnings are greater than they used to be, their wants are few, and their necessary expenses small. They will buy land at prices above its otherwise market value, as their habits and standard of living enable them to exist on land that is impossible for Europeans to farm on a small scale. There will be many administrative and social difficulties created by the multiplication of a number of Native lands scattered through a White population and owning the land of the country equally with them. It will be far more difficult to preserve the absolutely necessary political and social distinctions, if growth of a mixed rural population of landowners is not discouraged . . . (Report of the Native Affairs Commission, 1906, para. 192).

The Commission's recommendations exemplify the way in which the White polity was to subordinate market choices to ideological imperatives in the development experience of South Africa. It was unanimously recommended that:

it is necessary to safeguard what is conceived to be the interests of the Europeans of this country, but that is so doing the door should not be entirely closed to deserving and progressing individuals among the Natives acquiring land . . .

and resolved:

(a) that the purchase [of land] by Natives should be limited to certain areas to be defined by legislative enactment;
(b) that purchase of land which may lead to tribal, communal or collective possession or occupation by Natives should not be permitted (ibid., para. 193).

With respect to squatting and sharecropping, the Commission recommended the stringent enforcement of the existing laws against squatting, the taxation of Africans living on Crown lands and the enforcement of anti-vagrancy laws. It is clear that in this latter recommendation the Commission was responding to those of the White polity who had complained that the existing institutional arrangements with respect to African land occupation and utilisation were interfering with the supply of cheap African labour.

In 1913 the first Union Government responded to the findings and recommendations of the Commission by enacting the Native Land Act, which stipulated that no African could, without special permission from the Governor-General, purchase or hire land in other than "scheduled areas", i.e. those traditionally held by Africans as a result of the combined effects of military might, diplomacy and treaties. Almost without exception, it was acknowledged by Members of Parliament that the fraction of land allocated for African occupation was unjust and inadequate; therefore, the Act was passed with the added stipulation that a commission be created to investigate and recommend what further amounts of land should be "released" for African occupation in order to achieve a more "equitable" distribution of land between the two races. But nearly 25 years passed before any further land was so released. Under the Native Trust and Land Act, 1936, provision was made for an additional 6 per cent of territorial South Africa to be added to the Reserve areas and purchased with funds voted by Parliament for that purpose. Parliament, however, stopped voting funds in 1940, with the result that, to date, the Government has purchased only one-fifth of the land released for African occupation. The market still operates in the remainder of the released areas, although virtually all land is owned by Whites. The 1936 Act was severe also with respect to squatting and sharecropping; it led to the eviction of many thousands of Africans from White farms and their transfer to the Reserve areas or their placement as full-time agricultural labour.

Thus, in present-day South Africa, the African population owns about 8 per cent of the land and cannot legally increase this share beyond 13 per cent (7 per cent of the land is in the Reserves and the remaining 6 per cent in released areas). Consequently, population density has been increasing in the Reserve areas, accompanied by fragmentation of land holdings, overstocking, soil depletion and erosion. The land allocation under the 1913 Act has contributed to falling productivity per head in agriculture.

The sorry state of agriculture in the African Reserves was emphasised by the Tomlinson Commission, which in 1955 was to conduct an exhaustive inquiry into a report on a comprehensive scheme for the rehabilitation of the Native areas (Report of the Tomlinson Commission, 1955, p. xviii). The Commission expected that, by planned development, the agricultural sector of the African Reserves could reach a carrying capacity of 2.4 million persons. At that time there were 3.6 million Africans domiciled in the Reserves; at present, there are over 8 million.

Thus, growing population pressures in the Reserves, the under-development of reserve agriculture and rising conventional subsistence requirements, which required more and more cash to fulfil, help to explain the ability of the Chamber and White farmers to satisfy their ever growing labour demands without having to rely on wage increases.[3]

The industrial colour bar and African wage rates

The appropriation of African lands by Whites in southern Africa and the severe limitation placed on the acquisition of land by Africans largely precluded the development of commercial agriculture by Africans in South Africa. With rising cash requirements, Africans accordingly turned to wage employment and migration. However, the pressure to migrate from overcrowded and inaccessible Reserves was not the only factor operating to depress real wages in the gold-mining industry.

It was in the gold-mining industry that the integrating effects of uncontrolled competitive market forces first threatened to upset the traditional notions of what was supposed to be the White man's work and what was Africans' work. Africans had come to the mines as un-sophisticated and unskilled industrial workers but in the short span of a decade they were being substituted for expensive White labour. Reacting to this aspect of the profit-maximising behaviour of the Chamber of Mines, the Parliament enacted the Mines and Work Act, 1911. One section of this Act regulated the issuance of certificates of competency in skilled occupations by imposing the restriction that such certificates were not to be granted to "Coloured persons" in the Transvaal or the Orange Free State, in which territories any certificates issued in the Cape Province or Natal were not recognised (cf. Doxey, 1961 and Hutt, 1964). Thus, an African who might have received a certificate of competency in the more socially liberal Cape Province or Natal would not be able to use it in the former Boer republics of the Transvaal and the Orange Free State where the gold- and coalmines of the Chamber's members were located.

With the outbreak of the First World War the mines were faced with a situation in which they did not have enough White workers because of their enlistment for military service. With the consent of the Government and the White mineworkers, Africans were used in positions previously reserved for Whites. After the War the White miners' union pressed the Chamber to draw the job colour-line where it existed at that time. This was done under what came to be known as the Status Quo Agreement, 1918. However, within a few years the inflated costs of mining, combined with a fall in the price of gold, were threatening to close marginal mines. The reaction of the Chamber was to broaden its use of cheap African labour by placing Africans in jobs traditionally performed by Whites. White labour was understandably upset that its monopoly position was being encroached upon by this substitution of Black for White labour. Negotiations between the miners' union and the Chamber over a fixed employment ratio of Blacks to Whites and over job reservation for Whites broke down, precipitating the famous Rand strike of 1922. For over two months a minor civil war flared on the Witwatersrand. Interestingly enough, the slogan of the striking White mineworkers was "Workers of the world unite for a White South Africa".

The strike failed. Thousands of White mineworkers were laid off and replaced with African labour. The Chamber of Mines had won the battle; but the State was soon to ensure that the Chamber would lose the war. Two years after the strike, the "Pact" Government of Afrikaner ideology (personified by General Hertzog) and British trade unionism (represented by Creswell) was elected (Hertzog became Prime Minister and Creswell Secretary of Labour). From 1924 onwards the State was in indisputable control of the market. The Pact Government immediately acted against the Chamber of Mines by passing the Mines and Work Amendment Bill, 1926, which made a detailed listing of all jobs that could not be performed

21

by Africans. Thus, White labour in the South African gold-mining industry acquired a lease on all jobs designated as White. In addition to securing job reservation, the White union won its demand that a fixed ratio of eight Black to one White worker should obtain throughout the industry.

The implications of this "colour bar" and the fixed employment ratio for the pricing and employment of African labour in the gold-mining industry should be clear. Black wages are held down by legislation restricting Africans to jobs of low productivity. The growth in demand for African labour is stifled by four factors: *(a)* it is a function of the scarce supply of skilled Whites; *(b)* it is limited by the inability of the mines to substitute low-cost African labour for high-cost White labour; *(c)* because of the colour bar and fixed employment ratio, output is less than it would be in a competitive labour market; and *(d)* it leads to the adoption of production techniques using as little Black labour as possible so that the use of expensive White labour can also be reduced.

The period of increasing labour imports

By 1940 the forced industrialisation of the South African economy was under way. The diversification of the economy required massive public and private capital formation. This investment was reflected in a rapid expansion in employment in manufacturing, as well as in public and private construction. The percentage increases in private manufacturing and private construction employment between 1950 and 1970 were 143 per cent and 242 per cent respectively, whilst that for mining was 27 per cent.

This large increase in labour demand was also associated with rising African wages in the newly emerging sectors. As can be discerned from table 4, in 1935–36 the gold-mining industry offered wages which were equivalent to those offered in manufacturing. However, with the very rapid rate of growth of the manufacturing and other sectors, the wages offered by those sectors was rising. Between 1936 and 1973 current average annual earnings in manufacturing increased by 925 per cent. In gold-mining, over the same period, current average annual earnings rose by 391 per cent. Thus, the difference in average annual earnings between the two sectors increased from 18 per cent to 147 per cent over the same period. Agriculture, which draws heavily on African labour from abroad, was also able to maintain its traditional low wage rates. In 1973 wages in manufacturing were 466 per cent of those in agriculture.

Such substantial sectoral wage differentials caused South African Blacks to abandon mining employment in great numbers. As can be determined from table 1, between 1936 and 1973 South African Blacks as

Table 4. Average annual African earnings by sector, 1935–1978
(rands per annum) [1]

Industry [2]	1935–36	1945–46	1954–55	1964–65	1971	1976	1977	1978
Manufacturing	84	192	294	471	667	1 497	1 788	2 124
Construction	.	.	262	341	628	1 346	1 488	
Transport	.	.	.	379	611	1 300	1 572	1 656
Motor trade	.	.	.	.	643	1 251	1 512	1 692
Wholesale and retail trade	.	.	.	.	597	1 153	1 326	1 548
Public authorities	.	.	.	396	655	1 291	1 588	1 684
Gold-mining	71	88	132	176	221	950	1 244	1 476
Agriculture	.	.	70	81	119	.	.	.

[1] Cash earnings only. Payment in kind is an important source of earnings in both mining and agriculture.   [2] The industries selected were the largest employers of African labour outside agriculture. The average wage between 1935 and 1976 was calculated by dividing the total African wage bill in each industry by the corresponding number employed; the average wages in 1977 and 1978 were taken from ILO, 1979 and ILO, 1980.

Sources: Republic of South Africa: *Yearbook of South Africa*; Department of Agriculture: Publication no. 39 (1972); Chamber of Mines: *Annual reports*, various issues; Industrial census of the Bureau of Census and Statistics, quoted in Steenkamp (1962).

a proportion of the African mining labour force declined from 52 per cent to 20 per cent. In terms of absolute numbers this amounted to a decline from 165,932 to 86,172.

The Chamber of Mines responded in predictable fashion to its increasing inability to secure domestic supplies of Africans. Rather than compete with the secondary and tertiary sectors for domestic African labour, the Chamber simply went further outside South Africa to find its labour force. In particular, the Chamber began recruiting "tropical" Africans. These were recruited principally from Nyasaland (now Malawi). Tropical African labour became so important to the gold-mining industry that, by 1973, 127,000 workers, or over 30 per cent of the Chamber's African labour force, were recruited from tropical areas.

Only by using its recruitment area size variable was the Chamber able to maintain and expand its labour supply without incurring increased wage costs. Whereas most South African Blacks had access to the higher-paying secondary and tertiary sectors, Blacks from abroad were largely excluded from these sectors by legislative measures and distance. Such a division of the migrant labour force helps to explain the persistence of substantial wage differentials between mining and other sectors since, in theory, labour competition between industries tends eventually to reduce wage differentials between sectors.

Summary

In this section we have seen that actions by the Chamber of Mines in the African labour market, in combination with political factors affecting

23

labour supplies, have generated two distinct phases in gold-mining labour supplies. The first phase ran from the turn of the century to around 1940. It was characterised by a tremendous increase in the number of South African Blacks seeking employment in gold-mining, despite stagnant money wages and declining real earnings. The second phase began around 1940 and continued until 1973. It was characterised by a large decrease in the number of South African Blacks willing to work on the mines, despite a growth in money wages which prevented real earnings from declining. This phase was also characterised by very substantial increases in the number of Africans from abroad employed in gold-mining. The explanations of the first phase lie in: *(a)* collusion in the African labour market by affiliates of the Chamber of Mines; and *(b)* changes in the African subsistence sector which led to increasing cash requirements of the African population while there was a parallel decline in the ability of the African peasantry to secure that cash through the production of agricultural surpluses. The second phase, that of an increasing relative reliance on African labour from abroad, is ascribed to the ability of the Chamber of Mines to extend its labour recruitment area, thus avoiding wage competition with other sectors of the rapidly expanding South African economy.

RECENT CHANGES OF DEMAND FOR AFRICAN LABOUR AND FUTURE PROSPECTS

An inspection of recent data on the volume, sex and occupation of migrant Africans in South Africa indicates substantive changes in all three since the advent of independence in the migrants' countries of origin in the 1960s. The purpose of this section is to investigate the reasons underlying those changes and to explore their implications for the future demand for labour from abroad in South Africa. Understanding this process of change and its implications for future labour demand is directly relevant to the development strategies of the labour-exporting countries.

Recent changes in South African legislation have increasingly and effectively relegated Blacks from abroad to a supplementary supply position vis-à-vis South African Blacks. Combined with this development, there has been rising African unemployment in South Africa. This has been due to cyclical and structural factors that have operated on both the demand and the supply side of the South African Black labour market.

Not all the changes in the volume of migration to South Africa stem from developments within South Africa. Action on the part of the Governments of Malawi and Mozambique significantly reduced the

Table 5. Numbers of Africans from abroad employed, by country of origin, 1964, 1970, 1977 and 1979
(in thousands)

Country	1964[1]	1970	1977[2]	1979
Botswana, Lesotho and Swaziland	227	219	218	198
Malawi	101	107	36	36
Mozambique	121	145	76	62
Rhodesia (subsequently Zambia[3] and Zimbabwe)	22	12	24	22
Others	5	7	3	11
Total	476	490	357	327

[1] Figures for 1964 are from Leistner, 1967, but are corrected for his understatement of mining employment. [2] 1977 country figures are an estimate; the 1977 aggregate figure is official. Country figures for that year were obtained by adding the numbers employed in gold-mining by country to an estimate of non-gold-mining employment by country. The latter figures were obtained by assigning a non-gold-mining employment estimate to each country according to its proportion of total employment of Africans from abroad outside gold-mining in 1970. [3] Nil in 1970, 1977 and 1979.

Sources: Leistner, 1967, p. 49; Mine Labour Organisation: Annual reports, various issues; Republic of South Africa: House Assembly debates, 3–7 Apr. 1978, pp. 555–556, and 5–7 May 1980, p. 695; Department of Statistics: Population census, 1970 [02–05–01] (Pretoria, 1971).

number of migrants to South Africa from these countries and forced the gold-mining industry to look at its labour supply strategy. The result was what has been called the "internalisation" of mine labour supply.

Changes in the volume, sex composition and industrial distribution of Africans from abroad

Table 5 provides information on the numbers of Africans from abroad employed in South Africa since 1964. It is important to bear in mind that an unknown number of these Africans, especially from Botswana, Lesotho and Swaziland, are for all practical purposes permanent residents of South Africa.[4] Thus, the data give us pictures at various points in time of a labour supply which is partly comprised of a "stock", i.e. permanent residents, and partly comprised of a "flow", i.e. temporary migrants.

An inspection of the data in table 5 reveals a considerable decrease in the number of Africans from abroad finding employment in South Africa. Between mid-1964 and 1977 the drop was of the order of 120,000, or 25 per cent. However, these figures understate the impact of the decline on supplier countries. Using Botswana, Lesotho and Swaziland as an example, if we were to assume that the same *proportion* of the citizens of those countries who worked in South Africa in 1964 would have been free to work there in 1977, we could have expected 558,000 to be employed in South Africa, rather than 218,000.

Whereas the number of workers from Botswana, Lesotho and Swaziland in South Africa has declined since 1964, the figures for Malawi

Table 6.   Number and sex of migrants by country of origin, 1960 and 1970
(in thousands)

Country	1960			1970		
	Male	Female	Total	Male	Female	Total
Botswana, Lesotho, Swaziland	203.6	91.4	295.1	175.6	43.4	219.0
Malawi	60.9	1.4	62.3	106.6	0.1	106.7
Mozambique	157.0	5.2	162.2	142.8	2.1	144.9
Rhodesia (subsequently Zambia[1] and Zimbabwe)	31.5	2.2	33.7	11.1	0.6	11.7
Others	30.9	2.2	33.1	6.6	0.3	6.9
Total	483.9	102.4	586.4	442.7	46.5	489.2
Females as % of males	21.16			10.50		

[1] Included in 1960 figures only.
Sources: Department of Statistics: *Population census, 1960* (Pretoria, 1961); idem: *Population census, 1970,* op. cit.

show an increase between 1964 and 1970, followed by a significant decline. The growth and decline of Malawian, as well as Mozambican, employment is related to changes in these countries' contributions to gold-mining labour supplies and reflects causal factors different from those resulting in the Botswana, Lesotho, Swaziland reductions. These will be discussed separately.

In contrast with the trends in the employment of Africans from Botswana, Lesotho, Malawi, Mozambique and Swaziland, the number of workers coming from Southern Rhodesia (now Zimbabwe) shows an initial decline from 1964 to 1970 followed by an equal rise between 1970 and 1977. (The Zambian figures reflect a decision by President Kaunda in 1966 that Zambians were not to work in South Africa.) Combining all other countries, which are essentially Angola, Kenya, Namibia and Tanzania, we first see a small rise and then a decline in employment from 1964 to 1977.

To determine the number of workers from abroad one cannot use data on "foreign-born" Africans because of large discrepancies in numbers from various sources and because recent South African legislation has increasingly and almost wholly excluded the entry of dependants of these Africans. From July 1963 no women or families could be recruited from Botswana, Lesotho and Swaziland, nor accompany male recruits to South Africa (Breytenbach, 1972, p. 42). Neither, after 1966, could any domestic servants be recruited from these countries.

In 1960 a substantial proportion of "foreign-born" Africans must have been dependants of employed Africans from abroad. This would have certainly been the case for Botswana, Lesotho and Swaziland, whose citizens found it relatively easy to bring dependants to the locality of their work before the legislative changes of 1958–66. The 1960 census enumerated some 586,000 Africans born abroad; and yet, on the basis of reasonable assumptions, it is unlikely that more than 410,000 of these Africans were employed (see table 6),[5] since if this were so 30 per cent of "foreign-born" Africans would have been economically inactive. However, according to the 1970 census, only 7 per cent of "foreign-born" Africans were listed as not being economically active (Department of Statistics: *Population census, 1970* [02-05-01], Pretoria, 1971). The reduction in the number of dependants was one of the objectives of South African legislation during that period. The implications for welfare of prohibiting employees from abroad from bringing their families to the locality of their work need no elaboration.

Data on the sex of migrants since 1970 are not available. It is undoubtedly the case, however, that the forces which gave rise to the changes in the proportion of male and female migrants between 1960 and 1970 have continued to operate. It may be expected that up to the present there have been further absolute and relative declines in the number of African females migrating to South Africa.

Thus, not only has the number of migrants changed substantially during recent years but the composition of that migration by sex has been radically altered. In fact, it appears that women migrants have accounted for a very great proportion of the decline in the volume of migration to South Africa over this period.

Information on the industrial distribution of Africans from abroad is provided in table 7. The information clearly indicates a basic trend: the increasing concentration of these Africans in mining employment and the large decline in non-mining employment since 1964. Between 1964 and 1979 total employment of Africans from abroad decreased from 484,000 to 327,000, a decline of 32 per cent. However, during the same period non-mining employment decreased by 65 per cent. Thus, whereas in 1964 mining accounted for 58 per cent of the total employment of Africans from abroad, in 1979 it accounted for 78 per cent of the total.

Undoubtedly, mining has become the most important employer of African workers from abroad since 1964. In fact, South African mining, in general, relies heavily on them: in 1964, 51 per cent of all African miners were from abroad while in 1977 the figure was 45 per cent. With regard to the total non-agricultural African workforce, those from abroad accounted for 14 per cent of African employment in 1964 and 13 per cent in 1977.

Table 7. Sectoral distribution of African workers from abroad in South Africa, 1964, 1970, 1977–79
(in thousands)

Sector	1964	1970[1]	1977	1978	1979
Mining	281	352	288	258	255
affiliated to Chamber of Mines	231	267	208	.	.
non-affiliated mines and quarries	50	85	80	.	.
Agriculture	144	45	16	18	19
Manufacturing	23	12	10	10	10
Construction	4	6	9	8	8
Commerce	3	5	4	4	4
Government service	7	10	10	8	9
Domestic service	8	21	14	13	14
Other	14	4	6	7	8
Total	484	455	357	327	327
Mining as % of total	58	77	81	79	78
% change in non-mining since 1964		−49	−66	−66	−65

[1] The discrepancy in tables 5 and 7 between the 1970 data is accounted for by Africans from abroad listed in the 1970 census as "not economically active", "not specified" or "unemployed".

Sources: Leistner, 1967, p. 49; Mine Labour Organisation: *Annual reports*, 1964, 1970 and 1977; Republic of South Africa, *House Assembly debates*, 3–7 Apr. 1978, pp. 555–556; 7–11 May 1979, pp. 793–794 and 5–9 May 1980, pp. 694–695; Department of Statistics: *Population census, 1970*, op. cit.

Determinants of changing patterns of demand for Africans from abroad

There are essentially three substantive and, to a certain extent, inter-related determinants of the recent changes in the demand pattern. The first explanation is to be found in legislation which has fundamentally altered the legal status of Africans from abroad via-à-vis their employment in South Africa, particularly Africans from Botswana, Lesotho and Swaziland. Second, changing conditions in the South African Black labour market and changes within the South African "homelands" have reduced the need for South African industry to rely on African labour from abroad. Third, much of the change in the *volume* of migrant African employment was forced upon South Africa by actions on the supply side of the labour market by Malawi and Mozambique.

The impact of South African legislative changes

■ The changing legal status of migrants from Botswana, Lesotho and Swaziland: An alienation of historical rights

Until the 1960s there was practically no statutory difference between South African Africans and those from Botswana, Lesotho and Swaziland. All Africans from Botswana, Lesotho and Swaziland were subject to the same draconian laws controlling the movements of Blacks. So open were the borders between what were then the High Commission Territories and South Africa that it has been estimated that between 1911 and 1956 some 262,000 Basotho were permanently absorbed into South Africa (Leistner, 1967).

Before the mid-1960s unrecruited Africans from Botswana, Lesotho and Swaziland seeking work in South Africa either made their own way, obtaining the necessary documentation after they found employment, or registered with a district labour bureau in order to obtain a "pass" to seek employment.[6] Also, those who recruited Africans from these countries were not legally required to repatriate their recruits after the completion of their contract. As a result, many Africans from Botswana, Lesotho and Swaziland used the mines as an avenue to employment in the higher-paying industrial and tertiary sectors.

In 1958, probably as a result of the realisation by the Nationalist Party that the British Labour Party would not allow the incorporation of Botswana, Lesotho and Swaziland into South Africa as originally planned, Africans from these countries were declared prohibited immigrants. The Bantu Laws Amendment Act, 1963, prohibited Africans from these three territories from entering South Africa except for work in specified industries—essentially mining and agriculture. The Aliens Control Act, 1963 made it an offence for any such citizen to enter South Africa without a travel document issued by his own country, which meant that he could no longer obtain South African travel documents. (The deadline for the issuance of passport was, however, extended to 1966.) In addition to this legislation, from 1963 employers entering into service contracts with Africans from Botswana, Lesotho and Swaziland had to undertake their repatriation.

Thus, after 1963–66 the entry of Africans from Botswana, Lesotho and Swaziland into South Africa was severely circumscribed. This is not to say that much clandestine migration did not take place after this date; yet the effect of this legislation has been to reduce considerably the level of migration, to alter its composition by sex and to narrow its industrial diversity.

The South African census of 1960 estimated the number of Africans from Botswana, Lesotho and Swaziland residing in South Africa at 295,100 (table 6). This amounted to approximately 20 per cent of the estimated combined population of Botswana, Lesotho and Swaziland in 1960. However, in its report the Froneman Committee claimed that 431,000 Africans from these countries were in South Africa in 1960.[7] Thus, on the basis of the Froneman Committee's estimate, the percentage of the population from Botswana, Lesotho and Swaziland residing in South Africa in 1960 would have been about 28 per cent. In 1970 it was estimated that 219,000 Africans from these countries were in South Africa (table 6). As percentage of the combined 1970 population of the three countries, this amounted to about 11 per cent. If one were to presume that the same *proportion* of the combined workforce which migrated to South Africa in 1960 (based on the more believable Froneman Committee's estimates of migrant Africans in South Africa in that year) felt compelled and were free to migrate in 1970, the numbers of migrants enumerated in 1970 would have been 584,000. It seems fair to say that, without immigration restrictions, and given the progressively deteriorating rural conditions in Botswana, Swaziland and especially Lesotho during this time, the number of citizens of those countries who would have chosen migration would have certainly been at least 584,000 and probably much greater.

An inspection of the changes in Lesotho's rate of population growth between various censuses is also revealing in this regard. Between 1936 and 1956 population growth in Lesotho averaged 0.7 per cent per annum. Between 1956 and 1966 the average annual rate of growth was 2.9 per cent (IBRD, 1975). Although the usual caveat applies with regard to population data, the difference between these two growth rates is quite considerable. It can be deduced from this difference that between 1936 and 1956 considerable numbers of Basotho were permanently absorbed in South Africa. The large increase in population growth between 1956 and 1966 must in part be explained by South African "pass" legislation in 1952 and 1963 which made it more and more difficult for Africans from Botswana, Lesotho and Swaziland to settle in South Africa.

It would appear that the radical change in the status of Africans from Botswana, Lesotho and Swaziland as regards employment in South Africa, and the corresponding legislation controlling their movements, is at least partly responsible for the reduced numbers from those countries able to obtain employment in South Africa, as indicated in the tables.

■ Migration from Malawi and Mozambique before 1974: Business as usual

Citizens of Malawi and Mozambique have always been "prohibited immigrants". Consequently, they have never been permitted to seek work in South Africa on their own initiative. Employers of labour from these countries have always had to repatriate contracted workers upon completion of their contract, unless that contract was extended and the extension conformed to legislation regarding maximum length of stay.

In 1936 an agreement was concluded between the Government of Nyasaland (Malawi) and the Witwatersrand Native Labour Association (WNLA) under which WNLA was given permission to recruit labour for work in South African mines. At that time no other South African industry was allowed to recruit in Nyasaland. At first the agreement provided for an annual quota of 8,000 recruits on one-year contracts with an option to extend for six months. In 1946 the annual quota was increased to 12,750, and it continued to rise thereafter. By 1973 over 120,000 Malawians were employed on the gold-mines.

It is interesting to note that, whereas after 1963 Africans from Botswana, Lesotho and Swaziland were relegated to employment in "specified industries" (namely agriculture and mining), in 1967 Malawians were given the opportunity to enter a wide range of occupations.[8] The 1967 intergovernmental agreement aimed at increasing the employment of Malawians in various sectors of the South African economy, provided that a shortage of readily available indigenous labour existed. Whereas in 1960 virtually no Malawian found employment outside the mining industry, by 1970 23,200 Malawians, comprising 22 per cent of the number of Malawians working in South Africa, had done so. Yet, because of the supplementary character of migrant labour, and given the increasing unemployment in South Africa, this number has almost certainly declined since 1970.

One year after its formation in 1901, WNLA managed to obtain a monopoly from the Portuguese authorities for recruiting Mozambican Africans. The 1901 agreement was revised on numerous occasions and culminated in the Mozambique Convention of 1928. This specified a minimum level of recruitment of 65,000 Mozambicans per year and a maximum level of 100,000. In 1964 another agreement was concluded with the Portuguese authorities with regard to the recruitment of Mozambican labour by WNLA, which still remained the only South African body which could recruit in Mozambique (Breytenbach, 1972).

Before 1956 the recruitment of Mozambican labour was prohibited except for work in mines affiliated to the Chamber. However, from 1 July 1956 any South African employer (except employers in western Cape Province, manufacturing and domestic services) could use Mozambican labour; he could not, however, recruit that labour himself, and recruitment was undertaken by agents in Mozambique on his behalf. Although after 1956 the employment of Mozambican labour outside gold-mining became legal, it was not to have a positive impact on occupational diversity. Between 1960 and 1970 the number of Mozambicans employed outside gold-mining declined in both relative and absolute terms. In reality, the 1956 legislation affected only agricultural enterprises in border areas and legalised what had been going on for decades.

The legislation emanating from the Froneman Committee's recommendations has undoubtedly caused a severe short-run reduction in the current welfare of the labour-exporting countries. That reduction continues today and derives from two inter-related factors. First, with the 1963–66 legislation, the South African authorities began to apply strictly the principle of the "supplementary" nature of African labour from abroad. Second, unemployment among South African Blacks has been on the rise. The frequent sectoral labour shortages that had affected South Africa for many years are giving way to labour surpluses. As the Government accords a preference to South Africans, the implications for the labour-exporting countries of this growing labour surplus within South Africa are obvious.

Changing conditions in the South African labour market

In the preceding discussion the "supplementary" nature of migrant Africans was emphasised. In theory, local South African Blacks are given first preference for employment. Except for the Chamber of Mines, any firm wanting to employ Blacks from abroad has to seek approval from the relevant government labour office in South Africa. That office has to be satisfied that no South African worker is available before it will issue a "no objection" notice. Under these legal provisions it becomes apparent that conditions in the South African Black labour market have a bearing on the number and characteristics of African migrants. Let us now review those conditions.

■ Cyclical unemployment in South Africa and the demand for labour from abroad

After 1974 South Africa suffered from a recession lasting several years. Severe balance-of-payments difficulties (due in part to politically motivated capital flight) and continuing inflation have been met by conservative monetary and fiscal policy. These constraints reduced employment until the windfall gains from gold sales pulled the country out of its recession at the end of the decade. Under these circumstances one might have expected a rise in the rate of unemployment among South African Blacks, and both official statistics on unemployment and other independent studies of African unemployment do indeed present strong evidence of a rising rate of African unemployment during the second half of the 1970s. (The official estimates in the South African *Bulletin of Statistics* undoubtedly understate the level of Black unemployment. For recent attempts that try to estimate South African unemployment more accurately, see Simkins, 1976; Knight, 1976; and Knight and Loots, 1976.)

To some extent, the recession and its accompanying Black unemployment must be viewed as one factor underlying the decline in the volume of migration. Moreover, given that the mining companies are not subject to the "no objection" procedures of the labour bureaux, it becomes evident that this fact, combined with the implications of the recession for migration, to a large extent explains the recent narrowing of the occupational distribution of migrants.

■ Structural unemployment in South Africa and the demand
  for labour from abroad

It could be argued that if the African unemployment rate were brought down to its past average, as a result of a cyclical upswing, the demand for African workers from abroad would be revived. According to this line of reasoning, not only would the volume of employment of these Africans increase, but its occupational distribution and composition by sex could begin to reflect the migration patterns prevailing in the 1960s.

Such an argument implicitly assumes that rising African unemployment in South Africa during the 1970s is essentially short-run cyclical unemployment. It has been suggested, however, that the unemployment rate in South Africa has shown a secular rise. A proportion of the rises in the unemployment rate over recent years can be attributed to growing structural unemployment which will not be easily mitigated by short-run expansionary forces (see Simkins, 1976; Legassick, 1974; and more recently Clarke, 1977b).

Structural unemployment and underemployment have many sources. First and perhaps foremost, past legislation restricting African agricultural holdings to "homeland" areas and the removal of many Africans from "White" areas to the "homelands" in the 1960s (see Desmond, 1971) have greatly increased population/land and labour/land ratios in the "homelands". In view of the lack of development of "homeland" agriculture (which is itself a result of complex socio-politico-economic factors), the rising labour/land ratio has reduced agricultural productivity per head and has resulted in increases in the proportion of the African labour force finding it necessary to migrate in search of wage employment. This is a standard argument and is undoubtedly quite valid. Second (and this appears to have been disregarded in most studies related to this question), African conventional subsistence levels have risen considerably over the past few decades, above the levels necessary for the basic physiological requirements essential to "reproduce the labour supply". Africans have come to expect higher standards of living. But, given the manifest inability of the "homeland" agriculture to develop, this has necessitated a higher rate of migration. Third, rising wage rates in all sectors of the South African economy have increased the monetary rewards of migration while at the same time making owner-agriculture labour relatively less attractive. Such changes in the relative returns to time spent in wage employment and time spent in agriculture have undoubtedly exerted an upward pressure on the supply of labour wanting to take up wage employment.

The effect of these structural changes in the African labour market is to make the supply of African labour increase at a rate which exceeds the natural rate of increase in the labour supply.

There are also *structural* factors which have come to bear on the demand side of the labour market and which have operated in such a way as to reduce the rate of growth of demand for African labour. Essentially, these have resulted in increases in the capital/African labour ratio. First, the migrant labour system has not favoured the formation of the many types of skill needed in modern industry. The system has given rise to a relatively high rate of turnover of African employees and to extended periods of voluntary unemployment. In addition, the industrial colour bar has served to exclude Africans from access to many skilled occupations. This contrived shortage of skilled labour has impeded the development of skilled labour-intensive industries (e.g. machine-tool manufacturing, and engineering and fabrication) which could have increased the demand for labour. Second, the imperatives of modern manufacturing are such as to encourage the adoption of technologies and processes which maintain a uniform quality of product. This is often most easily achieved by mechanised production processes rather than labour-intensive, capital-saving processes. Third, South African industry has had to rely on imported technology purchased from countries whose factor endowments dictate relatively capital-intensive production processes. This reliance must, to some extent, be a result of South Africa's failure to develop its own alternative techniques, for the same reasons as those, outlined above, which prevented the development of skilled labour-intensive industries.

Thus, there has been and continues to be a combination of factors working on the demand and the supply side of the labour market to generate growing structural unemployment in South Africa. Given the supplementary nature of African labour from abroad, the declining demand for this labour in South Africa and the changes in its occupational distribution become understandable. Further, it becomes highly problematical whether future growth in labour demand will ever be sufficient to reverse the trend of decreasing demand for this labour.

Reductions in the supply of Malawian and Mozambican workers since 1974

We have been concentrating on developments inside South Africa which have resulted in a reduction in the demand for African labour from abroad. However, there have been considerable changes on the supply side of this labour market which have been imposed on South Africa from outside. These changes have altered both the volume and the source of labour supplies from abroad, and have affected the gold-mining industry in particular (see table 8).

In April 1974 a plane carrying Malawian recruits for the gold-mines crashed in Francistown (Botswana), killing 74 recruits. Life-President Banda of Malawi reacted by prohibiting any further South African

Table 8. Sources of African labour, by country of origin, employed at end of each year by affiliates of the Chamber of Mines, 1966–79 (in thousands)

Country	1966	1967	1968	1969	1970	1971	1972	1973	1974	1975	1976	1977[1]	1978	1979
Botswana	19.0	16.0	15.6	14.8	16.3	16.0	17.5	16.8	14.7	16.6	15.5	19.7	18.1	18.7
Lesotho	64.3	59.7	65.1	65.0	71.1	68.7	78.5	87.2	78.3	85.5	96.4	103.2	104.1	109.2
Swaziland	4.3	3.8	4.5	5.0	5.4	4.8	4.3	4.5	5.5	7.2	8.6	8.1	8.4	10.0
Malawi[2]	56.3	56.9	61.7	69.9	98.2	107.8	129.2	128.0	73.1	8.5	6.9	14.2	18.0	19.2
Mozambique	109.0	105.7	105.8	99.8	113.3	102.4	97.7	99.4	101.8	118.0	48.6	41.4	45.2	37.7
Southern Rhodesia (now Zimbabwe)	—	—	—	—	—	—	—	—	—	7.0	26.9	21.4	9.7	8.0
Total non-South African	252.8	242.2	252.7	254.6	304.2	299.7	327.2	335.9	273.4	242.9	202.8	208.0	205.4	204.3
South Africa	130.5	126.2	129.9	116.5	96.9	86.5	87.2	86.2	90.0	121.8	158.6	214.2	250.3	274.2
Over-all total	383.3	368.4	382.6	371.1	401.1	386.2	414.3	422.2	363.5	364.7	361.3	422.2	455.7	478.6

[1] Separate figures for Malawi and Southern Rhodesia (now Zimbabwe) not available for 1977. The figures are estimates.   [2] Malawian figures include a relatively small number of people recruited north of 22° S from countries other than Malawi—perhaps 10 per cent on average.

Sources: Mine Labour Organisation (WNLA): Annual reports, various issues; TEBA, Annual reports, various issues.

recruitment of Malawian labour. During the next two years practically all Malawians employed by the South African mines returned to their own country.

This sudden loss of a labour reserve which supplied the gold-mining industry with 25 per cent of its African labour had significant repercussions. At 31 December 1973 the gold-mining industry was employing 422,181 African workers. Such numbers permitted the industry to work at maximum capacity and, given the cost structure of the industry, most profitably. However, one year later the industry employed 364,658 African workers. Only by pulling substantial numbers off development work and putting them on to current production was the industry saved from very serious disruption and significant financial losses. Also, a significant increase of 65 per cent in the price of gold in 1974 certainly helped to compensate for the cost increases associated with decreased supply of labour. If the price of gold had remained at its 1973 level, the working profit per ton of ore milled would have been R 7.70 in 1974, compared with a 1973 working profit per ton of R 13.42. However, the large increase in gold prices in 1974 permitted working profit per ton in that year to be recorded at R 21.52 (Chamber of Mines: *Annual report, 1974*). The point to be emphasised is the significant contribution made by Malawian labour to the gold-mining industry by virtue of their large numbers. It took the gold-mining industry at least two years to fill the gap created by the withdrawal of Malawian workers.

The volume and origin of migrant labour in South Africa was similarly affected when, in 1974, Portugal relinquished Mozambique to the strongly socialist-oriented Mozambique Liberation Front (Frelimo). The export of labour to a country practising apartheid has been viewed by Frelimo as inconsistent with self-reliant socialist development, and consequently the policy adopted by the new Mozambique Government, together with the turmoil that followed the defeat of the Portuguese, have led to a reduction in the supply of labour from Mozambique to South Africa. As can be seen from table 8, after a short time-lag there was a radical drop in the number of Mozambicans taken on to work on the gold-mines. However, part of this reduction reflects a decreased demand by the Chamber of Mines for Mozambican workers. It seems readily apparent from the Chamber's action that it would not want to rely heavily on what it considers to be an insecure source of labour. Also contributing to the Chamber's reduced demand for Mozambican labour was the South African Government's decision in 1977 to make the individual mines (rather than the pooled resources of the Central Bank) responsible for the gold to be transferred to Mozambique to cover the deferred pay of Mozambican miners. This became an obvious disincentive for employing Mozambicans until the special gold agreement was ended altogether in 1977.

Implications of "internalisation" for suppliers of migrant labour

Background to "internalisation"

The action by Malawi on the "supply side" and the newly introduced uncertainty surrounding Mozambican supplies forced the Chamber of Mines to adopt a policy of "internalisation", i.e. to draw more and more of its workers from within South Africa. Admittedly, there had been a lengthy debate in the industry over this policy even before the 1974 changes. In the late 1960s the "rich" gold-mining groups, in particular the Anglo-Americans, were arguing for internalisation and the Black wage increases that were necessary to put such a policy into effect. The main reasoning behind their argument was that the industry's ever greater dependence on labour supplies from abroad could make it vulnerable. Of course, the reversal of this trend would require substantial African wage rises, given the very large differences between wage levels in the gold-mining and other sectors. The mines with relative low-grade ore hotly opposed wage increases because they saw their financial viability threatened thereby. However, the debate was to be resolved for the Chamber by a sequence of events such that any believer in divine intervention could only conclude that the gods were on the side of the gold-mining industry.

The considerable supply gap created by Malawi's action was not to be filled until well into 1976. The political uncertainty surrounding Mozambique placed great doubts in the Chamber's collective mind as to the reliability of future supplies from that country. Thus, the industry was virtually forced to recruit South African Blacks. The policy instrument it wielded to this end was, of course, wage increases (see table 3). Nominal African earnings (annual averages) quadrupled and real earnings trebled over the 1972 figures. What permitted the industry to impose upon itself such large increases in production costs, which had been so strenuously opposed several years earlier? Quite simply, incredibly large rises in the price of gold (see table 9). The price per fine ounce climbed from less than R 40 in 1972 to well over R 100 in the middle of the decade, and rose still higher subsequently. This pushed up profits per African employee from R 1,485 in 1972 to R 3,000–4,000 in later years, even taking into account the large rises in African wages over the same period (see table 10).

It is interesting to note that the wage increases up to 1974 were associated with virtually no increase in the number of South African Blacks taking up mine employment. Reflecting on this fact in the light of the Malawi-Mozambique supply reductions, the Chamber must have been in a quandary. Again, however, events were to occur which were to "bail out" the gold-mining industry. The continuing recession in South Africa was now accompanied by growing Black unemployment. This unemployment was beginning to do for the gold-mining industry

Table 9.   Price of gold, 1970–78

Year	Cost per fine oz. (rands)	Change in price over previous year (%)
1970	25.80	−4
1971	28.60	+11
1972	39.70	+39
1973	65.10	+64
1974	107.40	+65
1975	111.62	+4
1976	103.77	−7
1977	125.10	+21
1978	168.90	+35

Source: Chamber of Mines: *Annual reports*, various issues.

what the 1972–74 wage increase could not—that is, increase the number of South African Blacks taking up the least desired occupation in South Africa: gold-mining. This situation is continuing, in spite of the very much smaller increase in wages since 1976 (table 3). According to *The Star*, "the mining industry is experiencing 'an almost embarrassing flood' of Black workseekers owing to rising unemployment" (18 Mar. 1978). The paper reports the Chamber as saying: "It is obvious that this oversupply of labour can mainly be attributed to the current economic recession in South Africa which has led to growing unemployment and a shortage of job opportunities in most sectors."

"Internalisation" and the changing origin of migrant labour

The impact of the Chamber's "internalisation" policy on the number and origin of African workers from abroad employed in South Africa reflects the forced character of that process. As can be seen from table 8, the number of migrant African workers employed by affiliates of the Chamber declined sharply over the years 1973–77, from 335,900 to 203,500. Predictably, the countries bearing the brunt of this reduction were Malawi and Mozambique. Between December 1973 and December 1975 the decline in the number of Malawians was approximately 120,000. Fortunately for the Chamber, the decline in the number of Mozambican workers did not coincide with the Malawians' withdrawal; otherwise, the gap in the supply indicated by the fall in total employment from 422,200 in December 1973 to 363,500 one year later would have been even greater, adversely affecting profit rates in the industry. In fact, the reduction in the number of migrants from Mozambique did not commence until 1976. Whereas at 31 December 1975 there were 118,030 Mozambicans

Table 10. Tons of ore milled, working profit per ton, profit per African employee, and total working profits in gold-mining, 1966–78

Year	Ton milled per African employee[1]	Working profit per ton (rands)	Profit per African employee[2] (rands)	Total working profit (R '000)
(1)	(2)	(3)	(4)	(5)
1966	202.3	4.51	912.37	338 044
1971	207.4	4.48	929.15	352 353
1972	199.0	7.46	1 484.54	546 296
1973	197.1	13.42	2 645.08	1 020 970
1974	211.6	21.52	4 553.63	1 636 874
1975	225.3	17.74	3 996.82	1 332 600
1976	218.1	12.23	2 667.36	952 528
1977	197.2	18.62	3 671.86	1 387 800
1978[3]	185.0	22.50	4 162.50	1 750 000

[1] Separate figures on tons milled, average number of African employees and average annual earnings obtained from source below. [2] Calculated by multiplying (2) × (3); see also note 2 to table 11. [3] Estimates based on data for the first half of 1978. Given the continuing rise in the price of gold, it is most likely that profits for the full year will be well in excess of R 2,000 million and profits per African employee in excess of R 4,750.

Source: Mine Labour Organisation: *Annual reports*, various issues; *Financial Mail* (Johannesburg), various issues.

employed in the mines, at 30 June 1976 they numbered 72,315, and by the end of 1976 the number had fallen to 48,565.

The decline in labour supplies from Malawi and Mozambique has been offset, to some extent, by increased labour movements from Botswana, Lesotho and Swaziland. In 1973 these countries supplied a combined total of 108,500 workers. By April 1977 that figure stood at 136,600. Another source of labour to fill the supply gap created by Malawi and Mozambique was Southern Rhodesia (now Zimbabwe). By agreement, before 1975 the Chamber had not been allowed to recruit labour from that country. In 1975 this position was reversed, with a consequent rapid increase in the number of Africans from that country (see Clarke, 1978).

It should be noted that in 1977 the Chamber arrived at an agreement with the Malawian Government which permitted it once again to obtain labour supplies from Malawi (Böhning, 1977, p. 63). It was reported that at the end of 1977 some 17,600 men from Malawi were employed in the mines. It is expected that this figure will stabilise for some time at around 20,000 (Clarke, 1977a, p. 24).

Likely future developments

Given that the gold-mining industry is at present by far the largest employer of African labour from abroad, the current welfare of the labour-exporting countries is inextricably bound up with the

Table 11. Total net wastage,[1] average number of Africans employed by members of the Chamber of Mines,[2] and net wastage as a proportion of average number employed, 1971–79

Year	"Net wastage"	Average number employed	Wastage/employment
1971	330 591	406 066	0.814
1972	337 862	411 192	0.822
1973	354 708	435 671	0.814
1974	387 170	414 232	0.935
1975	472 135	385 160	1.226
1976	562 036	409 134	1.374
1977	584 684	435 024	1.344
1978	498 106	451 018	1.104
1979	437 390	468 776	0.933

[1] Net wastage is the sum of workers discharged after completing their contract, medical rejects, absconders, and those who died.   [2] The number employed by the Chamber of Mines is slightly higher than the number employed by the gold-mining companies who are its members.

Sources: Mine Labour Organisation (WNLA): *Annual reports*, various issues; TEBA: *Annual reports*, various issues.

"internalisation" policy of the Chamber of Mines. Two questions which loom large are, first, how far does the Chamber intend to pursue this policy; and second, over what length of time will it do so?

The Chamber is on record as assigning itself a 50 per cent "internalisation" target (Clarke, 1977a, p. 24). This target was decided upon early in 1976 and was attained by the first quarter of 1977. One year later, about 53 per cent of the 421,000 Africans employed on the mines were from within South Africa (including the Transkei and Bophuthatswana "homelands") (*Financial Mail*, 28 July 1978, mining survey supplement). At the same time it was claimed that the mines were turning away "considerable numbers" of Black workseekers (*The Star*, 18 Mar. 1978).

If the Chamber is in fact turning away "fit" South African Blacks, this has several implications for the future. First, the Chamber must be turning away South African "novices" in favour of experienced miners from abroad.[9] Hence, it might be argued that the Chamber has gone as far as it intends to do *in the short term*: that is to say, it no longer intends to replace experienced miners from abroad with novice South Africans. This strategy makes economic sense in the light of the dislocations and inefficiencies suffered by the industry during the period of rapid "internalisation" between 1975 and 1976. During this period the turnover of African labour rose dramatically (see table 11). Specifically, this was a reflection of shorter contracts, many more broken contracts and higher numbers of medical rejects. In general, it was a reflection of a less stable labour supply which revealed itself in a fall in efficiency and hence a rise in costs. Thus, for the next few years at least, the present level of demand for migrant African labour is likely to remain steady.

Second, given the oversupply of novices in South Africa, it is most likely that the Chamber, as stated, will give them preference over novices from elsewhere. Hence, as experienced migrant mineworkers retire they will be replaced by South African novices. Without an exceptionally strong and extended economic recovery in South Africa, it is unlikely that the level of demand for migrant labour will ever return to the level it had reached before "internalisation".

In addition to substituting local for migrant workers, the gold-mining industry is attempting to mechanise production, thus reducing its over-all demand for labour. According to the President of the Chamber of Mines in 1975:

A programme of research and development with emphasis on the mechanisation of gold-mining was begun in July 1974, a few months after the air accident (in which 74 Malawian mineworkers were killed) when it began to look as if this event might cut off Malawi as a source of labour, and at a time when events in Portugal and Mozambique made it clear that in the long term the industry might not be able to rely so heavily on foreign labour. Future expansion will require an increased labour force and the Chamber of Mines is doing all in its power to develop new recruitment areas and to safeguard the regularity and volume of labour supply from existing recruitment areas. However, it is clear that a reduction in labour dependency will be in the best interests of the gold-mining industry (Schumann, 1975, p. 4).

If the industry is successful in mechanising certain aspects of the production process, labour will most likely be displaced. One might speculate that workers from abroad would most probably be the first to find that they could not obtain further contracts on the gold-mines, in spite of the fact that the greater skill requirements that tend to go with mechanisation (Bardill et al., 1977) might favour them.

Finally, these developments must be viewed in the light of a projected incipient decline in gold production beginning in 1980. It is estimated that employment in the industry will fall to 148,000 by the year 2000 (Bromberger, 1978). Estimates of future employment in other sectors of the mining industry leave little hope that their expansion would be sufficient to maintain even current levels of demand for African labour from abroad.

Evidence also indicates that commercial agriculture, once a major employer of migrant African workers, reached its employment peak at the end of the 1960s. As a result of mechanisation and other changes, employment in that industry will decline. It is possible, but not likely, that opportunities for migrants will spring up elsewhere in the meantime.

Thus, the prospects for increased labour exports are dismal, and it is most probable that the demand for labour from outside South Africa will decline. However, some countries may be subjected to greater export reductions than others. The distribution of the industry's demand across supplier States is not easily clarified. It will be influenced by political factors as well as variations in recruitment costs.

Conclusions

We have attempted to explain recent substantive changes in international migration patterns within southern Africa and to explore the implication of those changes for future migration. Abstracting from the action by Malawi and Mozambique on the supply side, it is abundantly evident that recent developments in South Africa have been responsible for the much decreased demand for migrant workers in South Africa, as well as substantial changes in the proportion of male and female migrants and their occupational diversity. These changes can be attributed to, first, growing cyclical and structural unemployment in South Africa; and second, legislative changes which have increasingly and effectively relegated the Black worker from abroad to the position of being a labour supply supplementary to the South African Black labour force. Given the structural nature of an increasing amount of South African Black unemployment and declining future employment prospects in primary industries, it is unlikely that the demand for migrant African labour will return to past levels. In fact, assuming that the supplier States can do nothing to control the future demand for their labour, that demand will most probably continue to subside.

What are the implications of these past and probable future changes in the South African labour market for the supplier States? The governments of those supplier States have little choice but to design and implement development strategies to generate many more employment opportunities at home, both urban and rural. Total commitment to comprehensive development has become imperative.

Much can be done to generate local employment opportunities in the present supplier States. Agriculture can be diversified through the introduction of more labour-intensive crops of high nutritional value with large yields per hectare. Crops can be introduced which have forward linkages in terms of processing. Animal products such as wool, mohair and hides can be locally processed and transformed into final consumer products. For example, the Botswana and Lesotho weavers produce beautiful mohair and wool carpets and weavings, and yet they import all their wool and mohair from South Africa. Although Botswana slaughters hundreds of thousands of cattle each year, there is no factory to process the valuable hides. Leather for Botswana's growing leather handicrafts industry is imported from South Africa. Many workers can be productively employed on infrastructural projects in towns and villages. In Botswana much land is not utilised and virtually all is under-utilised. Many workers could be productively employed clearing thorn-bush and other scrub from potentially productive land. Hills in Lesotho's village areas, which are at present considered unsuitable for growing traditional crops, could be terraced with the many rocks to be found in the fertile soil, and these terraces could undoubtedly support vines, fruit-trees or even olive-trees, the oil of which could be processed locally. The many streams and rivers in Lesotho could be dammed to provide reserve water for the irrigation of vines and fruit-trees in periods of drought. Fish could be planted and harvested in such reservoirs.

Imagination and initiative can lead to the creation of innumerable small and large projects which could pay for themselves and employ much labour in setting them up and maintaining them. However, this is not to say that governments should be the national employer of tens of thousands of wage labourers working on projects which the workers cannot envisage as being of longer-run benefit to themselves. Plans and projects must be decided upon at the village level. People must see that improvements in their living conditions are a direct result of decisions which they make individually and collectively. The governments must assume the role of a provider of information about projects which can be carried out and how they can be carried out. Yet information should flow both ways. The village should be able to tell the Government what it thinks needs to be done and how it should be done.

Much can be achieved within the existing institutional structures. Still more can be achieved where these structures can be improved. Land tenure systems must become more flexible to permit the communal development of certain types of crop, e.g. fruit-trees and vine products, with future individual rewards being based on current investments of labour time and future labour inputs into cultivation. The functional allocation of currently communal grazing lands, as well as the maximum number of cattle per household, should be decided by the village. Individuals should be permitted to withhold their personal land from communal winter grazing if they intend to crop it, and to fence their land if the household undertaking the fencing reduces its cattle holding to compensate for the loss of communal winter grazing.

In short, with the loss of the "safety valve" represented by the export of labour, the governments of the present labour-supplying countries must implement an effective development strategy aimed at satisfying the basic needs of their citizens. In particular, this will mean pursuing a development strategy that will benefit the broad mass of the population. That, in turn, implies broad-based rural development.

Notes

[1] In addition to absorbing huge quantities of labour, the industry also attracted very large amounts of capital to South Africa. Foreign investment stemmed mainly from the United Kingdom, with some coming also from France and Germany. Between 1887 and 1932 the industry absorbed over R 296 million (Frankel, 1969, pp. 88–89). The importance of foreign capital in the development of the mining industry is highlighted by the fact that, over the same period, roughly 75 per cent of the dividends paid by the gold-mining industry went to overseas investors.

[2] Normally, a monopsonist must pay a higher wage to attract more workers. But the Chamber could now use the additional choice variable of size of recruitment area in its quest for the optimum amount of labour. Under normal circumstances it would have had to increase wages continually in order to attract workers living further and further away from its location. However, by paying for the worker's travel the Chamber could exercise its power with respect to price discrimination. Workers residing further away could receive the same wage as those nearer the gold-mines but, implicitly, would receive a higher subsidy to offset the expense of travelling further.

[3] It should be noted that the failure of the Reserves to develop agriculturally is not purely a reflection of increasing population pressures in combination with customary land tenure systems. One of the principal reasons for their failure to develop was their inability to compete with heavily subsidised White farmers. Lesotho, a long-term exporter of labour to the mines, also suffered from the subsidised development of White agriculture. Before the aided development of White agriculture, that country was a net exporter of grain. With a loss of its comparative advantage, but with a continued need for cash, it had to rely more and more on migrant labour. In Swaziland and Botswana the virtual confiscation of prime agricultural land also reduced the ability of the peasantry to satisfy conventional subsistence requirements through agricultural production.

[4] For purposes of simplification, data on migration from Botswana, Lesotho and Swaziland have been combined. As our chapter unfolds it will become evident that treating them jointly or separately does not alter the analysis or conclusions.

[5] On 30 June 1964 the total number of Africans from abroad employed in South Africa was 497,000. Hence the implicit assumption is that the increase in the employment of these Africans from 1960 to 1964 was around 5 per cent per year. Given the rapid increase in the number of South African Blacks employed over this period and the fact that controls over Botswana, Lesotho and Swazi Africans were not really consolidated until 1963–66, this would appear to be a defensible estimate.

[6] After 1952 Africans from abroad, like local Africans, found their movement into employment in urban areas circumscribed by strict enforcement of urban influx control legislation. After this time labour bureaux were set up and Africans from Botswana, Lesotho and Swaziland, as well as local Africans, had to obtain permits from district or local labour bureaux to seek work in urban or proclaimed areas. The legislation giving rise to further "influx control" was the Abolition of Passes and Co-ordination of Documents Act, 1952.

[7] The Froneman Committee believed that the discrepancy between its estimates and those of the census was due to Africans from abroad concealing their true origins during the 1960 census. The Committee "pointed out that urban influx control regulations became applicable to Africans from the High Commission Territories for the first time after 1952 and that this could have prompted many foreign Africans to conceal their identity out of fear that the system would be extended to rural areas" (see Owen, 1964, p. 5).

[8] *Agreement between the Government of Malawi and South Africa relating to the Employment and Documentation of Malawian Nationals in South Africa, May 10, 1967.* The agreement came into effect on 1 Oct. 1967 (Breytenbach, 1972).

[9] Indeed, as the General Manager of the Chamber's recruitment arm revealed in March 1977, "We (are) filling all vacancies for novices with South Africans and Transkeians while restricting foreign recruitment to the experienced men who have served the industry loyally in the past" (*The Star*, 18 Mar. 1977). The *Financial Mail* announced "bad news for foreign miners" on 10 June 1977, in a report based on an interview with the General Manager of the Mine Labour Organisation (MLO) and other MLO personnel, and also declared that "novices are no longer being recruited from neighbouring countries".

LABOUR MIGRATION IN SWAZILAND

F. de Vletter, in collaboration with M. H. Doran,
A. R. C. Low, F. D. Prinz and B. D. Rosen-Prinz

3

The impact and cause of migration in southern Africa have long been a subject of political and academic contention, but interest has largely been limited to those regions where the flows and effects have been most apparent. Trends in labour-supplying countries such as Swaziland have thus been overshadowed by those in countries where migration was the result of severe economic deprivation or blatant political artifice. Conclusions for the more extreme cases have often been conveniently applied to Swaziland also. Such conclusions are perhaps suitable for highlighting generic issues such as human rights and other moral issues; but they are dangerously misleading for country-specific recommendations. Swaziland, with a comparatively diversified and developed economic base and little evidence of serious population pressure, has options or opportunity costs of migration that are different from those of, say, Lesotho. And because of the lack of extremes in Swaziland—whether obvious underdevelopment, exploitation or conscious political collusion—the "natural" motives to migrate from the subsistence base may be better understood.

In spite of its prevalence, very little has been written about migration in Swaziland apart from the odd sociological and demographic commentary. Thus, in contrast with the picture in Lesotho—a magnet of migration research—there is little supporting literature, and virtually all the findings presented in this chapter are based on working papers emanating from the ILO/UNFPA project initiated in October 1976.

Owing to the paucity and unreliability of most of the available secondary data relating to migration, under this project several small-scale surveys were undertaken covering rural homesteads, outgoing and returning migrants working on the South African mines, Swaziland-based employers as well as workers, and secondary school students (for details see de Vletter, 1978; Rosen-Prinz and Prinz, 1978; also tables 14,

15, and 16). A survey of gold-mines was also undertaken (de Vletter, 1980) and this forms the basis of Chapter 4.

GENERAL CHARACTERISTICS OF SWAZILAND

The Kingdom of Swaziland, distinctly dual in economic structure, is also dual in government. It is administered by the State Council of Ministers and the traditional National Council (Libandla), with guidance from King Sobhuza II.[1] Policies have been conservative: ostensibly non-aligned and wedged between the diametrically opposed regimes of Mozambique and South Africa, Swaziland remains wary of the former and discreetly critical of apartheid, while cautious of disturbing its important economic bonds with South Africa. With its need to reduce its economic dependence on South Africa and for political reasons also, Swaziland enjoys an inflow of Western aid that could well place it among the countries receiving the most aid per head—and this in spite of its rapid growth through its relatively diversified economy and one of the healthiest trade balances in the developing world.

The smallest country of the region (about 17,000 square kilometres in area) with a population of only some 500,000, Swaziland has developed a sound economy, growing at a rate of about 12 per cent during the 1950s and 1960s in money terms, with a real growth of approximately 7 per cent during the 1970s, lately dropping to a little more than 3 per cent. Although the economy is reasonably diversified with sizeable contributions from sugar, forestry, mining, citrus and pineapple crops, manufacturing, tourism, cattle-ranching and other agricultural activities, it is showing signs of becoming highly dependent on the sugar industry, with the accompanying vicissitudes of a monocrop economy. The sugar industry directly employs 8,000 workers and is responsible for about 45 per cent of exports; the establishment of a third sugar-mill, which was expected to begin production in 1980, is expected to increase production by 80 per cent and employ a further 2,000 workers. Agriculture contributes about 30 per cent of GDP; the manufacturing sector has grown rapidly and now accounts for 22 per cent of GDP; while mining, having recently exhausted the reserves of high-grade iron ore, exports substantial quantities of asbestos and will be soon bolstered by the opening of large, rich coalfields.

Nevertheless, the economy suffers from some serious distortions. The JASPA Employment Advisory Mission, in its report (ILO/JASPA, 1977), mentions a highly skewed income distribution at three different levels: between rural, urban and expatriate populations. About 90 per cent of the population derive all or part of their livelihood from rural activities. Most of these live on what is known as Swazi Nation Land, which comprises about half Swaziland's total area; the remaining half is individual tenure land originally acquired under usufruct concessions during the 1890s but later appropriated as freehold land. Although much of the individual tenure land "owned" by absentees lies fallow, 90 per cent of the agricultural exports are produced from expatriate-controlled land. Estimates of real rural income growth over the past ten years range from negative to marginally above stagnation. Even with the assumed success of the Rural Development Areas (RDAs), real growth is unlikely to exceed 3 per cent. It is estimated that about 20 per cent of the land is arable, compared with 6 per cent and 15 per cent in Lesotho and Botswana respectively.

At the current real growth rate of the economy of 3 per cent, it has been forecast that, at best, only 1,700 of the 7,000 annual new entrants to the labour force will be absorbed by domestic wage employment. Up to 1977 labour shortages in lower-wage industries were common and great reliance was placed on imported labour, mainly from Mozambique. Recently, however, there have been indications of a serious labour surplus and open unemployment, aggravated by newly imposed restrictions by the South African gold-mines and the rapidly increasing numbers of school leavers unable to find employment. Because of former labour shortages and fiscal policies encouraging capital accumulation, capital/labour ratios are unduly high, resulting in technology incongruous with intrinsic factor endowments.

Swaziland's geographical position has inevitably engendered both institutional and economic dependence on South Africa. As a signatory to the Southern African Customs Union Agreement and the Rand Monetary Agreement, its trade and financial flows are virtually unrestricted. Approximately 90 per cent of Swaziland's imports originate or pass through South Africa, while South Africa absorbs 25 per cent of Swaziland's exports. Furthermore, as a member of the Customs Union, the Swaziland Government derived 62 per cent of its recurrent revenue therefrom in 1978/79. Through the Monetary Authority of Swaziland, some degree of monetary independence is exerted but the national currency is backed 100 per cent by the Rand—thus precluding fiduciary issue and subjecting foreign exchange rates to the movement of the Rand. Surplus institutional funds and government reserves are invested mainly in South Africa, while substantial industrial investments in Swaziland come from South Africa.

South Africa, until recently, has always provided a safety-valve outlet for the potentially unemployed through allowing access to job opportunities in the Republic—particularly the gold-mines where employment was guaranteed for those meeting the health and age requirements. Although there was a dramatic response to the 1974 wage increases in the mines, the importance of external migration has been decreasing. Approximately 40 per cent of the males in the 19–59 age-group are employed in the domestic economy and only 17 per cent work in South Africa, whereas in Lesotho 10 per cent of the same age-group are domestically employed and more than half work in South Africa.

EVOLUTION OF LABOUR MIGRATION IN SWAZILAND

Early migrant labour movements have been poorly chronicled. Important occurrences around the turn of the century influenced subsequent migration flows. Up to about 1894 the inhabitants were able to provide for their own food requirements, but in 1897 rinderpest decimated the Swazi cattle-herds and disrupted the rural economy. In the following year a substantial poll tax of £2 per adult male and 10 shillings per wife was imposed by the South African administration; however, because of the severe impact of rinderpest, the collection date was postponed, while the Boer Government specifically indicated that employment on the mines was available for earning the necessary cash. This conflicted with the attempts of King Ngwane V to retain his men, who were needed for military purposes and to replace lost draught animals in the production of subsistence crops. He was only partly successful in this, because there continued to be a fair outflow of men, mostly to the neighbouring Barbeton gold-mines.

Although an attempt was made during the 1890s to obtain recruiting rights, migration did not become institutionalised until 1912, with the formation of the Native Recruiting Corporation (NRC) and the enactment of the Native Labour Regulation Proclamation, 1913. External migration was disrupted during the South African War of 1899–1902 but, in its wake, Lobotsibeni the Queen Regent changed the previous regal attitude and actively encouraged Swazis to seek work on the Transvaal mines in her campaign to accumulate funds for the purchase of land from concessionnaires.

Following the War, the British Government reluctantly accepted responsibility for Swaziland and subsequently administered it with apathy, expecting its incorporation into the Union of South Africa to be imminent. "Government of the country was based on good administration rather than economic development and 70 per cent of the budget in 1913–14 was allocated to items such as police and the payment of Bantu chiefs" (Leistner and Smit, 1969, p. 2). Very little development occurred up to 1939, partly as a result of colonial neglect and partly because of the

First World War and of the depression that followed it.

At the turn of the century economic activity was virtually limited to the operations of a few European stock-farmers and traders. Before 1940 exports, consisting of small quantities of gold, tin, cotton and tobacco, never exceeded R 450,000 in value.[2] Not surprisingly, economic stagnation transformed Swaziland, as well as the other High Commission Territories and Mozambique, into "dormitory territories"—the original frontier reserves of cheap labour for the South African mining industry. Denoon (1972) points out that the colonial labour reserve policy required no capital investment to absorb labour nor any hard thinking about internal development policy, yet provided revenue for administration. Although the High Commission Territories were never incorporated into the Union, their nationals were subject to the same laws governing mobility as were South African Blacks; not surprisingly, Swazis working in South Africa far exceeded those domestically employed (see table 12).

Kuper (1947, p. 4) noted that "annual reports issued by the Colonial Office since 1908 stress the extent to which the Swazi are dependent on money wages earned primarily in industry". Not only was cash required for poll taxes, but also most peasants were forced to supplement their subsistence produce with food purchases from traders because, for the period from 1930 to 1934, only about one-fifth of the population's food requirements were grown domestically (in contrast, Lesotho had been a net exporter of maize until about 1930).

Traders, controlling virtually all the recruitment of Swazis for the gold-mines until the establishment of the first NRC office in 1928, enjoyed a dual benefit from the increasingly pervasive influence of the cash economy. The causation was ideal: having acquired recruiting licences for a nominal sum, they provided customers who had been given substantial credits with the means of repayment through employment on the mines, whilst simultaneously earning £1 10s–£2 per recruit. Traders in Swaziland recruited for the NRC not only Swazis but also a substantial number of immigrant Mozambicans seeking employment, and they continued recruitment until the early 1950s.

Irrespective of the need to acquire cash and the very low labour-absorptive capacity of the economy, external migration nevertheless had an inherent element of choice. Judging by the complaints of labour shortages of European farmers during the 1930s, many Swazis had shown a preference for work on the mines. Choice notwithstanding, many writers, referring to Labour Reserves with limited employment opportunities, often emphasise the monopsonistic power of the gold-mining industry by correctly pointing out that mine wages were less than

Table 12. Demographic data relating to external migration from Swaziland and South African census results

Year	Swaziland censuses							South African censuses		
	de jure African population	Absentees	Absentees		Absentees as % of population	Domestic employment	Absentees as % of domestic employment	Absentees[4]	Absentees	
			Male	Female					Male	Female
1911	104 533	5 800[1]	5 700	100	5.6	—	—	—	—	—
1921	110 295	5 990	5 839	151	5.43	3 094	193.6	29 177	17 285	11 892
1936	153 270	9 561	9 451	235	6.23	3 354	285.1	31 092	21 311	9 781
1946	181 269	8 677	8 254	423	4.78	4 835	179.5	33 738	21 768	11 970
1956	229 744	11 728	10 569	1 159	5.10	13 404	87.5	42 914[5]	26 721	16 193
1966	381 687	19 219	12 817	6 402	5.03	60 116 (36 815)[2]	32.0 (52.2)	38 892[6]	23 402	15 490
1976	520 184	25 650	18 903	6 747	4.93	108 237[3]	23.7	.	.	.

[1] The 1966 census gives a figure of 8,500 for "estimated" absentees, whereas the official 1921 census figure is 5,800. [2] According to the Manpower Information Unit, employment in Swaziland at December 1966 was 36,815, as against 60,116 in the 1966 census. [3] This figure includes those categorised as "self-employed", "irregular employees" and "full-time employees" in the 1976 census. [4] "Absentees" in this table refers to Swazi nationals present in South Africa at the time of enumeration. [5] 1951. [6] 1960.

the cost of reproduction. Kuper (1947, p. 20) observed: "Mine wages average £3 per month in cash, plus food and lodging in a compound. This wage is manifestly impossible for maintaining a family in town where in 1938 £6–£8 was estimated by different workers as an essential minimum wage for a Native man, his wife and three children; but £3 is considered enough to *subsidise* (my emphasis) the production from the land!" Regardless of how exploitive mine wages may have been, however, they still compared favourably with domestic wage rates.[3]

A further prominent, but perhaps overemphasised, factor influencing migration to the mines is the sociological importance for men to have worked at least once on the mines as a prerequisite for manhood (Schapera, 1947). External migration had undoubtedly made a strong impact on the life-style of the Swazi, causing Kuper (1947, p. 22) to speculate: "Nearly every Swazi male adult has been to Johannesburg or to one of the eight large Reef towns which depend primarily on the mines in the vicinity. *Egoli* (the Place of Gold) is better known to a number of Swazi than their own royal villages."

Many Swazis worked on the mines once only; but officials from The Employment Bureau of Africa (TEBA) claim that there has always been a hard core of Swazi career miners who often spend 15 years or more on the mines, while many others regularly took advantage of the deferred pay contract[4] to accumulate cash for specific purposes, particularly during bad crop years. Unlike their Zulu neighbours, Swazis reputedly took to mine work rapidly, showing a strong predilection for "machine boy" work.[5] They often also used the mines as a stepping-stone to industrial work in the urban centres on completion of their contract (Wilson, 1972a); but after 1948, with the introduction of influx controls, sectoral transfers of this kind were not possible. Regularity of return was underscored by the fact that novices recruited annually accounted for only 10–15 per cent of total recruits for most years before 1960 (Parsons, 1977).

From 1939 onwards asbestos mined at Havelock was a most valuable export product. Further stimulus to the economy came from the development introduced by the postwar colonial administration.[6] Employment opportunities grew at a continued rapid pace with the establishment of some of the largest man-made forests, sawmills and a pulp mill during the 1940s, sugar and citrus plantations in the 1950s and 1960s, and an iron ore mine in 1964. Secondary industries consequently registered impressive growth.

Nevertheless, in spite of this rapid expansion, many Swazis still preferred to work in South Africa either through habit or because of higher wages. This led to shortages of labour and resulted in substantial numbers of Black workers from outside Swaziland being imported. These workers either filled positions spurned by Swazis as being too hard and low-paying (such as cane-cutting) or were employed where Swazis were insufficiently trained (mainly in supervisory positions on the mines). Commenting on the prevalence of immigrant workers, Leistner and Smit (1969, p. 45) noted: "About 60 per cent of 4,166 non-local Black workers employed in December 1966 by establishments with ten or more workers were engaged in agriculture and forestry. . . . Non-local Black workers represented 20 to 22 per cent of all Black Africans employed by private firms with more than 50 workers during the years 1962 to 1964." Humphreys and McClelland (1964, p. 312), in attempting to detect any noticeable difference between immigrant and local contracts, found that: "No definite tendency is discernible for immigrant labour to be better or worse paid than local Swazi labour." There was also no apparent difference in the average length of contracts.

As noted earlier, Blacks from outside South Africa were subject to the same controls as South African Blacks. However, beginning in 1963, the South African Government began establishing controlled entry points for migrants and required would-be Basotho, Swazi and Botswana migrants to hold passports rather than reference books. These controls had a major impact on the number and composition of workers from abroad in South Africa: over the period 1960–70 the number of workers from Botswana, Lesotho and Swaziland fell by about one-third (see also Chapter 2). From 1946 to 1970 the effect of influx controls sharply reduced the number of women; at the same time, although the over-all number of men remained fairly constant, the number working on the gold-mines rose by some 70 per cent.

The number of Swazi mine recruits over the period 1936–74 remained remarkably stable (see figure 3 in de Vletter, 1978). However, late in 1974 major disruptions, precipitated by the withdrawal of Malawian labour as well as earlier labour unrest, led to a series of substantial wage increases by the gold-mines, following which the number of Swazi recruits doubled over a period of two years. There was similar response from the Transkei as well as Botswana and Lesotho, to the extent that, by early 1977 and again in 1978, restrictions were imposed on those recruits not in possession of re-engagement certificates, with a consequent fall in recruitment of Swazis in 1977.

Current labour migration to South Africa falls under the legislation of the 1975 Labour Agreement between Swaziland and South Africa, which provided for the appointment of a resident labour representative whose general function is to cater for the interests of Swazi migrant workers in South Africa. The agreement underscores South Africa's stronger bargaining position, by subjecting inflows to the lack of indigenous labour.

MAGNITUDE AND PATTERNS OF MIGRATION FLOWS

External migration

Data available on Swaziland's migration flows are inadequate, confusing and often contradictory. An examination of table 12 reveals an apparent substantial discrepancy between the figures for the number of Swazis working in South Africa reported by the Swaziland and South African censuses. Apart from the reliability of coverage, this can be partially accounted for by the fact that, first, the clandestine nature of some flows (especially since the inception of influx controls) may have influenced the responses by those enumerated; and second, before the 1966 Swaziland census, absentees recorded were only those who were employed outside Swaziland, and dependants were therefore excluded. This may account in particular for part of the discrepancy in the number of female absentees in the respective censuses. Furthermore, the South African recording of Swazi nationals may well be over-inflated in the sense that many of them—especially women—have no intention of returning to Swaziland.

Despite the vagaries of data, there is a clear declining relative importance of migration which—if pre-1966 censuses are adjusted for dependants and coverage—would be more dramatic than shown in table 12. Lord Hailey (1957, p. 1380) said of the 1940s: "Current estimates have placed at 25 or 30 per cent the proportion of able-bodied men who are away at any one time from their homes [externally]." Leistner and Smit (1969) estimated that 18.9 per cent and 17.9 per cent of the adult males were abroad in 1964 and 1966 (as against 34 per cent and 62 per cent respectively for Botswana and Lesotho in 1964). By 1976 the proportion had decreased to about 14 per cent. The decline is mainly the result of increased domestic employment opportunities: in 1956 domestic employment accounted for approximately 13 per cent of the resident working-age population (15–64 years); in 1966 this proportion increased to 34 per cent, while for 1976 it was 41 per cent. However, this impressive growth of labour absorption was not solely responsible for the diminished role of external migration: as noted earlier, influx controls had a significant impact on the number of migrants from Botswana, Lesotho and Swaziland working in South Africa.

The results of the 1976 census show that 25,650 of a *de jure* African population of 508,388 were living outside Swaziland (mainly in South Africa) at the time of enumeration. Approximately 23,000 were of working age and only little more than 25 per cent were female. This reflects the impact of stringent influx controls preventing wives from accompanying their husbands and limiting the employment oppor-

Table 13. Sectoral distribution of Swazi migrants in South Africa, by sex, 1956, 1964 and
1976

Year	Migrants	Agriculture[1]	Mining	Domestic services	Other labourers	Others occupations	Total
1956	Total	1 257	6 625	1 246	1 956	644	11 728
	Men	1 198	6 563	529	1 855	424	10 569
	Women	59	62	717	101	220	1 159
1964	Total	7 000	7 000	.	4 000	.	18 000
1976	Total	1 845	9 742	.	14 014	.	25 601
	Men	1 354	9 610	.	7 909	.	18 873
	Women	491	132	.	6 105	.	6 728

[1] "Farming" in 1956, "Agriculture" in 1964 and "Farms" in 1976.

Sources: Swaziland census for 1956; Leistner (1967) for 1964; and unofficial Swaziland census results for 1976 (not stated = 40).

tunities for women. Mainly because of the difficulties of re-employment in South Africa after temporary repatriation, about two-thirds of the female absentees were away for longer than one year, compared with only 38 per cent of the male absentees. The model age cohort was 20–29 years and this accounted for nearly 40 per cent of the absentees, with a mean age of 29.5 years for those assumed to be working (i.e. 15 years or over).

Although the 1976 census made some attempt to categorise the migrants in South Africa, relatively little is known about sectoral and occupational distribution (see table 13). According to the census, 9,742 Swazis worked on South African mines, 1,845 were employed on "Farms" while the remaining 14,014 were classified as "Other". The "Other" category encompasses a wide variety of activities, including services, manufacturing and agricultural activities such as forestry and cane-cutting, which absorb much labour in the Pongola, Piet Retief and Malelane areas. Very few of the workers in these border areas bother to attest themselves with local labour officers; they simply cross the border and face the consequences of contravening the South African influx laws, which show little sign of strict enforcement in these regions.

It has commonly been assumed that, because of the prevailing unemployment and recession and the recent tendency towards severer penalties for pass law infringement on both workseekers and employers,[7] relatively few Swazis would be able to secure employment outside mining and the border catchment areas. However, results from the secondary-school survey indicated otherwise: more than half the students had relatives or friends working in South Africa. In the survey the three most frequently mentioned sectors were services (34 per cent), manufacturing (16 per cent) and mining (16 per cent). Very few mentioned agriculture. These findings, supported by evidence from rural homesteads, indicate that a considerable number of Swazis are still working outside the "traditional" occupations in mining, forestry and agriculture and that employment in forestry and agriculture absorb proportionally much less than is generally believed.

The 1966 census data show (see figure 4 in de Vletter, 1978) that proximity to South African employment opportunities relative to domestic work is likely to be the most important factor determining the rate of migration. It was observed that Swazis living south of the Ingwavuma river gravitated to the sugar-fields of Pongola in South Africa whilst those living north of the river worked on the neighbouring domestic fields of Big Bend. This implies that the South African border and associated labour laws are of minimal hindrance to mobility. Thus, Shiselweni district in the south (the least developed of the four districts), with pockets of high population density in the border regions, has an external migration rate of 8.1 per cent of *de jure* population—almost twice the national average of 4.9 per cent. On the other hand, the distant Lubombo district has a rate of little more than half the national average; for the most part, these migrants are miners recruited through TEBA's head office in Siteki.

Internal migration flows

As a general rule, migrants come from the rural sector and move in either of two directions: internally, elsewhere in Swaziland; or to South Africa. The most dominant flow is clearly internal, even in many areas adjacent to the South African border.[8] Internal flows were mainly to the "urban" areas[9] and accounted for approximately 40 per cent or more of the rural homestead absentees, while about one-third were situated in other rural areas.

Information on internal flows is scanty at best, and only a very rough insight into patterns is provided by census data. But even these data are ambiguous, as they relate to a person's physical position at a particular moment; and because of the extent of "oscillating" migration (i.e. a pattern of migration characterised by more or less frequent movements, over varying periods, between a migrant's home and his place of work across the border) no concrete conclusions can be drawn about temporary or permanent migration. Thus, when the 1975 demographic survey reported that 30 per cent of Swazis born in Swaziland had left their place of birth, most of these were likely to have been away from their home base temporarily.

One very distinctive feature of migration, both internal and external, is the much larger number of males: more than two-thirds of the migrants from the rural homesteads were male. Of the total number of absentees,

50 per cent were males known to be working, while only 16 per cent were females known to be working; others were either scholars, spouses or persons with unknown activities. Highlighting our findings of male-dominated migration were the female/male ratios of the *de facto* population in the rural areas: for the age cohort of 20–34 years, females in rural homesteads for the whole country exceeded males by a factor of almost 2 to 1 (1.9:1); for the rural working-age population (15–64 years) the ratio was 1.6:1 (preliminary data, 1976 census).

The survey of Swaziland-based workers mentioned above showed that proximity of work to the homestead base was important and, predictably, most workers surveyed came from the immediate environs. Of the others, 10 per cent came from outlying regions within the same district and a further 20 per cent came from different districts: thus about one-third of the workers showed a high degree of mobility. Furthermore, it emerged from the homestead surveys that at least 50 per cent of the absentees could not be considered proximate to their homesteads, i.e. the distance between home and place of work would not enable the worker to return daily.

As regards inter-district flows, the results of the 1966 census demonstrate the strong pull of economic activity: Shiselweni, the least developed of the four districts, suffered a considerable loss, while others gained. Lubombo had by far the greatest inflow, perhaps mainly because of the development of labour-intensive projects as well as increasing population-land pressures of the Highveld and Middleveld.[10] Since 1966, however, Manzini and Hho-Hho districts have shown the largest growth in population (inter-district flows are not yet available), probably because of the large increase in employment absorption by the public and secondary sectors along the so-called Mbabane-Manzini corridor.

Urban growth has been surprisingly slow. According to Doran's (1977) model, this would be explained by the "safety valve" feature of employment in South Africa. The over-all urban growth rate was 3.7 per cent per annum over the decade 1966–76, with Mbabane and Manzini growing at just over 5 per cent per annum. The fastest growth was registered in the Manzini peri-urban area, with an annual growth rate of 6.5 per cent; this was influenced by the substantial development of secondary industry in the Matsapha region. Slow urban growth is unlikely to prevail, however: recently imposed restrictions by South Africa on employment opportunities, coupled with the propensity for secondary-school leavers to migrate to the urban areas,[11] will result in considerable rural-urban migration and the proliferation of squatter townships—unless the rural-urban income differential is reduced or employment creation is decentralised.

Although most migration in Swaziland is temporary in nature, urban growth is notably affected by many permanent rural-urban migrants. In a survey undertaken in conjunction with the American University in Washington, DC, the members of 282 low-income households were interviewed in Mbabane and Manzini; and although the results have not yet been fully analysed, it is quite clear that the newly arrived urban residents are abrogating many of their rural ties; many have no intention of returning to their former rural base.

Migration patterns from the home base

More than three decades ago Kuper (1947, p. 14) wrote: "Characteristic of [much of the local employment] is the fact that employees do not break completely from family or tribal life. They have families close by and keep in close touch with one another . . . their interests remain predominantly in the land." Our findings showed that virtually all external and internal migrants retained their home base in the rural areas. Two rural surveys were undertaken to examine the economic (de Vletter, 1978) and sociological (Rosen-Prinz and Prinz, 1978) perspectives of migration; these surveys were complemented by a more recent United Nations investigation into the rural homestead as an economic unit.[12]

Analyses of Swaziland's economy invariably mention the extreme duality and the inequality of income distribution between the so-called subsistence sector and the modern sector. Our three surveys, however, show conclusively that the subsistence homestead is likely to be closely tied to and very dependent on the wage sector. Three-quarters to four-fifths of the homesteads surveyed had wage earners absent, and half had at least two members engaged in wage employment away from home. Remitted wage earnings were clearly the main source of income for most homesteads, with more than 60 per cent receiving regular remittances, averaging approximately E 30 per month (Emalangeni and rands are interchangeable) (de Vletter, 1978). For the majority of homesteads agricultural income from crops and livestock is essentially derived from residual produce or the sale of a beast for a specific purpose. Most of the homestead-generated cash income is attributed to non-agricultural activities such as handicrafts and beer-brewing (see tables 14 and 15).

It is commonly assumed that migration is closely linked to the necessity to supplement subsistence requirements and therefore strongly correlated with such variables such as homestead size and the magnitude of income from other sources. However, Rosen-Prinz and Prinz (1978) found little or no relationship between these variables, nor any particular dominant characteristic influencing migration rates. In fact, quite contrary to expectations, it appeared that migration was most prevalent amongst those homesteads showing relatively more initiative in various

Table 14. Rural income patterns (excluding wages and remittances): results from three homestead surveys
(in percentages)

Homestead survey (Northern Rural Development Area) ($n = 125$)		United Nations Women in Development Project (Northern Rural Development Area) ($n = 60$)		Rosen-Prinz and Prinz survey ($n = 367$)	
Cash activities engaged in by homesteads		Cash activities engaged in by homesteads		Perceived ways of maintaining homesteads without relying on migration	
Activity	% of homesteads in activity	Activity	% of homesteads in activity[1]	Activity	% of homesteads in activity
Agricultural crops	35	Selling crops	52	Selling crops	33
Handicrafts	16	Other cash activities (for women only)	65	Subsistence	28
Beer-brewing	11			Handicrafts	16
Selling clothing	8	*of which:*		Selling beer	11
Selling prepared food	6	Handicrafts	64	Odd jobs	9
Poultry and pigs	4	Beer-brewing	26	Selling cattle	3
Dagga (marijuana)	2	Poultry	13		
		Pastry sales	10		
		Weeding	8		
		Harvesting	5		
		Resale of fruit and vegetables	5		
		Other	23		

[1] Figures do not total 100 per cent because homesteads could list more than one activity.

Sources: de Vletter, 1978; Rosen-Prinz and Prinz, 1978.

forms of income-generating activities. This tendency was also noted by Hughes (1964, p. 266) who found that there was "no definite evidence . . . that there is any direct causal relationship between high levels of wage earnings and agricultural inefficiency. In fact, there are some indications that higher wage earnings are more likely to be found in homesteads that are also relatively successful in the agricultural sphere." Clearly, a dynamic analysis would be necessary to establish any significant pattern between migration and wage remittances in effecting a "take-off" for other activities; but there was little indication from our findings of any noticeable change in attitudes and initiative amongst migrant workers towards the rural economy. Wealth and income distribution between rural homesteads showed great variation; income distribution was highly skewed and there was no greater inclination for the poorer homesteads to partake in migration than for the higher welfare homesteads.[13]

One factor emphasised by Rosen-Prinz and Prinz (1978) as contributing to the lack of relationship between migration and homestead welfare levels was the primogeniture system of inheritance. They point out that

Table 15. Magnitudes of cash flows by source (Northern Rural Development Area homestead study, $n=125$)

Crops			Remittances from absentees			Other sources (handicrafts, etc.)		
Annual income (Emalangeni)[1]	Homesteads		Monthly payments (Emalangeni)[1]	Homesteads		Annual income (Emalangeni)[1]	Homesteads	
	No.	%		No.	%		No.	%
10–50	9	20	0	17	20	0–40	2	3
50–100	21	48	0–10	13	15	40–80	9	15
100+	14	32	20	21	25	80–120	4	6
			30	15	18	120–160	2	3
			40	11	13	160+	11	18
			50	4	5	Don't know	34	55
			60+	4	5			
Total	44	100		85	100		62	100

[1] Emalangeni and rands are interchangeable.

Source: de Vletter, 1978.

the homestead is no longer the corporate unit commonly assumed. Junior sons and daughters are relegated to subordinate economic roles, having claim to little more than basic support for their labour inputs. For these members, migration from the rural base provides the only means of attaining individual wealth. Thus it was found that 80 per cent of the migrants were junior members of their respective homesteads.

The relationship of the migrant to his household was found to be important in determining the place of work and the amount of remittances sent home. The senior members or those with greater family commitments tended to be internal migrants, while external migrants were younger with considerably fewer dependants. The survey of Swaziland-based workers found that, for many of the senior homestead members, proximity to home was more important in job selection than higher wage levels. Internal migrants, although on average earning less than external migrants working on the South African gold-mines, were found to remit more regularly and in greater amounts than their compatriots on the mines.

Although almost one-quarter of the household population was found to be absent, the degree of contact with their home base was strong. Internal migrants, particularly senior household members, visited their homesteads regularly, with most of them visiting every weekend or monthly. External migrants working on the South African mines, on the other hand, rarely visited their families before the end of their contract. Because of the nature of internal employment, visits tended to be limited to weekends and holidays only, and only 14 per cent of the wage-earning absentees stayed longer than a month when returning home. Miners averaged a homestay of 3.4 months.

The recruitment of most miners follows a distinct seasonal pattern (see figure 5 in de Vletter, 1978) which underscores the importance of the agricultural requirements of the rural base during the ploughing and planting season. Albeit strong, the pull of agricultural duties is dominated by the urge to return to the family. Approximately 60 per cent of outgoing and returned miners stated that their main reason for returning home was to see the family. Although it is admittedly difficult to quantify or rank, the importance of the family could be easily observed from the response to the question whether the miner would stay longer on the mines if the TEBA offices were to provide tractors for ploughing: only about one-quarter of both the outgoing and returned miners said yes. Of those who said no, more than two-thirds specifically mentioned that they wanted to see their families. The importance of the family is further emphasised by the positive replies made by about half the miners when asked if they would work longer on the mines if their families were allowed to visit them or if trips were made available for brief visits home. But, when asked if they would like their families to live with them on the mines, only 15 per cent of the outgoing miners said that they would.[14]

CAUSES OF MIGRATION

Forces "compelling" the migrant to leave his home base are the most contentious of issues in the literature on southern African migration. Clarke (1977b) has drawn attention to the fact that most of the literature skirts the root causes of migration, stating (p. 3) that "modern models have isolated the 'causes' of migration at the level of behaviouralism and psychologism". Thus the Todaro, Lewis and push-pull models of migration are felt to be superficial, historical and "indifferent to the specific structural circumstances of the Labour Reserve economy" (p. 7). There can be little argument against the analyses of Clarke and of Bardill et al. (1977), whose basic theme is that the juxtaposition of the dominant capitalist mode of production with the pre-capitalist "natural economy" initially induced migration through strategic force (hut taxes, conscious underdevelopment), subsequently leading to the disintegration of the subsistence base. This reinforced the migration process in Labour Reserves where "primitive accumulation"[15] ensured that subsistence agriculture and migratory wage labour could not be mutually exclusive for the survival and reproduction of most of the population. The dialectic has been particularly evident in the more pronounced Labour Reserves such as Lesotho.

Notwithstanding the importance of understanding the fundamental causes of migration, the less broad parametric models are more useful and relevant for current policy considerations. Doran's (1977) extension of the Todaro model, which relates wage differentials, perceived employment opportunities and migration flows, may (as Clarke claims) be nothing more than a "paradigm"; but it none the less provides a useful insight into the magnitudes of change through significant movements of variables, as has recently occurred. Push-pull analyses are, as Wilson (1972a) points out, flexible and therefore useful in evaluating changes in attitudes, relative importance of remuneration, living and working conditions, and so on.

Perhaps the most important consideration when an attempt is made to relate causes and flows of migration in southern Africa is the degree to which flows are predetermined within the institutional framework and subject to changes in political and economic strategy. Thus, Clarke (1977b) highlights the folly of extrapolation based on empirical evidence and long-term trends in a region prone to volatile change.

Economic influences

Kuper wrote in 1947: "The causes of migration are many and of unequal force. The economic drive is undoubtedly the most effective" (p. 18). Rosen-Prinz and Prinz (1978) found that 84 per cent of the migrants left for economic reasons; furthermore, in the same study, in answer to the question whether they could be self-supporting without sending members out to work, 46 per cent of the homesteads said no.

The importance of cash for supplementing agricultural production, aggravated by comparatively high hut taxes, made it necessary for most Swazi males to seek formal wage employment. Although there is little evidence of deteriorating rural agricultural productivity, differentials between incomes in the rural sector and those in the formal sector have widened (Doran, 1977; Funnell, 1977) in parallel with the increasing pervasiveness of the cash economy. "Subsistence income" has consequently become a misnomer which can no longer be associated with nutritional and survival minima: it has adapted to changing expectations and consumption behaviour and cannot be supported by the "natural economy" alone. Thus, education is now generally regarded as a necessity, while diet fashions and household requirements have altered radically from the former traditional norms. Expenditure patterns of internal migrants show that the main items are food, household goods, clothing and school fees. The combination of increased wants and progressively higher formal sector remuneration has therefore gradually decreased the effort price of subsistence agriculture and increased the attractiveness of migration.

61

Opportunity and choice

Doran's simulation and regression studies suggest that the key determinant in the decision to migrate to the South African mines is the differential between real incomes in rural Swaziland and on the South African mines. Movements in either of these income variables may have a significant impact on the rate of external migration; and marked increases in number of the Swazis recruited during recent years have been closely associated with sharp changes in South African mine income relative to rural income and production: a multiple regression analysis showed that 96 per cent of the variation in recruitment between 1970 and 1976 is explained in terms of annual variations in rural income (the push factor) and annual changes in mine wages (the pull factor). Of this 96 per cent, one-quarter can be attributed to rural income changes and seven-tenths to mine wage levels. Thus, while alternative forms of income are needed in poor crop years (the mines providing one of the more popular alternatives), results indicate that the *relatively* more attractive economic opportunities afforded by South African mine employment have been the major determinant of migration flows. In other words, migration has been mainly the consequence of "pull" rather than "push" factors.

Urban income and employment prospects prevailing in Swaziland at or near the time of migration do not appear to influence the decision significantly. Several reasons may account for this: many men intending to migrate to South Africa do not at first consider a long-term absence from the home area desirable; the nature of the mine contract not only makes short-term contracts possible but is convenient and popular from the point of view of housing, food and deferred pay arrangements; and, most of all, it allows the peasant to return for several months to work on the land without marring his employment record or his chances of re-engagement. Moreover, weighted by the low probability of high wage employment, expected modern-sector or urban income may be relatively so low, compared with mine income, that it receives virtually no consideration in the decision to migrate.

Predictably, most external migrants prefer to work in Swaziland *given the right conditions*. In one survey of outgoing mineworkers, 80 per cent of the respondents said they would prefer to work in Swaziland but that the lack of job opportunities (69 per cent) and inadequate wages (41 per cent) stood in their way. However, it should be noted that the lack of job opportunities basically referred to *suitable* job opportunities, because, at the time of interviewing, many lower-wage sectors were suffering from severe labour shortages; and when outgoing miners were asked if they would consider working as manual labourers on farms, forest plantations, sugar fields and citrus groves, the majority—often more than two-thirds—would not, generally on the grounds that wages were too low and the work too hard. In another survey of outgoing miners (before recruiting restrictions were imposed) almost 90 per cent of the novice recruits had held previous jobs in Swaziland and 41 per cent of those with previous jobs claimed to have left their work because of poor pay, while 57 per cent said that they did not bother looking for work elsewhere in Swaziland after leaving their previous job.

Secondary-school students displayed a surprisingly realistic perception of the factors influencing migration to the mines: asked by open-ended question what they thought of the men who work in the South African mines, most mentioned that they went there for higher wages; but it is interesting to note that the second most frequent opinion was that uneducated Swazis would find it difficult to find *suitable* work in Swaziland and therefore turn to the mines.[16]

"Surplus" and wealth

When one compares the expenditure patterns of internal migrants and of those working on the South African mines, one immediately sees that the majority of mineworkers accumulate a surplus for the purchase of cattle while the Swaziland-based worker limits his spending to basic support (see table 16). Responses from outgoing and returning miners, as well as the internal migrants' opinions, suggest that cattle are amongst the two or three predominant expenditure items of the mineworker. Rosen-Prinz and Prinz (1978) supported this and found that cattle ranked as the second most important expenditure item. In their study, a simple attitude test found that 64 per cent of their respondents disagreed with the statement that a person goes away to work because he has no land, while 47 per cent agreed that a person goes away because he has no cattle.

The acquisition of assets has for most mineworkers probably been only a recent possibility. As a Mozambican study points out: "The wages of the mines before the 1970s were not sufficient in themselves to permit the purchase of expensive consumer goods (like sewing-machines) or to pay for cement brick houses or to finance the beginning of a process of accumulation through the acquisition of small shops or through transport."[17] The recent wage increases, coupled with the deferred pay system, has enabled "forced" savings to accumulate for relatively substantial purchases. Mine wages *per se* may not, or may barely, cover the costs of reproduction, but the dual income patterns (or, in the case of many miners, lack of family commitments) allows the accumulation of a surplus.

Target income—as unfashionable as it may be in the literature on southern Africa—still appears to be significant for the external mine

Table 16. Intended, perceived and actual expenditure patterns of main expenditure items by migrant type and household (various surveys) (in percentages)

A	B	C	D	E
Outgoing migrants, Survey I Intended expenditure (n = 222)	Returned migrants (n = 102) I = actual expenditure II/III = intended expenditure	What Swaziland-based miners thought money spent on (n = 229)	Swaziland-based workers: Actual expenditure (n = 229)	Rural homesteads (Rosen-Prinz and Prinz) asked for 2 most important expenditure items (n = 367)
Cattle 59	I. Expenditure while in South Africa	Cattle 79	Clothing 89	Household necessities 35
Food and clothing 41	Clothing 99	Clothing and food 71	Food and household goods 88	Cattle 20
Building and household requirements 40	Trunk 24	Blankets 44	School fees 65	School fees 13
Agricultural requirements 20	Blankets 16	Radios/bicycles/ cars, etc. 37	Building 12	Luxury items 11
School fees 16	Radios/record players 11	Entertainment and beer-drinking 35	Agricultural requirements 2	Entertainment 10
		Agricultural goods 6	Cattle 1	Agricultural implements 6
Outgoing migrants, Survey II (n = 165)	II. Expenditure during transition from TEBA to home	Don't know 12		
Food and clothing 61	Nothing 52			
Cattle 58	Food 22			
School fees 14	Clothing/blankets 20			
Building only 12	Drink/women 4			
Agricultural requirements 13	III. Expenditure while at home			
	Cattle 50			
	Support family 20			
	Bank earnings 15			
	Building 13			
	Agricultural equipment 8			
	School fees 8			
	Furniture 4			

Source: de Vletter, 1978.

migrants. Evidence of this is seen in the classic example of a worker's going to the mine to secure *lobola* (bride-price), a custom which continues to be of great traditional importance. *Lobola* has usually been in the form of cattle (still common in Swaziland) but there is a growing tendency to replace cattle by cash. Apart from specific cases where miners go to the mines with the intention of purchasing a particular item, the concept of target income can be extended to include those who work until they feel they have accumulated sufficient funds for their short-term needs and possibly for a residual investment. Interviews with returned mineworkers showed that there was a marked correlation between the expected length of homestay and the period during which they expected their money to last. Swazis tend to have the shortest contract lengths of all the major ethnic groups. Preliminary investigation shows that on average they have the shortest inter-contract homestays as well. For the industry as a whole, van der Wiel (1977) observed that, since the wage increases of 1973, the average length of contract has decreased significantly, from 12.6 months before 1973 to 10.6 in 1976, while the number of premature contract breaks rose from 9 per cent to 17 per cent during the same period.[18]

Sociological influences

Schapera (1947) and others have attached great importance to the bond between manhood and migration. This may have been true when minework was still a mysterious novelty and a new frontier for the brave. Wallman (1972) feels that the only relevance of "manhood" is the capacity to afford *lobola* after a contract on the mines. Natrass (1976) points out that aggregate models of migration assume that migrants are homogeneous and that migration should realistically be seen as a process of differentiation where the process is selective, involving those who are outward-looking, venturesome and not averse to change. This difference in character of those more prone to migrate may well have led to the importance of the "virility" element becoming attached to migration. To assess whether there were noticeable differences of opinion regarding men and their work experience, Rosen-Prinz and Prinz (1978) asked whether men who have worked in South Africa are more important than those who have not, to which only 16 per cent of the respondents agreed. Furthermore, 67 per cent disagreed with the statement that "women prefer to marry men who have worked away from home".

As pointed out earlier, the household rank of the migrant was influential in determining the place of work, mainly because of family commitments. Internal migrants, when asked why they worked for their company, emphasised proximity of work to their families; external migrants proceeding to the mines gave high wages as the main attraction.[19] The probable difference in status and family responsibility emphasised the marked difference in the numbers of dependants between the two types of migrant: internal migrants averaged 6.9 dependants (median 5.8) and external migrants 4.5 (median 3.4).

A further fairly important influence on migration from the rural sector is the relative attractiveness provided by the formal sector for young males in particular, when compared with parochial rural life. Van Drunen's (1978) work in Lesotho and the Swaziland surveys showed that the technological and cosmopolitan environment of the South African mines was a significant pull for many respondents. Migration also seemed to provide a convenient route for escape from one's society: Rosen-Prinz and Prinz (1978) found that 16 per cent of the migrants left their homes because of personal problems such as causing an illegitimate pregnancy, being involved in a crime or disagreements with the chief or indunas (overseers).

ECONOMIC IMPACT OF MIGRATION

Migration and the labour market

On the basis of the response by Swaziland-based employers and the attitudes expressed by both internal and external migrants, migration appears to have had serious repercussions on formal sector labour supplies and labour stability, as well as on the technologies adopted and on productivity. The political and economic events of the 1970s highlighted these effects and revealed Swaziland's vulnerability to exogenous changes.

Labour supplies: shortages versus surpluses

As indicated earlier, there is strong evidence that many external migrants choose to work in South Africa rather than be without alternative domestic opportunities. In 1974 two important developments underscored this tendency: first, with Mozambique's independence, most of the sizeable Shangaan labour force was withdrawn; and second, events in the gold-mining industry led to substantial increases in Black wages. The Shangaan withdrawal caused severe shortages in industries with arduous unskilled manual labour requirements (sugar in particular), while at the same time Swazis responded to the higher remuneration offered by the mines, thus further exacerbating the labour shortage.

These developments prompted the King to convoke employers in February 1977, appealing for an adjustment in wages to the levels prevailing in South Africa, in order to stem the tide of migration. A subsequent report submitted by the Federation of Swaziland Employers (Bevan and de Vletter, 1977) investigated the wage differentials between Swaziland and South Africa and found that comparative rates were much more similar than was commonly assumed. It was not a difference in wage structure that was responsible for the outflow to the mines, but rather intersectoral wage differentials that led to shortages in those sectors unable to compete remuneratively with the relatively high-wage mining sector. Farms and agro-based industries, which were found to pay higher or competitive wages, suffered shortages, whilst high-wage sectors (such as manufacturing) with rates considerably lower than in South Africa had no labour supply problems. Similar shortages in low-wage sectors, particularly agriculture, are avoided in South Africa through influx controls.

The results of an employer survey undertaken in December 1976, i.e. at the end of a record recruitment year for Swazi miners to South Africa, showed that shortages were fairly widespread in agricultural and agro-based industries but were not felt in high-wage sectors. Of the 17 companies in this category, 13 had suffered from shortages over a period of at least five years; however, the response was split as to whether the situation was worsening. The citrus industry claimed to have been so badly hit by labour shortages in recent years that it had to resort to hiring old women and schoolchildren on holidays and free afternoons during the picking season. Eleven of the 18 agricultural or agro-based firms thought they were adversely affected by the recruitment of Swazi labour to South Africa and a further 11 of the 15 who responded felt that some sort of control on migration should have been imposed by the Government. Asked whether wages and salaries in South Africa affected their firms, seven of ten sugar companies said they did not, claiming that their rates were competitive; while those who were affected alleged that they were hurt by the recent increase in mine wages.

The acute labour shortages which prevailed up to 1976 dramatically turned into labour surpluses during 1977. Employers who had suggested that migration to South Africa should be controlled by quotas then claimed to be turning away labour. Although the reasons are not entirely clear, several contributory factors explain at least some of this about-turn. In February 1977 restrictions were imposed by the gold-mines owing to the unprecedented demand for minework. These restrictions were lifted from October to December, when mines traditionally face troughs in their labour complements, but were reintroduced in January 1978. The impact on the recruitment of Swazi miners was considerable: recruitment dropped from 20,743 (all South African mines) in 1976 to 15,491 in 1977, 14,284 in 1978 and only 10,397 in 1979. TEBA officials claim that, in terms of numbers seeking minework, 1977 would have been a record year, implying that well over 5,000 men were frustrated in their attempts to find work. Moreover, there are strong signs that many more Swazis are responding to minework through a lagged demonstration effect, as the vast majority of mineworkers interviewed said they were influenced by returning friends and relatives and were unaware of changes through recruitment propaganda.[20]

A further contributing factor to the recent labour surplus is the effect of climate and rural subsistence production. Officials in the sugar companies, unaware of the recruitment restrictions, attributed the increase in labour availability to poor crops in 1976, stating that there has traditionally been a strong inverse relationship between crop production and the necessity to seek wage employment. Finally, clerical and administrative posts which have so far absorbed most secondary-school leavers are saturated and many school leavers now turn away from urban areas in their quest for employment.

Labour absorption

Complacency over migration and the continuing dependence on the convenient safety-valve of South African employment opportunities have led to serious distortions. By not planning for necessary internal employment creation, Swaziland has left herself exposed to the effects of changes in South African policies, such as the recruitment restrictions, while at the same time the free flow of migrants has caused internal shortages forcing industry to adopt perverse technologies. These developments, accompanied by high population growth, a very high student population and stagnating employment growth, point to an impending unemployment crisis.

Formal-sector employment absorption, until recently, has been impressive. Figures indicate that about 13 per cent of the population hold regular jobs within the country—more than in any other majority-ruled country in southern or central Africa. However, employment statistics show a marked decline, if not stagnation, in employment growth during the past few years. The recently published manpower plan (Wingfield Digby and Colclough, 1978) warns that, even on the optimistic assumption of a growth rate of 7 per cent up to 1982 (but in reality more likely to be 3–4 per cent), there will be formal-sector job opportunities for no more than 3,000–4,000 workers annually from the expected yearly increment of 7,000 to the active domestic labour force. The consequences of this limited absorption are aggravated by the fact that well over 19,000 students are at present enrolled in secondary schools.

With a shortage of employment opportunities, many are likely to remain in the rural sector while others will expand the relatively underdeveloped informal sector. Nevertheless, urban squatter growth and unemployment seem inevitable unless rural development strategy can successfully stifle aspirations for wage employment.

Seasonal fluctuations in labour stability

One of the striking features of external migration to the mines and, to a certain extent, of internal migration is the distinct seasonal pattern arising from the close ties with rural agricultural requirements. January and February are peak recruitment months for the mines, while November and December are trough months when many mines have repeatedly suffered labour complements as low as 65 per cent of requirements (see figure 5 in de Vletter, 1978). Domestic companies also face seasonal fluctuations. The total number of employees of companies surveyed in 1975 ranged from a low of 12,646 to a high of 15,615. Much of the fluctuation is accounted for by changing seasonal requirements for labour, but a sizeable proportion is due to the seasonal subsistence requirements of the workers themselves. Few of the high-wage industries complained of turnover or absenteeism. This contrasts with many of the agro-based industries: sugar companies claimed to have turnover rates of about 12 per cent per month, peaking at 35 per cent during the months of October–December when many workers return home for ploughing. Absenteeism over weekends or at the end of the month also plagued farms and agro-based industries. This was often attributable to workers returning to distant homesteads for visits and to leave remittances after pay day. What was particularly striking about the responses was that companies within similar industries were very differently affected by turnover and absenteeism.

Few of the underlying factors explaining the differences in turnover and absenteeism are immediately evident, but there is little doubt that relative wage levels and the nature of the work have an important bearing. Humphreys and McClelland (1964, p. 291) observed that "when the labour force in general has a relatively high average period of employment, the wage level, too, tends to be above the average". Most employers dismiss turnover and absenteeism as inevitable when traditional rural ties are so strong, but there is sufficient evidence that many Swazis are not averse to abrogating many of their rural ties and are willing to reduce the degree of oscillation between the traditional and modern sectors—given the right conditions.

Despite its isolated location, the Havelock mine was the first major industry successfully to stabilise its labour force, mainly because it provided family housing units. Further insight into labour stability has been provided by two of the largest forestry companies in Swaziland, with similar working conditions and wage rates but widely differing turnover rates, namely 1 per cent and 85 per cent.[21] The company with the high turnover provides barrack-style bachelor housing for 90–95 per cent of its employees in units dispersed throughout the forest, while the other offers married quarters for most employees in a township with centralised social amenities. The larger sugar companies are now also attempting to stabilise their labour force through the provision of permanent employment and improved housing and social facilities for many former seasonally employed workers. It seems fairly clear that, when working conditions are offered which enable detachment from the dual income patterns of most migrants, oscillating migration can be effectively dampened. It should be noted, however, that regardless of the type of work many Swazis maintain rural ties or homesteads. Personal involvement in agricultural production will depend on its necessity.

Migration and the quality of labour

Men with greater initiative and ambition will usually have a greater propensity to migrate. This not only applies to those who are physically and psychologically more adaptable but also to those with better educational and skill backgrounds. Evidence from the 1976 census showed a very high rate of male migration from the rural area. Furthermore, as suggested by the sociological factors influencing migration, the younger males tend to work in South Africa. Thus the average age of the mineworkers surveyed was 28.5 years (median 25), with 70–80 per cent under the age of 30, while Swaziland-based workers in the survey averaged 31.5 years (median 28.8), with only 52 per cent under the age of 30.[22]

It is commonly assumed that most miners are illiterate and uneducated. This is indeed true for a significant proportion: 40 per cent of our survey respondents had no schooling. Until very recently there has been little change in the educational background of the miners. De Bruyn and Levitas (1975) found that for the gold-mining industry the distribution of the mean level of education did not change between 1961 and 1975, claiming that over 50 per cent of the Black workers had no education. Mauer (1976) confirmed these findings in a later study, stating that the common belief that the miners seemed better educated arose from their increased sophistication through urbanisation. Nevertheless, TEBA officials in Swaziland believe that there has recently been a definite tendency for proportionately more educated men to enter the recruitment offices. Survey results showed that 10 per cent of those interviewed had received secondary-school education. This trend was also evident in Lesotho, where in 1975 some 9 per cent of the recruits had secondary education; the proportion rose to 11 per cent in 1976, while during 1977 it appeared to be rising further (van der Wiel, 1977). The Human Resources Laboratory of the Chamber of Mines noted in a recent report [23] that "the less experienced men tended to be the better educated. This suggests that the level of education is rising"; but added that "men with little or no formal schooling tended to stay longer in the industry". In relation to education and type of work, the report observed that "the occupation held by a man did not seem to be related to the level of education he had attained" and that "length of experience appeared to be closely related to the level of job performed". These findings suggest that, apart from seeking clerical or administrative work, educated workseekers are being attracted because of the higher wages or because of the lack of suitable domestic opportunities. There appears to be some truth in both.[24]

The level of experience of minework was found to be widely distributed, and it would be difficult to generalise about the extent to which minework could be considered a career. The average number of previous contracts held by Swazis was 4.5 (median 2.8). In surveys of outgoing miners and returning miners, it was found that 12 per cent of the non-novices had been to the mines ten or more times. Although it is quite clear that Swazis are not generally the career miners that the Basotho or Mozambicans are,[25] a significant proportion of Swazi recruits are likely to regard minework as their only source of wage income and have devoted a major part of their working life to the mines.

The skill drain from Swaziland has been a bone of contention but has not been subject to quantification. Leistner and Smit (1969, p. 49) noted: "According to some observers, many well qualified Swazis prefer employment in the Republic where wages are usually higher and where there is wider scope for the exercise of their talents." The same sentiment was expressed by the JASPA Employment Advisory Mission (ILO/JASPA, 1977). In spite of strict influx controls and the severe recession, many Swazis are still employed in sectors outside mining and farming, and a high proportion of them are skilled.[26] Bloch (1978) and others have shown that there are severe shortages of Black technicians in South African industry and foreign Black skilled labour should have no problems here in circumventing the strictures of influx controls.

The skill drain, whatever its extent, is somewhat counterbalanced by the positive effects of working experience in South Africa. Our employer survey showed that about two-thirds of the respondents felt that those returning from South Africa would be noticeably more productive. Students who conducted surveys on the mines also generally agreed that, although the type of work on the mines is largely irrelevant for subsequent employment in Swaziland, the work discipline and exposure to the concept of production targets, teamwork, and so on, contributed to the making of an improved industrial labour force. Largely on this basis, Stahl (1975) pondered the idea of using the South African mines to save some of the considerable costs of internal industrial training. In addition to providing normal work experience, most mines offer free training courses in various fields such as masonry, carpentry, literacy and apprenticeship in various artisan trades. Unfortunately, to date relatively few miners have taken advantage of these training programmes (see Chapter 4). The extent of skill acquisition and training is, however, constricted by the restrictive colour bars of the Mines and Works Act, 1956.

Migration and the rural economy

There has been much discussion of the cause and effect of migration in relation to the rural economy. Is migration the result of "push" from deteriorating and insufficient subsistence production, or has migration led to the disintegration and stifling of the rural sector? There is, of course, interdependence of causality, and the direction of impact will vary by region and magnitude of migration. Migration engenders a vicious circle of mutual support between the modern capitalist sector and the traditional rural sector. Rural production is no longer sufficient to meet the changing norms of "subsistence," but wages (even following the recent substantial increases) are barely adequate for the maintenance of the family during the period of employment[27] and cannot sustain the migrant and his family after retirement. Thus, although the tie to the land is undoubtedly traditional in nature, it is also an inescapable necessity for most.

Migration for many is simply a means of family support. This was particularly evident from the response given by internal migrants who indicated that they spent money mainly on food, clothing, household goods and education. There was little evidence of internal migrants accumulating any "surplus" for the purchase of cattle or any substantial agricultural investment. External migrants also emphasised the importance of family support, but gave equal or greater emphasis in all our miner surveys to the purchase of cattle, with 50–60 per cent variously stating that they intended to buy cattle.

External migrants tended to spend more money on agricultural inputs than internal migrants, but nevertheless the importance attached to such expenditures was relatively insignificant. In Mozambique there is considerable evidence that middle- and upper-income peasants spent much more of their surplus earnings on expanding the productive capacity of their land or on the necessary capital requirements for establishing an artisan trade, etc. In Swaziland there was virtually no evidence of migrants returning with new ideas about cropping methods or alternative income-generating initiatives.

Rutman (1974) points out that the type of wealth formation in indigenous economies is largely determined by the institutional environment and by prevailing attitudes. The behaviour of the Swazi miner would be seen as rational in a communal society where usufruct agreements are not likely to induce many to improve the capitalised value of land through irrigation, planting trees, and so on. Although at present there is much disagreement over the issue, agricultural officials have drawn attention to cases of chiefs expropriating or reallocating land from farmers who have "done too well". Spaarman and Diphoorn[28] have noted a distinct reluctance among the more motivated farmers to plant trees and to make substantial agricultural investments, ostensibly because of insecurity of tenure; however, there are many other underlying and complex factors here, inter alia ostracism and witchcraft. Cattle, in this rigid traditional framework, remain the only easily accessible and realisable asset for the peasant. The individual miner is probably optimising his resources; but on a macro level, continued purchases and growth of cattle stock will have serious repercussions on a country which is already highly over-grazed.

Surveys indicate that perhaps only 5 per cent of the farmers in rural homesteads engage seriously in any form of cash cropping. Others are basically subsistence farmers who earn cash from the sale of residual produce. For the latter, Low (1977) points out that the marginal opportunity cost of external migration is virtually zero, as mining contracts complement the agricultural requirements of subsistence farming, allowing miners to return for ploughing and planting. Agricultural improvement is therefore impeded not only by institutional factors but also by the very nature of migration itself. Low argues that traditional crops (maize, in particular) are much less labour-intensive than alternative cash crops such as cotton and tobacco (by one-half and one-fifth, respectively) and demonstrates that a considerable increase in migration would in fact be possible between January and September before any loss in production was incurred. This conclusion stems from farm survey observations showing that the adult male input is greatest at ploughing and planting time (October–December), that weeding and harvesting are traditionally carried out by women (January–May) and that, of the total work input on crop enterprises, 70 per cent is contributed by adult females and children between 9 and 15 years of age. The introduction of high-potential cash crops (particularly cotton and tobacco) would, however, both increase the total male labour contribution and alter the seasonal distribution of effort, leaving considerably less scope for migration.

An interesting pattern appears to be developing between internal migrants and external migrants in relation to their direct physical input into agricultural production. Previously, many internal migrants simply left work for several weeks to attend to ploughing and later returned confidently to their jobs. Under the present conditions of high unemployment there is no longer any assurance that jobs will be kept open. Only one-third of the internal migrants stated that they returned home for ploughing; a surprisingly high 26 per cent said they relied on tractors (mostly hired) to do their ploughing; the rest depended on their family and relatives. External migrants leaving during the peak months of January and February were much more directly involved in physical inputs when they returned during the ploughing season; and very few miners mentioned that they used tractors for ploughing.

Migration and the state sector

The Swaziland Government has so far not fully realised the potential of migration for revenue purposes. While other countries had attestation fees of R 10 or more, Swaziland's fee remained at R 1. Late in 1976 personal discussions with TEBA officials in South Africa revealed that they would hardly be averse to increasing the fee to R 10 and in fact were surprised that this had not already occurred. Yet in 1977 Swaziland sought to raise it only to R 5. It was not until 1980 that legislation was enacted to raise the fee to R 10, in harmony with the practice in Botswana and Lesotho.

The earnings of Swazi miners in South Africa in 1976 were put at E 12.9 million by the Monetary Authority of Swaziland. If this figure is to be believed,[29] it follows that a considerable amount of goods are bought externally, as only about E 4.5 million were deferred or remitted. Survey results show that main expenditure items in South Africa are clothing, radios, trunks, blankets and food. It is likely that records of these expenditures—which are entitled to a considerable rebate through the customs union revenue-sharing formula—are grossly understated, if indeed they are stated at all.

CONCLUSIONS AND POLICY RECOMMENDATIONS

Conclusions

Migration to South Africa has been described by Hobart Houghton (1960, p. 189) as "an evil canker at the heart of our whole society, wasteful of labour, destructive of ambition, a wrecker of homes and a symptom of our fundamental failure to create a coherent and progressive economic society". Strong words, but apt for a system where the movement of labour is circumscribed by discriminatory laws and involuntary separation of the family. However, in the case of countries such as Swaziland, where domestic employment conditions are considerably more accommodating than in, say, Lesotho, work in South Africa is for many a conscious choice, and migration therefore cannot be so easily characterised.

Migration is the vital link between the wage sector and the rural homestead, providing the main source of cash income for approximately two-thirds of the homesteads at any given time; yet it is much more complex a factor than a simple "push" to provide the necessary support for the dependent family. Our findings have to some extent delineated the distinguishing characteristics between internal and external migrants. Domestic labour shortages before 1977 demonstrated the decision by most external migrants to work in South Africa, in preference to taking up local employment—the preference being due to such factors as higher wages, short-term contracts with re-engagement guarantees, deferred pay schemes and free food with lodging. External migrants tended to be younger, with fewer dependants, and were able to accumulate a surplus for the purchase of "luxuries" and, very often, cattle. Internal migrants, on the other hand, appeared to be much closer to their families, to have greater responsibilities and to spend virtually all their money on items of basic support.

With pressure mounting inside South Africa to raise the wages of the Black mine workers, it may be extremely difficult to prevent the real Swaziland-rural/South African-mine income differential from widening. External migration is therefore likely to increase, particularly with mounting internal unemployment, unless institutional restrictions are imposed. Doran (1977) demonstrated in his model that without these restrictions all eligible Swazi rural males could conceivably be seeking short-term mine contracts within the next 15 years, barring a significant growth in rural incomes. The sharp increase in recruitment for the mines, in response to the wage increases of 1974, underlined the importance of the "pull" of wage levels, with further increases in the number of migrants being obstructed only by the externally imposed restrictions of 1977 and 1978.

External migration has played the role of a "safety-valve" in terms of residual unemployment and has provided a seemingly popular source of quick savings. It has not done so, however, without considerable cost. Recent labour shortages have led to the introduction of inappropriate technology, while complacency towards migration has precluded any serious policy for improving the labour-absorptive capacity of the economy. Perhaps most serious is the obvious vulnerability of Swaziland to externally imposed dictates on migrant flows which, overnight, can switch a comfortable labour position into serious domestic unemployment. Furthermore, expenditure patterns by external migrants with accumulated surpluses, contrary to popular opinion, have shown little evidence of productive investment. Rather, they tend to exacerbate the serious over-grazing problem. There is also no indication that external migrants have improved their cropping patterns. In fact, there seems to be much support for the hypothesis that migration stifles the development of cash cropping because of the nature of the migrant contract, which perpetuates the patterns of subsistence agriculture and works against the relatively labour-intensive cash crops.

From the internal political perspective of Swaziland, perhaps the most important consideration is the individual himself. Suggestions that migration to South Africa can be stopped by simply providing the would-be migrant, somehow, with the means to satisfy his basic needs or by providing domestically located employment, can only be described as naive. To replace external migration with any simple form of internal work is unlikely to satisfy the many (if not the majority of) migrants who have consciously opted for external employment. A *natural* absorption of external migrants, i.e. the voluntary choice of the individual to work in Swaziland, will require attractive conditions such as family housing, competitive wages (which may be difficult in low-wage sectors such as agriculture) and possibly contractual innovations such as deferred pay and short-term renewable contracts for those with rural commitments.

Policy recommendations

Migration in southern Africa has, until recently, evoked little more than ethical solicitude, but much interest is now being shown in its strategical potential, through concerted efforts by labour-supplying States. The need to examine such possibilities was foreseen in the original project outline of the ILO/UNFPA research (see Wilson, 1975, p. 4); Böhning (1977, pp. 52–57) and Stahl (1977), contributed further thoughts on the subject; in November 1977, ministers and labour commissioners from supplier States met in Lesotho and issued a paper entitled *Migrant labour to South Africa: The need for a common approach*, and a follow-up meeting was convened in February 1978; in April 1978 the United Nations Economic Commission for Africa, with ILO support, staged in Lusaka the major Conference on Migratory Labour in Southern Africa, which discussed the feasibility of establishing a common labour policy in southern Africa; Stahl and Böhning (1979) co-authored the most far-reaching analysis and proposals made to date; and at the beginning of 1980 Botswana, Lesotho and Swaziland agreed to set up the Southern Africa Labour Commission, which was also to be open to other labour-supplying countries (Mozambique and Zimbabwe have since become full members, Malawi and Zambia observers). Unfortunately, this awakening to the problems and potentials of the migrant labour system is the result not so much of predictive acumen as of tardy afterthought. The South African Chamber of Mines took the strategic initiative through "internalisation" and subsequent restrictions on supplier States (Clarke, 1977a) beginning in 1976–77.

The major proposal emanating from the 1977 ministerial meeting concerned the establishment of permanent joint consultative machinery to meet at least once a year to discuss contractual arrangements, general conditions of employment, the redistribution of benefits from the migration system, the securing of markets for commodities produced in supplier countries, the general treatment of migrant workers in South Africa and research into the migratory system. Further proposals recommended inter alia the "payment of compensation analogous to that under the Customs Agreement" and negotiations for better working conditions and rates of pay.

At the ECA conference the intention was to take these proposals further and to offer concrete guidelines for action by supplier States. Instead, the debate underlined the sensitivity of the migration issue, becoming a confrontation between those whose views were morally appealing and those who were influenced by practical reality. Non-supplier States and individual militants called for the immediate abolition of migration, feeling that gradual abolition implied a tacit acceptance of apartheid. Others, more directly affected by migration, accepted the need to abolish what some referred to as a form of slave labour but hoped to solicit more substantive counsel in tackling the problem. Apart from rhetoric that was appropriate for International Anti-Apartheid Year, little of direct use for dealing with repatriated workers was forthcoming.

Resolutions often prove easy enough to adopt at the conference table but are difficult to transpose into direct action. This problem in particular threatens to undermine the recently adopted recommendations for government-initiated action on migrant labour. From the internal political perspective of Swaziland the reason appears simple enough: the replacement of migration by a suitable alternative represents a formidable and perhaps idealistic *challenge* rather than an obvious *necessity*. To date, migration has been a convenience for both the Government and the migrants: it has absorbed the potentially unemployed, provided the means of direct or indirect support for at least one-fifth of the population[30] and has been traditionally accepted for almost a century. Any physical interference by the Government, no matter how necessary from the moral or economic perspective, unquestionably bears considerable political risk. Even in Mozambique, where two large hostels for mine recruits in transit have recently been constructed, there appears to be little evidence of a binding commitment towards withdrawal. Any committed policy by a supplier State would, however, be an historical milestone. Höpfner and Huber (1978) note that, although policies regulating immigration are in most cases an integral part of economic policy, no supplier State has introduced a comprehensive long-term strategy concerning emigration.

In recognition of the necessity to abolish migration because of its demeaning nature as well as of the urgent need for peripheral States to reduce their dependence on South Africa, the recommendations that follow complement the core objective of withdrawal from the South African labour market, co-ordinated with a schematic growth of labour-absorptive capacity of the Swaziland economy. A scheduled withdrawal implies transition, and over this transition period it is felt that efforts should be made to extract the maximum benefits from the system while at the same time alleviating the more pernicious aspects of work as a migrant labourer in South Africa. Policy proposals will therefore first deal with the possibilities of extracting greater benefits for the country as a whole and then turn to the question of withdrawal and internal absorption. Although our recommendations are devised with Swaziland in mind, many of them are considered to be sufficiently broad for general application to other labour-supplying States. Recommendations for the improved welfare of the migrant are considered in Chapter 4.

Increasing the benefits from migration

- **Migration and government revenues**

Attestation fees. In future, all agreements relating to attestation fees should be negotiated jointly by all supplier States so as to improve their bargaining leverage, much of which has been lost as a result of mounting internal unemployment in South Africa and increasing pressures to reduce the number of migrant workers.

Customs Union revenue. If better records of external migrants' spending in South Africa were kept, this would probably have a noticeable effect on Customs Union revenue (calculated on the proportion of goods imported by the country or purchased in South Africa by its nationals). The importance of these records is emphasised by the fact that, in addition to basic revenue sharing, Botswana, Lesotho and Swaziland are entitled to a substantial compensation factor.

Taxation. Swazi miners working on the South African mines do not pay income taxes in South Africa or in Swaziland. This *de facto* exemption increases the income differential between domestic alternatives and external employment—the main "pull" factor. Although the Swaziland Government cannot technically impose income taxes on returning miners, it could justifiably introduce a surrogate tax in the form of a levy on the length of contract or type of work, to be collected on their return through recruitment offices or by the Swazi Labour Representative based in South Africa.

Taxation and the rural sector. A tax on mine earnings would obviously lower the prospective miner's perceived level of remuneration from mine employment. It would also tend to alter the regional distribution of mine recruits. As Low (1977) demonstrates, returns to labour from *traditional agriculture* are higher in the Lowveld ecological zone (where land is the relatively more abundant resource) and lower in the Highveld/Middleveld zones (where labour is the relatively more abundant resource). Given a reduction in the remuneration level, we should expect the percentage decline in the migration rate to be greater in the Lowveld than in the Highveld/Middleveld and the over-all proportion of migrants from the Highveld/Middleveld to increase. Since productive potential is greater and climatic variability is lower in this latter zone, a tax on mine earnings that would in the first instance increase the proportion of Highveld/Middleveld recruits could result in a redistribution of income which would further favour this zone.

Furthermore, the long-run effect on the regional distribution of income might be even more marked since, as the level of remuneration declined, the incentive to adopt new cropping practices would be greater in the Highveld/Middleveld than in the Lowveld. Marginal returns to labour from *improved cropping* would be greater in the Highveld/Middleveld zone and the gap between Lowveld homestead income and Highveld/Middleveld homestead income would, in time, tend to widen.

In either case, however, a lower level of perceived remuneration would tend to increase incentives to adopt new cropping practices. Conversely, an increase in the perceived remuneration level would tend to reduce incentives to adopt new techniques. Potential policy conflicts therefore exist since, whilst a tax on mine earnings would almost certainly reduce incentives to migrate from rural areas and increase incentives to adopt improved cropping techniques, it would also tend to result in a redistribution of rural income which further favoured the country's zones of higher potential. These are, therefore, crucial considerations which should influence the use of tax revenue in fostering the internal changes necessary before withdrawal could be envisaged.

Compensatory payments. The sharing of revenue amongst members of the Southern African Customs Union Agreement explicitly recognises the spatial disadvantages for peripheral trading partners and attempts to compensate for these by a factor of 42 per cent of their respective revenue shares. Similarly, there is no reason why labour-supplying countries cannot claim similar compensation for the use of their labour resources, so crucial in the development of mining industry.

The World Bank (IBRD, 1978) estimated that supplier States contributed 7.1 million man-years over the period from 1946 to 1975 and felt that these countries "would seem to have some legitimate claim on the resources generated by the mining industry over and above the amounts paid in wages to their migrants". The argument appears to be as convincing as that for trade compensation; but successful negotiation may be more difficult because compensation would have to be extracted from the mining industry alone, unless the South African Government recognised the political ramifications of the demands of the supplier States.

With the prevailing high levels of South African unemployment and underutilised labour reserves in southern and central Africa, the success of such demands would depend on the harmonisation of efforts by supplier States. In Chapter 7 Stahl and Böhning demonstrate a possible means of approach, suggesting the formation of an "Association of Home Countries of Migrants" (AHCM) which would wield sufficient control over labour supplies and have sufficient political influence to make compensatory payments conceivable. They further suggest that, on the basis of exigency for withdrawal, a United Nations fund could be set up to provide further leverage in such negotiations by guaranteeing the funds necessary for immediate withdrawal if these negotiations should fail and if compensatory payments should not be forthcoming.

■ Trade agreements

As a possible alternative or supplement to outright compensation, marketing agreements between the mines and supplier States for the provision of various types of input appear to be feasible (IBRD, 1978). These arrangements might initially (or perhaps indefinitely) prove financially suboptimal for the mines but would be seen as a form of compensation injecting a demand stimulus for peripherally located industry. Much potential lies in the supply of meat, vegetables and timber from supplier States, while further secondary linkages could be promoted in the manufacture of boots, clothing, plastic helmets, and so forth. Guaranteed markets would benefit these economies, but are likely to advance rather than diminish trade dependence on South Africa.

To take advantage of the economies of scale which could be promoted through such agreements, supplier States could mutually support each other's economic expansion through more intensive regional trade. In the short and perhaps medium run this trade might be disadvantageous in terms of cost, but it would provide a key instrument through which to absorb displaced migrant workers as well as reducing the overwhelming trade dependence on South Africa.

■ Industrial training

Many mines provide free or subsidised formal education as well as comprehensive artisan training with certificates or diplomas issued on successful completion. The response by the miners to such services has been poor; but the encouragement of greater participation would be of great benefit both to Swaziland and to other supplier States where training facilities are scarce and expensive and vocational skills are at a premium. Governments could stimulate greater interest by offering bonuses to returning miners who had acquired some proof of training during their absence.

Disengagement from migration

■ Scheduled withdrawal

Withdrawal from the South African migrant labour system has been rationalised from both the moral and the practical perspectives. High rates of South African unemployment combined with the predictable policy of "internalisation" of the mining labour force (Clarke, 1977b), changing modes of production in gold-mining which point to a greater degree of labour stability (Bardill et al., 1977) and the eventual reduction of gold production during the next few decades (Bromberger, 1979) underline the urgent need for a co-ordinated strategy as supplier States find themselves in an ever weaker bargaining position.

Ironically, the South African Government itself has noted the likelihood of the withdrawal of supplier States, and a recently leaked report (of an interdepartmental committee appointed in 1975 to investigate the causes of mine riots) has drawn attention to the fact that South Africa could expect imminent requests for "royalties" paid by the mines to be used for the creation of domestic job opportunities "so that their [supplier States'] ultimate objective of total withdrawal of labour may be realised", and added that "co-ordinated action in respect to these demands could be expected in the future". Yet, to date, migration policy has proven to be little more than a paper issue. Any government deciding *individually* to withdraw will be politically vulnerable; and on the economic front, other countries may simply fill the void with their own unemployed. The prerequisite for withdrawal must be *joint action*. But a common approach, although easy enough to decide upon, might be fraught with practical difficulties. Beyond the common effects suffered from the South African economic and political hegemony, there is little to bind supplier States, with their diverse ideologies and economic structures, closely together. Furthermore, because of their varying degrees of dependence on migrant labour (Böhning, 1977), a concerted withdrawal strategy would obviously have to treat each country separately as regards rates of withdrawal, the distribution of compensation, and so on. Mutually acceptable criteria for measuring migration dependence and absorptive capacities would be a probable source of contention, as the various indicators would probably affect countries in different ways.

In any such agreement, there would be the danger that one country might abrogate the pact. This danger was implicitly recognised at the previously mentioned ministerial meeting on migratory labour in November 1977, whose paper stated "that there is a risk of South Africa playing one country against another in individual negotiations". In fact, the absence of Malawi from the 1978 ECA Conference on Migratory Labour in Southern Africa was interpreted by some observers as an obvious tactic to dent the migration market. The danger of such breaches could possibly be overcome through a "devil's advocate" arrangement between supplier States and the South African Government and/or the Chamber of Mines. Supplier States, on the strength of their collective political leverage (and with possible support from United Nations funds), could demand co-operation from the South Africans in controlling migrant flows according to withdrawal plans.

The principle of withdrawal has by and large been accepted by supplier States, but so far no attempt has been made to investigate the actual implementation of such a strategy apart from the work by Stahl and Böhning as expounded in Chapter 7. As mentioned above, it would also be necessary to agree on the criteria to be used to determine rates of withdrawal and, by implication, absorptive capacities for repatriated workers. Once unity of approach had been achieved, the success of the withdrawal strategy would lie with the individual supplier countries in their efforts to provide suitable alternatives for the displaced migrants.

■ National employment policy

The creation of domestic employment as an integral complementary policy to withdrawal would have to receive high priority attention, rather than the passive concern exhibited by the Swaziland Government in the recent past. "Employment", however, should not be understood as simply wage or formal job opportunities. Only a fraction of the growing labour force (probably no more than one-half, in the most optimistic of circumstances) could be taken up by the formal sector, while the rest would have to be *productively* absorbed into the rural sector. One of the primary objectives of the policy would therefore be to raise the almost negligible marginal opportunity costs of out-migration from the rural sector; this would require radical changes in cropping patterns as well as the promotion of non-agricultural rural activities.

Absorption in the formal sector. Fundamental to a national employment programme for Swaziland is the realisation that external migration is not simply the movement of residual labour forced to seek work in South Africa because of the lack of domestic opportunities. In establishing "suitable" alternatives for the repatriated workers, the following observations should be taken into consideration:

1. For many, South African minework is preferable to domestic employment because of the relative ease of obtaining work, the comparatively high wages and the nature of the contract.

2. Proximity to home is given prominence by senior household members in choosing work, and lower domestic wages would be somewhat compensated by this factor.

3. Accommodation and general living conditions have been found to be important in determining the stability of the labour force. In Swaziland there is ample evidence of workers who are willing to break physical (input) ties with their rural base if they are provided with family housing, adequate social amenities, and so forth.

4. For the foreseeable future many workers will probably continue to retain strong rural ties and use formal-sector employment as a convenient means of supplementing their subsistence income, returning to their base regularly after having accumulated sufficient funds or when they are required for agricultural activities. Industry and the Government should therefore investigate the possibility of introducing schemes similar to those of the mines, which would not only make it possible to accumulate earnings through deferred pay arrangements but would also allow workers to make lengthy visits to their homes, while at the same time assuring their re-employment if their work under the previous contract had been satisfactory and if they returned within a specified time.

The Government has now apparently recognised that unemployment is perhaps the most critical development problem faced by Swaziland, but serious distortions resulting from a lukewarm attitude towards employment creation will make the maximising of labour absorption in the formal sector difficult in the future. The promotion of capital-intensive investment through generous capital cost allowances and other incentives have led to distorted factor use, recently culminating in the establishment of a sugar-mill expected to employ workers at a capital cost of E 60,000–70,000 per head. Adherence to the British system of education has resulted in an excessive output of secondary-school leavers with high job aspirations and a rural exodus of educated manpower seeking jobs in an already saturated formal sector, while centralised industrial development along the Manzini-Mbabane corridor has left serious regional disparities that have led to further outflows.

Doran's (1977) experiments emphasise, however, that policies aimed at simply maximising the rate of job creation may in fact not alleviate urban unemployment rates. He points out that, unless these policies are complemented by an effective incomes policy which would prevent widening rural/urban earnings differentials, rural-urban migration would cause urban employment ratios to remain virtually unchanged or perhaps decline in the long run. The limited absorptive capacity of the formal sector and the general tendency for formal sector earnings greatly to exceed rural earnings underscore the importance of co-ordinated sectoral employment policies to stem both external and internal flows.

Rural development strategy. Doran's model draws attention to the importance of rural development and the maintenance of rural income growth to reduce migration flows. Low (1977) further demonstrates how the types of employment opportunity available through different cropping patterns are significant in determining the likelihood of migration. Rural development strategy in accordance with a national employment programme would aim at the basic objective of promoting activities providing sufficient returns to maintain *satisfactorily* that proportion of the labour force not absorbed by the formal sector. This implies both considerably higher returns to labour input (basically higher crop yields) and a much wider use of labour.

The Swaziland Government has since 1970 mounted the ambitious Rural Development Areas Programme (RDAP) to increase the income and general standard of the inhabitants of Swazi Nation Land. The programme is scheduled to cover 14 areas by 1982, encompassing 55 per cent of the population of Swazi Nation Land. The growth of farm incomes per head for the Rural Development Areas has been optimistically projected at 5 per cent per annum, but even at this rate the over-all average income growth for Swazi Nation Land is not likely to be more than 2–3 per cent per annum.

On the basis of observed migrant behaviour and response, a significant proportion of the labour force is likely to remain at the rural base if the economic opportunity avails them. In determining suitable opportunities, it can be assumed that income levels generated could be noticeably lower than wage employment alternatives. This is because of

(a) the differential arising from the imputed values attached to housing and subsistence production derived from essentially "free" land; (b) the proximity of the family, which has been specifically mentioned by many as being more important than higher wages; and (c) the home base, which is likely to provide a safer working environment than most industries, with a considerably reduced risk of death, injury, disease, assault, and so on. There will nevertheless be many who continue to leave the rural sector because of the special attractions of urban life.

Economic opportunities should not be limited to agricultural activities alone. Rural informal sector activities such as beer brewing, handicrafts, the sale of prepared food and vehicle hire provide the most important source of cash income after wage remittances. To date, the promotion of such activities has been minimal and there is much scope for government encouragement through the provision of credit facilities, extension services and distribution networks.

In spite of the persuasive arguments for high-yield, labour-intensive activities to stem rural out-migration, current government policy, in its campaign to attain self-sufficiency in maize and thereby reduce dependence on South Africa for its staple food, may be reinforcing a more foreboding form of dependence. The production of maize (a relatively low-yield crop, low in labour intensity and highly seasonal in husbandry) complements the flow of migrants—particularly to the South African mines which, by the nature of the migrants' contracts, makes it possible for the workers to move to and fro according to agricultural labour requirements. Low (1977) estimated that the cost of achieving self-sufficiency in maize production over the next ten years would be an extra 4,500 adult male migrants. Successful withdrawal (implying that priority be given to the reduction of labour dependence) would therefore require a change of emphasis in cropping patterns, from self-reliance on staple foodstuffs to the production of commercial crops such as tobacco and cotton. Such a shift might, however, affect the nutrition of the subsistence population in the short run.

Rural Swaziland continues to be highly traditional in its institutional and socio-economic structure. For many, migration remains the only option available for accumulating sufficient cash income. One of the most formidable hurdles in the creation of adequate rural income-generating activities is therefore likely to be persuading the traditional leaders that the need for the changes required to make possible the commercialisation of the rural sector is an urgent one. Once this can be overcome, the following considerations should influence policy designs for providing rural employment opportunities:

1. The capricious behaviour of some tribal authorities and the consequent insecurity of the communal land tenure system in some areas

of Swaziland is hardly conducive to the substantial capital investments needed for successful cash cropping.

2. Smallholder schemes similar to that found at Vuvulane[31] could be used to change radically the low labour-intensive plantation systems found in the sugar, citrus and pineapple industries. The Vuvulane scheme in sugar production has proved very successful and is highly remunerative for participant smallholders. Nevertheless, there are no apparent plans to introduce other similar projects. Although smallholder crop production would perhaps be less economical in the short run, the long-run political, social and economic benefits of productively employing the rural population on a self-employment basis could prove to be the fundamental key to successful withdrawal.

3. The current investment behaviour of rural-based migrant workers shows an extremely high propensity to purchase cattle, which is not only detrimental to grazing as a whole but represents a relatively unproductive channel for surplus funds.

4. Credit facilities available to smallholder farmers are felt to be inadequate in spite of the recently introduced "hypothecation" facilities.[32]

5. Poor marketing facilities for crops other than cotton and tobacco, as well as inadequate distribution centres for agricultural inputs, have dampened cash cropping initiatives. There would appear to be much scope for co-operative ventures.

6. The widespread ignorance of cropping alternatives and of the techniques necessary for efficient husbandry calls for a considerable broadening of the extension services, which, even in their present limited operations, seem not to be as effective as they might.[33]

7. During off-season periods, rural residents could be mobilised to engage in the provision of rural amenities such as clinics, schools, irrigation systems and boreholes, so as to improve rural living standards. Studies have shown a strong willingness on the part of the rural population to partake in such community development.

Finally, in view of the transitional nature of withdrawal, government policy should not neglect to attend to the adverse effects of migration. In economic terms perhaps the most pressing issue is that of overgrazing and the predilection of returned miners to purchase cattle. Because of the abnormally low cow/oxen ratio, it was thought that cattle were held largely for draught purposes and that the intensive large-scale introduction of tractors would reduce the need to hold oxen. There is, however, scepticism over the probable impact of this proposal on destocking. Moreover, the introduction of tractors would reduce male input requirements during the ploughing season and would further encourage migration. Recent recommendations have proposed an intensified mixed farming system, involving dairy cattle and fodder production to encourage destocking, as fewer cattle would lead to higher income. However, Doran et al. (1979) have demonstrated (inverse relationship between cattle price and destocking) that cattle are not held mainly to generate income but rather as a store of wealth. Meanwhile, the pervasive investment in cattle will probably continue as long as migrants remain ignorant of other productive investment opportunities—an ignorance that can largely be overcome by effective extension services. Finally, alternative agricultural investments are likely to be stifled by the risks of uncertainty inherent in the traditional communal land tenure system.

Notes

[1] In 1973 the King suspended the constitution on the grounds that the British model seemed inappropriate, and has since ruled by decree. In the meantime constitutional committees are drafting proposals for a system of government based on approximately 40 community committees (tinkhundla). Although the King's rule has been remarkably stable, with the minimum of official or underground opposition, there is considerable speculation about the successor to the King (who is now 80) and the future balance between the traditionalists and the modernists.

[2] By 1938 domestic employment creation was still insignificant: Kuper (1947) noted that 15,000 Swazis (including families) were living as squatters and farm labourers on individual tenure land, while another 2,000 were hired on a temporary basis by European farmers; 785 Swazis worked on three tin-mines.

[3] Kuper (1947) found that in 1938 public works labourers earned between 27s 6d and 40s per month, most domestic workers earned less than 30s per month, farm labour earned 15s to 40s per month and local nineworkers earned between 8d and 2s per day.

[4] The deferred pay system in Swaziland enables the worker to draw a specific monthly allowance while accumulating the rest to be collected at the termination of work (not necessarily contract), either at the mine or at the TEBA office where he was originally recruited; 95–99 per cent of the Swazi recruits opt for this system of payment.

[5] "Machine boys" are drillers at the stope face who, as well as being paid at a base rate, earn bonuses according to the number of holes they drill per day. According to both local employers and mining officials, Swazis have shown a strong preference for task work, which is a set amount of work paid at a basic rate with any production thereafter being paid at bonus rates.

[6] Postwar development was supported by considerable grants-in-aid and Commonwealth Development and Welfare funds, as well as substantial investments by the Commonwealth Development Corporation, notably in sugar and pulp.

[7] Swazis wishing to work legally in sectors other than mining must find an employer who is willing to verify by affidavit that he cannot find a South African citizen to fill the job. This must then be attested by the South African police. The Swazi is then responsible for getting an attestation from the Swaziland Labour Department. Previously only those workers found contravening influx laws were subject to imprisonment or heavy fine; but employers now face even stiffer penalties.

[8] A recent unpublished survey by de Vletter found that for the Northern Rural Development Area about one-quarter of the homestead absentees were located in South Africa and the rest were elsewhere in Swaziland. Internal areas surveyed showed that only about 8 per cent of the absentees were to be found in South Africa.

[9] Although, strictly speaking, only Mbabane and Manzini may tenuously be considered urban areas, the term "urban" was defined for the purposes of the survey to include the so-called Mbabane-Manzini corridor and any of the larger towns such as Piggs Peak, Havelock and Siteki.

[10] To date, there have been few traditional homesteads on the Lowveld because of the capricious and often oppressive climate, the less fertile soil and the relatively high incidence of disease.

[11] In the Shiselweni district it was observed during a field trip that emigration of a permanent nature was evident amongst the majority of the secondary-school leavers who, according to headmasters, were attracted to the urban areas. Secondary-school leavers, when questioned in a survey as to why people left rural areas to live in Mbabane or Manzini, felt basically that they represented the best places to find employment (77 per cent); 10 per cent cited the lack of money in the rural areas; 5 per cent mentioned a more exciting or better life; and 3 per cent felt that the urban areas provided better education.

[12] This investigation was commissioned by the United Nations Women in Development Project (Swaziland) to determine major economic characteristics such as income flows and sources, asset holdings, agricultural inputs and outputs and migration patterns.

[13] Welfare categorisations of homesteads were somewhat arbitrarily based on income (determined only by cash income) and asset holdings circumscribed to cattle holdings (de Vletter, 1978) but later expanded to include the ownership of motor vehicles, tractors, bicycle or plough (in the unpublished survey mentioned in footnote 8).

[14] This figure was derived from the response by 105 returned mineworkers in relation to their expected homestay based largely on previous experience. It is important to note that these miners were interviewed during February 1977—a period when most miners leave for the mines rather than return; thus the sample may not be representative and is likely to underestimate the length of homestay.

[15] Clarke (1977b) notes that reinvestment in an economy reliant on Labour Reserves not only occurs on the basis of surpluses arising from within the capitalist sector but is also dependent on the labour supply conditions, especially when labour can be obtained at below the cost of reproduction. He writes: "The over-all level and rate of reinvestment in such economies is thus a function of two forms of accumulation. The form which is dependent on intersectoral articulation can be understood as primitive accumulation" (p. 11). In relation to "primitive accumulation", he continues: "The following points appear essential: firstly, labour must exchange at a wage below its cost of subsistence and reproduction; and, secondly, means of meeting the labour costs of subsistence and reproduction which are not provided from wage-labour must exist and be directed towards this purpose" (p. 12).

[16] There was no strong criticism of employment in South Africa; students tended to be aware of the difficulty that both educated and uneducated had in finding work in Swaziland and regarded South African employment opportunities as a natural and, in some instances, preferable alternative to employment in Swaziland.

[17] Centro de Estudos Africanos, Universidade Eduardo Mondlane: *The Mozambican miner*, published under the directorship of Ruth First (Maputo, 1977; mimeographed).

[18] The decreasing length of contracts for the mining industry as a whole can be largely attributed to the changes that have occurred in the composition of mineworkers and their respective contract lengths. Malawian and Mozambican workers, who have had the longest minimum contracts in the industry, have been mostly replaced by South African Blacks signing the shortest contracts allowable (six months).

[19] In the surveys of outgoing and returned miners, high wages accounted for 55–63 per cent of all reasons given for working in the mines, while 50 per cent of the responses of Swaziland-based workers mentioned proximity to home as the principal reason for working at their particular company, and about one-third stated that no work could be found elsewhere.

[20] Potential recruits who had been turned away following the restrictions of 1977 were asked what they would do: only 14 of the 35 respondents said they would continue to seek work in Swaziland, while the remainder said they would return to their homesteads to tend their crops and hope for a future opening of the mines. Of the returned miners, almost 80 per cent said they would definitely return to the mines; and when asked what they would do if they could not be re-engaged, 63 per cent said they would continue to seek work in Swaziland.

[21] "Turnover" in the second case also included absenteeism when workers leave for ploughing and then return with the hope of getting their previous job back.

[22] The age difference was more marked in Lesotho where the average age of mine recruits was found to be somewhat higher, at 33 (van der Wiel, 1977), but with a similar modal group in the 20–24 age cohort. Migration rates in Lesotho drop appreciably after the age of 39: the average age of those men remaining in Lesotho was found to be 45. Natrass (1976) noted that in South Africa domestic migrants bunch in the age cohort of 25–29 with a weighted average age of only 25, compared with 35 for the non-migrant labour force.

[23] See Human Resources Laboratory, Chamber of Mines, 1977. This report by the Laboratory's Monitoring Division is the first of a series of monitoring reports. Over the past few years the Monitoring Division has conducted continuing interviews with more than 2,000 mineworkers on the various groups' mines.

[24] Reactions from the survey of secondary-school students indicate that there was a general prevailing assumption that wage levels were higher in South Africa. Although relatively few students said that they would directly seek work in South Africa, many said they would if they could not find suitable employment in Swaziland.

[25] Van der Wiel (1977) found that the average length of time the Basotho migrant worker (mostly miners) spends outside his own country is between 13 years (for those in the mountain zone) and 16 years (for those from the more proximate lowlands). The Mozambique study found that the worker-peasants interviewed spent, on average, 42–49 per cent of their working life on the mines with only about one-quarter spending less than 30 per cent, while another quarter spent nearly two-thirds of their working life on the mines.

[26] Secondary-school students, in response to the question about friends and relatives working in South Africa, stated that one-quarter held unskilled jobs, one-quarter were in semi-skilled employment, and approximately one-tenth were in each of skilled, clerical and professional (mainly teacher) capacities, the rest being unspecified.

[27] For Lesotho, van der Wiel (1977, p. 90) wrote: "The starting wage paid by the mines is about 70 per cent of the income an average rural household requires per annum to satisfy their basic needs. It is estimated that approximately 55 per cent of mine labourers in 1976 received a salary in cash and kind below the poverty line."

[28] Two MA students from the University of Utrecht attached to the University College of Swaziland for six months while working on a marketing survey of agricultural produce.

[29] Official figures on the gross earnings of Swazi miners in South Africa are not yet available from the Chamber of Mines, and TEBA officials based in Swaziland feel that the figure of E 12.9 million is too high. However, on the basis of approximately 20,000 mine recruits in 1976, with an average contract length of six months and average monthly earnings of about E 100, the figure appears to be realistic.

[30] Assuming that approximately 20,000 workers depend on South African employment and that they in turn support on average more than four dependants, about 100,000 Swazis would be directly affected by withdrawal.

[31] Vuvulane, a limited area within the Swaziland Irrigation Scheme financed by the Commonwealth Development Corporation, is composed of small farms under leasehold arrangements. Farmers independently grow sugar-cane which is guaranteed a market at the nearby sugar-mill. Although the scheme has proven very successful and there are many farmers who have expressed a strong desire to engage in similar smallholding ventures, sugar continues to be grown on expanding plantations requiring comparatively little wage labour.

[32] "Hypothecation" allows farmers—particularly those who do not legally own land or buildings, i.e. who live on Swazi Nation Land—to pledge cattle and other chattels as security for loans. There is, however, a general feeling that small farmers still find it unnecessarily difficult to obtain loans.

[33] Rural surveys conducted in the Northern Rural Development Area showed a very strong reaction concerning extension officers, who, it was felt, *(a)* covered too few homesteads; *(b)* did not follow up as necessary; and *(c)* spent too little time in the fields. Only 25 per cent of the homesteads surveyed were satisfied with the work of the extension officers and only about one-third actually made use of the services of an extension officer.

CONDITIONS AFFECTING BLACK MIGRANT WORKERS IN SOUTH AFRICA: A CASE STUDY OF THE GOLD-MINES

4

F. de Vletter

This chapter gives the salient points of a survey undertaken in the summer of 1977 under my direction by 16 students of the University College of Swaziland. They observed and interviewed Swazi miners on four South African gold-mines (Vaal Reefs and Western Deep Levels of Anglo American Corporation, and Kinross and Winkelhaak of Union Corporation) for a period of seven to ten days and subsequently recorded what they saw and heard in individual reports. It must be accepted that views expressed by Swazi migrants and observers do not necessarily reflect those of Basotho, Xhosa or others. I should like to express my deepest gratitude to the students and merely add that they undertook their assignment with a mixture of apprehension and enthusiasm. I have rarely seen students' reports written with such dedication!

RECENT DEVELOPMENTS

The sharp rise in the price of gold in 1971 heralded several significant developments in the mining industry. The subsequent jump in profits enabled White workers to extract a 14 per cent wage increase, while Black wage increases were negligible. Black miners' wages had hardly changed since 1944, whereas Black wages in manufacturing had increased more than threefold and White miners' wages more than quadrupled. The question of wages for Black miners became extremely sensitive, leading Anglo American and Johannesburg Consolidated Investments to break the inviolable code of conduct between members of the Chamber of Mines[1] by rejecting the "maximum average clause" (payment of a minimum of 90 cents for underground shifts compared with the industry minimum wage of 72 cents).[2] Although a compromise was reached in the following year, Anglo American continued to press for higher wages.

In 1973 widespread unrest swept through the mines and other industries. Management, caught unawares, was obliged to re-evaluate labour relations frameworks, to increase wages and to improve living and working conditions. More problems arose when a mine aircraft crashed, killing 72 Malawian recruits and inducing Life President Banda of Malawi to ban further recruitment of Malawians, who at that time made up almost one-third of all mineworkers. Furthermore, Mozambican independence led to a drastic cut in recruitment.[3] The mines were caught in a quandary. TEBA officials aimed through internal recruitment to raise the proportion of South African Blacks employed on the mines from the 1973 level of 20 per cent to 50 per cent. Mine wages subsequently jumped and labour was rationalised. In spite of the initial panic, the severe recession, which left between 1 and 2 million Blacks unemployed (along with a level of remuneration which became competitive with the manufacturing sector), led to a surplus of workseekers from Botswana, Lesotho, Mozambique, Swaziland and Zimbabwe as well as South Africa itself; as a result, restrictions were imposed in 1977. Ironically, only three years after Malawi's withdrawal, an attempt to renegotiate re-entry left that country with a limited quota of 20,000–25,000 workers. The aftermath of disruption led to a significant reduction of workers from abroad and notable increases in productivity through the rationalisation of labour. By 1980 South African Blacks accounted for more than 54 per cent of the Black labour force on the gold-mines.

RECRUITMENT AND INDUCTION

Signing up

In the early years the recruitment of miners was characterised by coercion and chicanery, and until fairly recently "runners"[4] were extensively used in most labour-supplying areas. Recently, recruitment has relied mainly on the demonstration effect of returned miners and the lack of employment alternatives to provide the supply. At present the number of candidates exceeds the requirements. Before the restrictions were imposed in early 1977, virtually anyone of sufficient age, weight and health was guaranteed employment. Nowadays, novices (who accounted for one-third of the recruits in 1976) are turned away except during what were formerly "trough" months,[5] while only those in possession of valid re-engagement certificates[6] are assured re-employment. On "signing" a contract by fingerprint at any of the recruiting offices, recruits are attested by government officers and undergo a superficial medical examination before being transported by bus or rail to depots either in Johannesburg or in Welkom, depending on their destination. There appeared to be a marked contrast in recruitment conditions between countries.[7]

Before proceeding to their respective mines, recruits are further registered and subjected to more rigorous medical attention. Miners complained bitterly of the humiliation they suffered from the treatment by officers (mainly Black) who seemed hard pressed to maximise the flow of recruits. Those who erred or obstructed the flow were often kicked or beaten with no compassion nor respect for age. Medical examinations entailed the herding of naked recruits past unsympathetic medical officers. Public nudity was abhorred by many of the ethnic groups.[8]

Orientation

The ethnic heterogeneity of the mine workers makes some rudimentary form of communication necessary. This need is met by the bastard language, Fanakolo,[9] which is taught to neophytes. Newly arrived recruits are addressed by hostel managers and senior Black administrators who explain mine regulations, workers' rights, banking facilities, and so forth, with emphasis on the importance of deference and respect for discipline. Information that is very important for the miner is compacted into a brief and confusing talk. It was felt by our students that subsequent misunderstandings and the bitterness found amongst many of the miners arise largely from the inadequate dissemination of information.

Induction

Because of the high costs inherent in turnover and recruitment, mines seek to optimise the time between recruitment and production. All recruits perform sequential aptitude tests which place them into different types of work falling within eight wage bands. Subsequent training varies in duration: novices will have from two to six days, while training for more experienced workers such as team-leaders or artisan-aides can last up to six weeks.

Those wishing to work underground, where pay is considerably higher than for surface work, must take the dreaded acclimatisation exercises to sift heat-intolerant men and to condition others for underground work. The exercises are endured for four hours per day for from four to nine days in a heat-controlled chamber. Observed treatment by supervising officers was unduly harsh and unnecessarily drove men to physical extremes. There is prevailing resentment that Whites are inexplicably exempt from similar exercises.

WORK ON THE MINES

The work day

For the main shift, Black workers rise at about 3 a.m. to reach the shaft head at approximately 5 a.m. If a worker is late, according to a predetermined schedule, the day's work is forfeited and on some mines the tardy worker is severely punished. Owing to the congestion at the shaft and the distance between shaft station and workplace, workers commonly spend one or two hours "commuting". Until recently, unpaid inactivity was extended by the need to wait for White supervision, but concessions have been made by the Mine Workers Union (MWU) allowing Black team leaders to supervise preliminary clearing before the arrival of the White miner and shift boss.

The work shift spans eight hours and there is no allowance for an official break. This hardly deterred the Whites, who were observed often to sit and chat whilst delegating orders. Black workers had to take advantage of a lull in work (if any) to eat, drink or rest. White miners and their team-leaders—both of whom were substantially increasing their incomes by production bonuses—were frequently found to push the Black teams to physical extremes, although most Black members are kept to a simple basic rate. At the end of a shift Black workers complained of further prolonged waiting while Whites ascended (last to arrive, first to leave).

Many ethnic groups, such as the Zulu, have traditionally viewed minework as demeaning, there being no doubt as to the exertions it requires; but a majority of Swazi respondents, both on the mines and at recruitment centres, felt that the hours were shorter, the work less arduous and the remuneration much higher than for alternative domestic work in the sugar-fields, forests, citrus plantations and farms (de Vletter, 1978).

Danger of work

Underground work is considerably more taxing than surface work. The wage differential reflects the much greater danger. As evidenced by the response from surveys of rural homesteads and non-mine workers (de Vletter, 1978), stories of the risks of minework are legion. The workplace death rate for 1977 was 1.41 per 1,000 workers, while 47.6 per 1,000 were injured in one way or another. In spite of the fatality rate having dropped from 4.15 per 1,000 in 1903, the current rates imply that 500–600 workers die each year (587 in 1977) on the gold and platinum mines. Safety standards on these mines are said to be among the highest in the world; but the Witwatersrand is the most dangerous area for the rock-bursts that account for the highest proportion of deaths and accidents.

Our students observed that safety awareness had been inculcated in most miners and that they took maximum precautions—pervasive superstition and fatalism notwithstanding. The Chamber of Mines cannot dictate standards of safety on individual mines, but every mine manager is required to attend a course at the International Loss Control Institute in Atlanta. Nevertheless, many miners complained that their team leaders—and, by implication, White miners—forced them to work under dangerous conditions.

Equally pernicious is the prevalence of occupational diseases arising from minework. During the period from 1968 to 1974 an annual average of 2.8 per 1,000 workers were certified as suffering from a compensable occupational disease other than tuberculosis.[10] Over the same period 3,486 Blacks and 48 Whites or Coloured were listed as suffering from tuberculosis. An average of 5,775 Blacks, as against 693 Whites or Coloured, died each year from occupational diseases during these seven years.

Furthermore, there are indications that the impact of diseases contracted on the mines is much more pervasive than figures suggest. Studies have found abnormally high rates of pneumoconiosis and tuberculosis in areas known to supply labour to the mines.[11] Although there is as yet no conclusive evidence, the unusually high differential of life expectancy at birth between males and females found in both Swaziland and Lesotho may stem directly from mine work.[12] The medical treatment of workers on contract was found to be of high standard; but, once they have returned home, miners are virtually left to their own devices.

Migrant workers or professionals?[13]

In spite of the oscillating nature of their work and the factors militating against proficiency, minework is, for many, a career. Regularly returning mineworkers strive to attain recognition and prestige, not only amongst fellow workers but also at the home base. Three major obstacles—the inability to transfer work records, the colour bar and pay—frustrate career advancement.

Workers' records. Surprisingly, even under conditions of repressive labour controls, Black miners' records are not transferable from one mine to another, whether moves are made within the same company or between companies. A miner dissatisfied with conditions on one mine must weigh the cost of revoking his previous work records before considering relocation. Also, miners who have been laid off from their former mine because of, for example, an expired re-engagement certificate may have to start from scratch on another mine. Miners often related instances of former team leaders being relegated to the abject duties of a spanner boy after having switched mines.

The system is not only grossly unjust; it is also an effective mechanism for the conservative companies' opposition to the improvement of conditions. At the time of writing the issue of records is a source of bitter dispute between the relatively progressive and the reactionary members in the Chamber of Mines. If Blacks were given the same inter-mine work recognition as White miners, the increasingly divergent working and living conditions would have a noticeable effect on the labour supplies between unpopular and popular mines similar to the effects of "crimping" through pay differentials in the early mining years.[14]

Colour bars. In 1978 the Minister of Labour claimed that South African labour laws were not discriminatory.[15] The sophistry of this statement is readily apparent in the colour bars prevalent on the mines. Mobility in underground work is impeded by *(a)* the legal requirement of holding a "blaster's certificate" or "certificate of competency" obtainable only from White mining schools, or *(b)* closed shop agreements awarded to recognised trade unions. The tenuous arguments about colour bars, the level of skill and rates of pay are pointedly absurd when one notes that White neophyte immigrants undergoing training are paid more than Black team-leaders with years of mining experience. Secular adjustments made for Blacks taking over White jobs—previously defined as skilled work—for health, economic or political reasons have underscored the fact that "the division of work between African and White has less to do with skill and experience than with convention, vested interests of White miners and their determination to defend their access to sheltered well-paid employment".[16]

The escalating political and economic costs of the colour bar culminated in a confrontation between the Anglo American Corporation and the Mine Workers Union, sparked off by the leaking of an internal Corporation document stating that the mining industry could no longer tolerate the admission of Whites "who are either unable or unwilling to outpace the ambitious Black and who are likely to prove an embarrassment in the future". The document also suggested that the long-term objective of the industry should be the elimination of job reservation and the acceptance of the principle of negotiation by all employees. The Mine Workers Union saw this as a move to oust the White miner in favour of cheaper Black labour. The threat of Black worker advancement and prospective labour reforms assumed to emanate from the Wiehahn Commission were felt to be important contributory factors to the widespread Mine Workers Union strike during March 1979.

Pay. One of the most distinguishing characteristics of apartheid is the Black/White pay differential. Although, relatively, the gap has been closing (from 1 : 24 in 1971 to approximately 1 : 8 in 1979), the absolute gap (currently about R 900) continues to increase. The gap itself, because of the ratio of Black workers to White, is unlikely to become very narrow, given the high weighting of unskilled Black workers; but it will remain contentious until miners—regardless of race—are remunerated according to the principle of equal pay for equal work. Although over the period from 1971 to 1976 Black miners' wages increased by 400 per cent—twice the national average increase for Black workers—the jump in wages reflected the combined influence of gold prices, labour disturbances and sectoral labour competition, and was not a conscious protracted policy by the industry to improve the relative welfare of the Black worker. Wage increases in 1977 were only 6 per cent, and subsequent increases would appear to be tied to cost-of-living indices.

THE MINE HOSTEL

Accommodation

Accommodation was the facility most subject to variation between the mines, reflecting the mine's age, profitability and expected lifespan and, most important, company policy. Compounds or hostels are composed of blocks of rooms with barrack-style accommodation. Older rooms house 20–22 occupants in bunks which are still of cement on some mines and were heated by a grimy, smoky coal stove. Newer accommodation offers a sharp contrast: "rooms" are now divided into three—two sleeping-rooms each with bunks for four men and a sitting-room for the eight boarders. Following the spate of so-called "faction fights", dormitory blocks are now "integrated" but rooms maintain ethnic homogeneity.

For permanent family housing, mines are legally restricted to a limit of 3 per cent of their Black labour force. Delays on the part of the government administration have effectively curbed this to about 1.5 per cent. Recently, however, a change in attitude has empowered the mines not only to provide 3 per cent of their Black workers with permanent housing but also to house any worker in Black townships. The costs of doing so, however, will ensure that the "permanent" residents will be key workers only.

Attitudes towards accommodation varied considerably. Swazis, who are mostly illiterate and come from traditional homesteads on comparatively short contracts, seemed on the whole to appreciate their accommodation. More cosmopolitan workers from Zimbabwe and South African urban areas, and those with longer contracts, were less tolerant. The increasing sophistication of and the parallel demands from these workers have been recognised by a recent Chamber of Mines report, which warns:

Present conditions both at work and in the hostel, suggest a reasonably contented workforce, but the current economic climate [i.e. high unemployment rates] may be underplaying the true state of affairs. Evidence continues to gather that a more sophisticated man is entering the gold-mining industry. For this reason, the avenues of advancement open to him need to be clearly demonstrated so that he can measure against his levels of aspiration. Furthermore, the improvements in work and hostel conditions over the past few years need to be maintained if the industry is to retain the services of this higher calibre man. (Human Resources Laboratory, Chamber of Mines, 1977.)

Food

Food tended to be the most contentious general issue. The nutritional requirements of the ingredients could, according to dietary schedules, hardly be faulted, but the quality on some mines was deplorable. These mines used the lame excuse that excessive numbers affected the quality of the food, but the largest mines surveyed by our students unequivocally provided the best food.

Our students observed strong behavioural patterns correlated with environment and amenities. Miners eating in the cold, cavernous dining-halls displayed great contempt for their surroundings, deliberately dumping left-overs on the tables, while miners in the small and more intimate modern cafeterias were comparatively urbane. Similar attitudes were noted in respect of toilet facilities.

Leisure activities

The workers' prolonged absence from their family and the rigours of work make it very important that entertainment should be available. Each mine provided distractions for the miners but the quality of the activities varied.

Sport and entertainment facilities. Sports facilities were abundant and the arenas, stadiums and tracks were of professional quality. Most mines actively encouraged promising sportsmen to the point where they became professional and were only marginally engaged in minework. Although the expenditure on sports is considerable, many amenities are basically of European appeal only. Thus, tennis courts and cricket fields, for example, remain largely unused.

Entertainment facilities were also impressive but varied from mine to mine. Capital outlay, promotion and variety notwithstanding, one official commented: "I doubt very much if more than 25 per cent of the labour force on any mine participate directly in such activities or derives any entertainment from the participation of others."

The lack of participation in these sports activities contrasts sharply with almost universal attendance at the mine beer hall—the social focal point of the mine hostel. Drinking and socialising are considered by most miners as their most important pastimes. Gordon (1977) observed: "Drinking together is one of the most important rituals of Brotherhood and friendship. . . . The buying and sharing of beer is one of the common opportunities available for engaging in these transactions."[17]

The "locations". For many miners, sophisticated facilities and subsidised drinks[18] are not enough to induce them to remain within the confines of the hostel. The "locations" or nearby Black townships offer a welcome escape from the strictures of mine life—at the risk of frequent assaults and arrests.[19] Locations are convenient for heterosexual relations and prostitution is rife. Gambling and the availability of drugs are also important attractions. Mine regulations do not debar miners from residing in the locations but few do so.

The subject of homosexuality was extremely difficult to broach, but its practice pervaded the hostels despite the immediate dismissal of those found engaged in such activity. Its occurrence (given the all-male environment and the prolonged separation from spouses or mates) is not surprising and, short of full family housing, more frequent home visits or legalised prostitution, there is no obvious solution. What requires immediate attention, however, is the abuse of power in soliciting homosexual favours. Indunas, team-leaders and some of the more powerful clerks were often accused of threatening young recruits who refused to comply with their demands.

Education and training. For the more serious and aspiring miners, virtually all mines offer free education up to the junior certificate level; thereafter many mines offer to pay up to 87.5 per cent of educational costs on proof of successful examination results. Furthermore, for those wishing to pursue vocational training, some mines provide comprehensive instruction in such areas as masonry, carpentry and driving. Miners aspiring to become artisan-aides are also provided the opportunity for part-time training. Unfortunately, the response has so far been disappointing, mainly because most miners are too tired after a rigorous day's work. Most of the illiterate peasants who regard mine work as a convenient means of acquiring a certain amount of income appear to have little incentive to upgrade their vocational competence.

POWER STRUCTURE AND SOCIAL CONTROL

Power hierarchy

The tangible realms of power for most Black miners interviewed did not go beyond the hostel manager for day-to-day activities and the mine overseer at the workplace. But even these lower echelons of White management (supposedly in close contact with the Black worker) are shielded by Black clerical, supervisory and disciplinary officers. Interesting attitudinal patterns were reported by our students, who perceived the general disillusionment and resentment felt by Black workers toward fellow Blacks in authority, who were often regarded as the corrupt and brow-beaten stooges of Whites, afraid of thwarting management policy.

The mine hostel is administered by the hostel manager, supported by White personnel officers and deputy personnel officers. Black personnel assistants act as the go-between for White management and the Black workers. The pinnacle of the Black hierarchy is the induna—a type of headman controlling each major ethnic group, supported by tribal representatives (formerly called "police boys"). At the bottom of the ladder, and the only democratically selected position in the power structure, is the isibonda—an elected representative for each room.

The induna. Predictably, in a system using Blacks to enforce White dictates, the induna is the most censured link in the hierarchical chain. Criticism is so vehement that an immediate examination of the problem is imperative. The selection of indunas is based on their mine experience and, no doubt, on their degree of compliance with management. Although management has the final say in the selection, some tacit approval from prospective subjects is essential to ensure a modicum of authority. Nevertheless, the induna, who exerts considerable power over the miners in respect of discipline and career, is the target of bitter attacks denouncing him as unabashedly corrupt, management-fearing, partial in disciplinary and promotion decisions, harbouring young sycophants and fostering homosexual activities, and so on. The fact that the induna is invariably uneducated (an experiment with educated indunas failed dismally) and often embarrassingly inept in diplomacy, makes the dextrous task of toeing the management line, while maintaining an element of respectability in his constituency, almost impossible and rarely well executed. Anglo American Corporation, experimenting with the system, has "detribalised" the induna, who is now called a "unit supervisor" and is assigned to an integrated block rather than an ethnic group. At the same time Anglo American Corporation ensures a reasonably ethnic balance of unit supervisors so as to enable miners with ethnic-oriented problems to air their grievances. Although only in its early stages, the system is felt to be a marked improvement.

The hostel manager. The hostel manager is ultimately responsible for the maintenance of a high and stable labour complement. Before the supply disruptions of 1974 and the repeal of the Master and Servants Act, absenteeism and desertion were of minor concern. However, there has recently been greater pressure on the hostel manager to improve labour relations and conditions because *(a)* workers can now break contracts without serious legal repercussions, and *(b)* there is more dependence on South African Blacks with comparatively short contracts. A distinct change of attitude has been borne out by the miners' response, which acknowledged that there had been an improvement in grievance procedures over the past few years, with a similar improvement in racial relations in the work environment. Before 1974 assaults by Whites on their Black workers were a matter of course. Nowadays the Black worker is more likely to retaliate and, furthermore, has recourse to a more sympathetic ear from a grievance tribunal.[20] There are some mines where assaults still occur, and many Black miners complained of partiality in decisions; but recent dismissals of Whites for assault have nevertheless left a more favourable impression on Black miners.

Workers' representation

Gold and platinum mines are exempt from the Bantu Labour Relations Regulation Act as well as the Industrial Conciliation Further Amendment Act and are therefore not required by law to allow works or liaison committees to be set up. This notwithstanding, the industrial relations structures have been in a state of flux since the labour unrest of 1973. Mines are currently experimenting with different forms of representation and all have some form of committee system. It is unlikely that any uniform system will be considered by the mining industry before the appearance of the recommendations of the Wiehahn Commission on the mining industry.

There is at present considerable controversy within the mining industry as a result of two leaked "internal working documents" prepared within the Anglo American Corporation (to one of which reference has already been made), which attack the Mine Workers Union for its role in stifling the mining industry through closed shop and statutory restrictions obstructing job advancement for Blacks. The documents call for Black union rights, emphasising the importance of and need to have integrated unions.

Albeit late and slow, some companies are making headway in improving the channels for workers' representation, though still falling considerably short of allowing full bargaining rights. The committee system varies between companies: the degree of concession usually reflects the extent of a company's progressiveness. Anglo American Corporation operates a two-tier system covering production or the work situation on the one hand and hostels on the other. Committees are pyramidal. On the production side, one worker is elected to represent a body of about 60 colleagues, to form a committee of ten to meet with the mine overseer (White). From this base committee, a representative is elected to sit on a mine committee which meets with section managers, and finally a representative from the latter committee sits on a council composed of representatives from other sections (engineering, metallurgy, administration, etc.) who sit with the mine management. This particular arrangement has been in force since 1976, with a parallel structure for White workers which Anglo American hopes ultimately to integrate with the structure for Blacks. There is a similar structure for hostels, with the base committees composed of elected representatives from amongst the isibondas.

Survey findings from different mines show little awareness of or interest in these activities by the Black workers: those concerned often claim that the recent developments were cosmetic and that there was no real effective shift in bargaining power from management to the worker. It is perhaps too early to assess the change which has in fact taken place; but the many problems which plague the committee system are also likely to hinder the work of trade unions. With the high turnover inherent in the migrant labour system and with the apathy of the many transient workers, effective bargaining will be hampered. Anglo American Corporation have full-time Black councillors working with committee representatives to advise them on representation and dissemination. Union Corporation runs a three-day course for all isibondas as training for committee work. To ensure the effectiveness of the negotiating machinery, the training of Whites has been introduced. In 1977 Anglo American Corporation introduced an industrial relations course centred on the theme "the utilisation of labour". It is compulsory for all Whites, from managers to miners, and one of its declared purposes is to convince the Whites of the need for collective bargaining rights for all racial groups. Union Corporation operates a five-day course for shift bosses and miners dealing with work relationships between Blacks and Whites, three days of which are devoted to understanding certain aspects of the Black workers' culture with the objective of fostering better inter-racial tolerance.

The failure of the committee system to channel workers' grievances effectively was highlighted after extensive damage and rioting by miners in 1979 on the new Elandsrand mine, considered to be a showcase for the accommodation and facilities it offers Black workers. An investigation found that the uprising was linked with over-ambitious production targets, the attainment of which was hampered by teething problems with newly installed equipment, a shortage of accommodation because some hostels were not finished and other problems, all of which could have been solved if management had been made aware of them. Rather than use existing channels of communication, the workers preferred to take the more direct approach and to vent their frustrations on the main sources of irritation, such as the computer which allegedly miscalculated bonus pay.

POLICY RECOMMENDATIONS

Following private consultations I had with managers of Union Corporation on the students' reports, a number of reforms were introduced in 1978. They include increased privacy for Black workers by reducing the number of occupants per room; better washing and toilet facilities; more careful and varied food preparation, now undertaken by private catering firms; and separate accommodation for senior Black staff. It is encouraging to see concrete results arising from recommendations; but, to date, they represent only ad hoc company-specific reforms affecting basic creature comforts. More fundamental changes within the industry as a whole are needed if the lot of the migrant worker is to be significantly improved.

With the imminent publication of the second Wiehahn Commission report dealing, inter alia, with the mining industry, one can only hope that the ineluctable pressures of political and economic development will create a more enlightened legislative framework relating to migrant workers, whether from abroad or domestic. Many of the recommendations which follow are within the capacity of the mining industry itself; they do not require legislation. This is particularly apt since the so-called "gold bonanza", which has been generating windfall profits that should be spread more equitably among the factors of production.

The following policy proposals will centre on four areas: *(a)* the concept of the Black worker being regarded as a professional rather than a migrant; *(b)* changes necessary to improve working and living conditions on the mines; *(c)* changes in racial attitudes inherent in the present framework under the aegis of apartheid; and *(d)* the role of supplier States in determining the fate of their workers on the South African gold-mines.

The Black worker as a professional

As noted earlier, the labour laws of the apartheid regime militate against the Black migrant's pursuing a career in the White economy. Many Blacks may be migrants by choice but few have any choice but to be migrants. Although a significant proportion of the mine labour force undoubtedly regard their contracts with the mines as transitory, there is a large core who should fairly be recognised as career miners.

103

Centralisation of employment records. One of the basic reasons for the formation of the Chamber of Mines was to introduce centralised recruitment and standardised wages, so as to avoid self-defeating intra-industry competition for labour. Yet only superficial efforts are made to ensure that minimum working and living conditions are provided. Consequently, in an effort to maintain some measure of labour stability in spite of the great variations between conditions on the different mines, workers' records still cannot be transferred from one mine to another. Mines where working and living conditions are relatively poor, so that they are unable to retain workers without artificial barriers to movement, should not be protected in this way. Black workers must be entitled to the same privileges of transferability as White workers, who can make an intra- or inter-company transfer within the Chamber of Mines and retain all their previous records and benefits.

The centralisation of records would facilitate the administration of pension and long-service benefits which are at present subject to gross injustices and the whims of company policy and ad hoc discretion.[21] Pension funds must also be provided on a much more equitable basis, and the compulsory period of 15 years of service before eligibility for benefits is acquired should be substantially shortened. Centralised records would make it possible for workers to accumulate benefits proportionate to their service.

A further important factor to be taken into account in any centralisation of records is the potential effect on workers' compensation and rehabilitation. Workers' histories could be related to the incidence of disease and accidents; and the most negligent mines would pay the highest premiums. Rehabilitation centres for Black workers, similar to the one recently introduced at the Ernest Oppenheimer Hospital in Welkom, are vital for those who have depended on the mines as their sole source of income. Because of the extremely high rates of employment injury and incapacity for work, the mines must shoulder the responsibility of rehabilitating injured workers and guaranteeing them re-employment rather than relegating them to their rural homesteads with a compensatory pittance. This greater financial responsibility for the mines would promote greater safety consciousness.

Freedom and recognition of association. The Wiehahn Commission is likely to recommend the establishment of recognised Black unions and the abolition of job reservation; but, as Anglo American Corporation has noted in an internal working document, "An integrated union remains the only real and viable solution to the Mine Workers Union problem." In other words, as long as unions remain segregated, White unions will inevitably protect their "minority" rights through some form of implicit or explicit colour bar. Collective bargaining must be pursued according to conditions of employment, and remuneration must follow the principle of equal pay for equal work. As long as the attainment of "skill" is adapted to genealogical artifice, plurality and friction will plague labour relations. Many Black mineworkers with oscillating or erratic involvement are unlikely to take more than a peripheral interest in workers' representation, but the unrestricted opportunities for all those miners who devote a great part of their life to the mines will have an important psychological impact on workers' morale in general.

Equal opportunities in employment imply equal accessibility to training facilities. The President of the Chamber of Mines echoed this sentiment in a recent report and—seemingly in contradiction with the prevailing attitude within the Chamber—went on to say: "If the mining industry is to make optimum use of available human resources, it is essential that the potential work effort of all race groups is fully mobilised. . . . Inevitably, this must mean a concerted and progressive move away from racial discrimination in the workplace."[22]

Working and living conditions

The Chamber of Mines seems to have become aware of the implications of the recruitment of increasingly sophisticated Black workers. It is important to adapt conditions to meet the expectations that go with sophistication. At this stage, a radical change in the infrastructure seems unlikely because of the mines' expected life, which in most cases does not exceed 20 years.

Working conditions. To reduce the hours of commuting and waiting that Blacks must endure in addition to the normal shift hours, a more sophisticated scheduling of staggered team-work is necessary, although the implications of mobilising and co-ordinating, say, 10,000 workers through one shaft are admittedly formidable.

Official breaks during the shift are imperative for health and welfare reasons. If as a result the shift has to last longer so as to maintain production, this is likely to be only slightly inconvenient to the Black worker, who in any case spends so much extra time going to and from his workplace.

Physical exploitation by White miners and their team-leaders in order to maximise production must be checked. Furthermore, to promote better working relations between Blacks and Whites, teams as a whole should be paid production bonuses.

The practice of petty apartheid in work and on the mine premises unnecessarily irritates the Black worker, and evidence from companies which have abolished regulations such as those on segregated toilets suggests that there is little likelihood of government intervention. Although much of the petty apartheid is written into mine regulations, the habits on some mines, such as discrimination in the lift cage, are simply a matter of attitude.

Accommodation. Most critics of the migrant labour system feel that migrants should be given the option of bringing their families to their place of work. This, of course, would be the ideal; but it is unlikely, given the circumstances. To set up Black townships within the mines would be financially prohibitive, and the miner himself would probably be against the idea, since in various surveys, both in Swaziland and on the mines, miners almost unanimously balked at the suggestion of having their family living with them.[23] However, there is a great need for more opportunities for the worker to stay in touch with his family and for the mine to encourage such contact while the worker is on their pay-roll. Permanent family housing for all skilled Black miners who view the mines as a long-term career must be regarded as a minimum. Housing for short-contract miners should follow the example of the more modern mines in concept, while old marginal mines should make appropriate renovations.[24]

Food. The cost of providing better food is negligible. The provision of better food ranks among the highest priorities raised by the miners. Improved quality, greater variety and more ethnic balance seem to be the major demands. Furthermore, eating is an important social pastime for the Black worker, and calls for a much more intimate environment than the halls offered on most mines; in the event, these are shunned by many miners who prefer to eat in their rooms.

Entertainment. Entertainment facilities, though impressive, were used by only a minority of workers. If the five-day week were introduced,[25] workers might have two days for leisure. The prospect of inadequate attractions apart from the beer hall is a source of considerable worry to the miners who fear renewed "faction fighting" set off by drunkenness. One Chamber of Mines official has suggested the establishment of "leisure centres" for the Black worker. These centres would offer shopping complexes with a wide range of goods which are popular with the Black workers. There would also be cafés and restaurants, but the main emphasis would be on entertainment and live shows where workers would be allowed to take girl-friends. It is crucial that, before ideas such as this come to fruition, Black workers be consulted on what *they* want, and that the wastefulness of preconceived benevolence be avoided.

Attitudes

The ingrained attitudes which were found to prevail in Lesotho (Agency for Industrial Mission, 1976), the WNLA depot, the acclimatis-ation chamber and underground derive from the intrinsic nature of the mining industry in its use (or rather, abuse) of cheap Black labour. Unfortunately, the simple changing of company policy and rules is not likely to have any significant impact on those Whites who are the most hardened products of the racist constitution of apartheid. Only through intensive exposure to remedial programmes designed to demonstrate the social, economic and moral costs of racism could these attitudes *genuinely* change. Of course, there is much superficial change. The strict measures imposed on Whites who assault Blacks account for what is interpreted by Black miners as "improved" racial relations underground.

Anglo American Corporation has programmes which emphasise the importance of harmonious industrial relations. Union Corporation stresses the promotion of better understanding between Blacks and Whites. Both claim to have had considerable success. This kind of approach is commendable, but it could be several years before significant results are achieved.

The most serious problems of attitude are likely to arise amongst the administrative officers. Our survey showed that, although some hostel managers were sympathetic and paternal in outlook, others were steadfastly colonial and racist and were unable to adapt themselves to the abolition of the Masters and Servants Act. Miners' treatment by hostel managers was consequently observed to have a strong influence on the "popularity rating" of a mine and on their decision to return. Those officers who remain inflexible in their attitudes even after "rehabilitation" programmes should be dismissed, while personnel officers recruited in future should hold degrees in sociology, anthropology, psychology or a related discipline, as well as have some experience or training in labour relations. There is evidence of such a move by some companies,[26] but the trend is by no means universal.

The role of the migrant-supplying State

The improvement of the welfare of migrant workers employed in South Africa is a delicate issue and is felt by some to place the supplier States in a compromising position which implicitly gives credence to the migrant labour system. Rhetoric and declarations notwithstanding, the immediate withdrawal of labour from South Africa would be too costly both politically and economically for these countries. Migrant labour is a current reality and for some countries, such as Lesotho and even

Mozambique,[27] the phenomenon is likely to be of protracted duration. Given the desirability of breaking these countries' dependence on the apartheid regime, a conscious strategy which seeks to withdraw workers over a predetermined period, complemented by an effort to improve migrant workers' conditions of life and work, would not be contradictory.

Joint action. The notion of a cartel type of agreement between supplier States may rhetorically be dismissed on the grounds that it implies negotiation with the apartheid system. However, the continuance of migrant flows—for whatever period—is by implication a tacit acceptance of the system, albeit through exigency. The reality of the matter is that, if concerted action is not pursued, the pressure on South Africa is reduced while ad hoc efforts by individual States such as Lesotho[28] will continue separately and less effectively. "Negotiation" with the mines and the South African Government should perhaps be regarded as a "confrontation".

The issue of phased withdrawal through joint action is discussed in more detail in Chapter 7. In my view it is important that the countries should press for workers' rights now as well as during any period of withdrawal. Demands by the supplier States (by virtue of the proportion of labour supply controlled and the sensitive political relations between South Africa and peripheral States) would carry significant weight both in the mining industry and in Parliament. The degree of "confrontation" and the forcefulness of demands would, however, be tempered by the extent of prevailing unemployment in South Africa and the surplus labour in countries which may not join the collective body of supplier States.

Botswana, Lesotho and Swaziland have recently established the Southern Africa Labour Commission.[29] This aims to fight for workers' rights and to develop workers' consciousness. In the Commission government officials, representatives of labour movements, representatives of migrant workers based in South Africa and social scientists meet together. Whilst maintaining the ultimate desirability of withdrawal, the Committee concentrates on the rights of workers still employed during the transitional period and of "career" miners falling out by attrition.

Supplier States could help to ensure that minimum conditions are maintained by operating a monitoring team of labour officials and researchers who would survey mines and interview miners to assess conditions and make the necessary recommendations. Mines assessed as suboptimal could be boycotted by the supplier States. Furthermore, an agreement could be struck with the Chamber of Mines to allow the governments of supplier States direct access to the research findings of the

Human Resources Laboratory.[30] A pragmatic working relationship between the governments and the Laboratory would ensure confidentiality while at the same time enabling the governments better to understand the many problems faced by their citizens.

Health, compensation and other benefits. As long as the supplier States are unable to provide sufficient employment opportunities to absorb migrant workers, they will be morally obliged to oversee their workers' welfare. The most pressing matter requiring government action is the monitoring of occupational diseases and injury. Returning migrants should be subjected to a thorough medical examination to assess whether any compensable disease had been contracted while under contract. Anyone found to be in need of medical treatment should be treated locally but at the mining industry's expense. Examination centres would be best situated at the TEBA recruiting stations and operated by the Chamber of Mines under the supervision of government doctors. It is expected that the medical examination of outgoing migrants would be more centralised at the point of recruitment, implying an improvement in the medical facilities at the TEBA offices. This system could also be used for returning miners.

Finally, governments should play a much greater role in the surveillance of fair compensation and retirement benefits. There is little recourse for miners who have been unfairly treated in this respect. To this end government labour departments should provide appropriate machinery similar to that for locally employed workers. The labour representatives of supplier States stationed in South Africa—except perhaps for those of Lesotho—are basically little more than administrative officers. They must be trained effectively to investigate complaints raised by their nationals and be provided with the necessary staff to deal with any malpractices by the mines or other employers.

Conclusion

Given the volatility of southern Africa, any recommendations relating to the apartheid regime are the certain target of severe criticism. The recommendations presented in this chapter could justifiably be rejected as being piecemeal, though it could not be said that they are apologetic to a country whose basic constitution is fundamentally perverse. Some observers simply demand a basic charter of workers' rights, which I would regard as naive idealism for which only a revolution could provide the requisite clean slate. Radical reform voluntarily undertaken by the South African Government seems a remote possibility. Mounting external and internal pressure for change may be effective; but we can only speculate. Although internal upheaval may provide the solution, the above recommendations are presented in the spirit that the mining industry wields the potential power effectively to defy stultifying government policy which is also becoming increasingly vulnerable to external political pressure. Furthermore, South Africa can no longer afford to annoy its Black neighbours, and the time is now ripe for the labour-supplying States to consolidate their demands.

Notes

[1] The Chamber of Mines is in many respects a *de facto* cartel of South Africa's major mining groups. One of the strongest bonds tieing the mining firms together is the monopolistic control of labour, which hinges mainly on agreements that labour supplies would fall under the jurisdiction of recruiting bodies of the Chamber and that companies would not diverge from the general prevailing wage structure.

[2] Fierce competition between the mines for labour at the turn of the century through wage differentials almost crippled many mines and led to the adoption of the "maximum average clause", which basically allowed a range of wage levels to be paid to Black workers but limited this range by a maximum average based on the total wage bill divided by the number of workers. Thus, although it gave some flexibility in wage structure between levels of skill and former experience, it allowed very little variation for the unskilled manual work which occupied the overwhelming majority of Black mineworkers.

[3] The reduction of post-independence recruitment from Mozambique was the result of various factors and not only of ideological considerations. Radical changes in the recruiting system led to initial administrative problems which apparently led to a substantial drop in outflow, while at the same time many mines—particularly Anglo American—were trying to reduce the size of their Mozambican complements following an amendment in the Mozambique convention which put the onus of the considerably higher recruitment costs of Mozambican miners on the mines themselves; in the past the cost had been shared out through the Chamber of Mines. Although the Mozambican Government has condemned the migrant labour system and stated its commitment to absorb migrant workers in its economy, migrant flows have recently increased.

[4] Runners were used by recruitment offices to solicit potential recruits from rural areas by extolling the mines, their contracts and their wages. The runners were given commissions based on the number of recruits brought in. Nowadays it is evident from the queues of recruits outside the recruitment offices that runners have become redundant. Nevertheless, recruiting offices (in Swaziland at least) maintain informal communications systems and agreements with bus-drivers, rural storekeepers and the like for such services as transporting recruits from rural areas and informing potential recruits of vacancies on particular mines.

[5] Traditionally, all mines faced serious labour shortages over the last three months of the year, when complement levels often dropped to about two-thirds of requirements. The exodus of miners from most areas of southern Africa is related to the seasonal requirements of agriculture when, during this period, men are usually required for ploughing and for planting subsistence crops. Even for those not involved in agriculture, there is a pervasive tendency for miners to return home to visit their families over Christmas.

[6] Two types of re-engagement certificate are issued: the 26-week and the 45-week certificates. The first is issued, at the discretion of the mine concerned, to those who have worked underground for a period of between 26 and 45 weeks, allowing the miner to stay at home for one week for every four worked. If he stays at home for longer than the entitled period, the privilege of re-employment on the issuing mine expires. The 45-week certificate allows the miner to stay at home for six months on completion of 45 weeks of service.

[7] Student impressions of recruitment conditions in Lesotho, as presented in Agency for Industrial Mission (1976), were of shocking conditions and ill-treatment, contrasting with the relaxed

atmosphere of recruitment centres in Swaziland, which are run by White Swazi nationals who are held in high regard.

[8] Many tribes have strict traditional codes which forbid close relatives—particularly fathers and sons-in-law—to encounter each other naked. Furthermore, many miners complained of being taunted and ridiculed by tribes such as the Xhosa for not being circumcised—a prerequisite to manhood for the Xhosa and other tribes.

[9] Fanakolo is basically a command language derived from adulterated Zulu, Afrikaans and other vernacular expressions. Because of the ethnic heterogeneity of the mine labour force and the high turnover of workers, this appears to be the most efficient mode of communication. However, it is demeaning and often results in serious misunderstandings because of the superficiality of the brief language courses. Some observers feel that the usefulness of Fanakolo will wane as the labour force becomes more stabilised and workers become progressively more sophisticated in an increasingly mechanised industry.

[10] Report of the South African Commission of Inquiry into Industrial Health, 1975, as quoted in SACTU, 1978, p. 6.

[11] Pneumoconiosis is a recently coined generic term covering all forms of dust disease, such as silicosis, phthisis and asbestosis.

[12] Unofficial results from the 1976 Swaziland census show that there is approximately an eight-year difference in life expectancy between Swazi males and females. Although age may not have been recorded entirely accurately by the census takers, demographers feel that the differential is significant. Similar patterns also emerged from the Lesotho census results.

[13] I am grateful to H. J. Simons and R. Simons who first broached this issue in their paper presented at the 1978 ECA Conference on Migratory Labour in Southern Africa, and for their subsequent enlightening thoughts and suggestions given to me on workers' conditions (see Simons and Simons, 1978).

[14] "Crimping" was the term used for methods of attracting or poaching another mine's labour before the major mining houses agreed on controlled recruitment and wage policies.

[15] Addressing the congress of the Trade Union Council of South Africa (TUCSA), the Minister of Labour claimed that labour legislation specifically prohibited discrimination or differentiation on the basis of colour in the prescription of wages or any other conditions of employment. He declared: "Wages are . . . prescribed on an occupational basis and the person performing a certain class of work should be paid the wage prescribed for that class of work irrespective of his race or colour." (*Rand Daily Mail* (Johannesburg), 6 Apr. 1978).

[16] Simons and Simons, 1978, p. 14.

[17] Gordon's (1977) comprehensive coverage of what he terms "Brotherhood" is illuminating and, although undertaken on a Namibian mine with less ethnic diversity, is relevant to the South African mines. "Brotherhood" is the natural upshot of affinity, but does not necessarily encompass all those within the same environment. Gordon states: "It emphasises respect, trust, consultation, dignity and delineates a distinct moral universe which specifically excludes all Whites and Blacks who by their actions have proved to be non-Brothers."

[18] Drinks are subsidised as a direct attempt to dissuade miners from going to the locations, yet many miners still prefer to go there at the weekend to buy drinks (which, our students said, were exorbitantly priced). It is commonly claimed that the mines offer cheap drinks as a way of retrieving wages from their workers. Mine managers stated that beer hall profits were closely monitored and, under the regulations, must be used for improving workers' welfare and/or "homeland" development.

[19] Miners often talked to our student interviewers about the hazards of visiting the locations. It appeared that the greatest threat was that of assault by young men from the locations, often jealous of the miners who flaunted their money and monopolised the young women. The second fear was to be caught by the police, drinking in illegal shebeens, smoking dagga or gambling.

[20] On Anglo American Corporation mines, if a miner chooses to bring his case to a tribunal, a medical examination is undertaken and witnesses called in for statements, with reports being sent to the relevant section manager, chief hostel manager and mine overseer. A date is set for the inquiry, which is chaired by the section manager and attended by the hostel manager, personnel assistant (Black), deputy personnel officer and a representative for the accused as observer. If found guilty, the section manager and the deputy personnel officer are responsible for disciplining the accused: discipline, depending on the offence, ranges from "severe reprimand" through "final warning" to "discharge".

[21] Miners who transfer from one mine to another face the strong possibility of forgoing their accrued long-service benefits. Some mine officials have admitted the gross injustices in the system and claim that in many cases long-service benefits are granted when the miner can simply relate events

which took place in mining during his previous contracts or refer officials from the new mine to those of his previous mine who are willing to testify to his service.

[22] From the Chamber's March 1978 report, as quoted in *The Star* (20 Apr. 1978). The same sentiment was later expressed in President L. W. P. van den Bosch's annual report of 27 June 1978. These statements were quite surprising, as they largely reflected the more liberal attitudes expressed by Anglo American Corporation earlier in the year, which caused dissension within the Chamber and led to Anglo American's submitting a separate report to the Wiehahn Commission in addition to the Chamber's recommendations for labour reform.

[23] The main reason for this attitude would seem to lie with the very close ties that most miners maintain with their rural homestead. It provides a relatively secure base to return to but is subject to possible reallocation by the chief if it is left neglected. It also provides a high proportion of the family's food requirements. Many miners also complained about the extra financial burden they would have to bear if their family lived on the mine premises, while others felt that the mine compound and/or apartheid did not provide a suitable environment for their family.

[24] Renovations could be along the lines of those recently introduced by Anglo American Corporation in the old hostels of Western Deep Levels mine. Fewer occupants were accommodated in the same room, electric wall-heaters were installed and each man was given his own personal locker.

[25] The five-day working week, although still under trial in the form of an 11-shift fortnight and under evaluation by the Franszen Commission, is the subject of bitter debate. The Mine Workers Union feels that the 45 per cent increase in mine profits during the second quarter of 1978 can be partly attributed to the 11-shift fortnight. The mines, on the other hand, claim that the increase is due to the cancellation of the Mozambique labour agreement and the new pay system. The President of the Chamber of Mines stated that as a result of the 11-shift fortnight the total wage bill increased by 15 per cent, working costs increased by R 30 million a year, capital cost increases were approaching R 8 million per year and the drop in productivity was over 6 per cent.

[26] The following excerpt from a recent advertisement for a compound manager on a De Beers diamond-mine reveals management's growing awareness of the need for a new breed of hostel manager and personnel officer: "Applicants should preferably be graduates with anthropology or applied anthropology as majors. A prerequisite of the person appointed will be a keen interest in Black employees and the ability to interact with them and management on hostel affairs" (advertised in the *Rand Daily Mail* appointments section, Oct. 1977).

[27] The recent completion in Mozambique of two large hostels to accommodate migrant workers travelling to and from the mines would suggest that the Mozambican Government has accepted migration at least in the medium term.

[28] The Lesotho Government holds biannual meetings with the TEBA executive and representatives from non-Chamber mines employing Basotho workers. Meetings are attended by members of the Lesotho Labour Department, the permanent secretaries of the ministries affected and labour representatives stationed in South Africa. Negotiations have covered such issues as workmen's compensation, inter-mine record transfers, family visits and paid leave.

[29] Malawi was the first supplier country to attempt immediate withdrawal on its own in 1974 but has successfully tried to re-enter the South African mine labour market since 1977. The country is currently restricted to fairly small quotas because of adequate supplies from more proximate sources. It was a conspicuous absentee from the 1978 ECA Conference on Migratory Labour in Southern Africa, as well as from the 1979 and 1980 follow-up meetings. Malawi at present stands on the sidelines, watching other supplier States and for any opportunities which may allow her to fill any void.

[30] The Human Resources Laboratory, a branch of the Chamber of Mines Research Organisation, not only examines matters such as physical tolerance levels and the effect of heat on mineworkers but also conducts many sociological investigations. Through its Monitoring Division it has interviewed more than 2,000 miners on a variety of issues. Officers of the Human Resources Laboratory have expressed their willingness to circulate their findings but have so far been prevented by a Chamber of Mines regulation requiring unanimous agreement to the release of such information. Unfortunately, one or two of the more reactionary mines have objected to the release of the Laboratory's findings.

EASING THE PLIGHT OF MIGRANT WORKERS' FAMILIES IN LESOTHO

5

Elizabeth Gordon

This chapter concentrates on a particular aspect of the life of migrant workers' families in Lesotho: their present unstable income base, which significantly limits their standard of living. Greater income security could improve their lives considerably. We shall first describe the way in which the migrants' families obtain their income at present and then suggest how that income could be made more secure.

The discussion is based on an investigation into the present conditions of labour migration in Lesotho and on the results of an extensive study of migrant workers' households conducted throughout the country. Particular reference will be made to the survey of 524 wives of men working in South Africa that was undertaken within the household study. This part of the research concentrated on discovering the problems that such wives were experiencing in their husbands' absence and on identifying those wives who were having the greatest difficulty and experiencing the greatest strain in living without their husbands. To that end they were asked about their demographic characteristics, family structure, attitudes towards their situation and greatest problems, and their answers were also sought to a group of ten questions that attempted to explore their feelings of strain in living without a husband. The resulting "strain score", based on responses to the ten items, was then cross-tabulated with other variables to develop a picture of the factors related to strain and of the wives experiencing it the most. Although the results of this research will not be reported in detail here (see Gordon, 1978), they helped to shape the underlying concerns of this chapter and will be referred to where appropriate.

No attempt will be made here to describe the entire gamut of problems that beset the families left behind: nor will problems of the prevailing institutions of labour migration be dealt with in their entirety. Only those elements that pertain to the income sources of the families and to possible changes in their structure will be discussed (for the more general problems, see Wallis, 1977).

Our discussion accepts that the prevailing situation is one of overwhelming labour migration. Recommendations will be made within that framework. There can be little argument that the ultimate improvement in the lives of the migrant workers' families would be achieved by returning their men permanently to them, with adequately paid jobs in their home areas. However, it is felt that, rather than wait until the dawning of that improbable day, it is possible to make changes in the existing structure of labour migration that would significantly enhance the lives of the families left behind.

LABOUR MIGRATION AND ITS IMPACT ON FAMILY LIFE

The specific conditions of labour migration in Lesotho ensure that its impact on family life is profound. When a man crosses the border to work in South Africa, he leaves his family behind. By law, he must migrate alone, as women and children are prohibited from living with him. South African law also dictates that the worker cannot stay in South Africa for more than two years. He must return to Lesotho, for at least a period of leave, when the two years are up.

These conditions give rise to a type of migration described as "oscillating". The usual pattern is for the migrant to leave his family in the village, to work across the border for a period of time, to return to his family for as long as he feels is economically feasible and, once again, to cross the border to work.

The extent of migration in Lesotho is such that almost every family in the country has at least one member conforming to this pattern at some time. It has been estimated that close to half the adult male labour force are absentees working in South Africa, with a much higher percentage working there at some time in their lives.

To gain an understanding of what this means for marriage in Lesotho, we shall attempt to estimate the number of married women who are the wives of absent migrants at any one time, by determining the number of migrants working outside the country and the proportion of these who are married.

The exact figures for men working outside Lesotho are difficult to obtain, except for mineworkers, on whom statistics are kept by the South African recruitment offices and the Lesotho Department of Labour. Figures for 1976 indicate that an average of 121,061 Basotho are working on the mines in South Africa at any given moment. If we apply a marriage rate of 70 per cent[1] to this figure, it transpires that the miners leave close to 85,000 wives behind them in Lesotho. If the wives of between 30,000 and 80,000 men working as migrants in agriculture, construction and other industries are added, the number of wives left behind rises to between 100,000 and 140,000. The census gives a figure of 234,159 married women residing in Lesotho in the same year. Thus, approximately 40 to 60 per cent of married women in Lesotho live as wives of absent migrants at any one time.

Not only are the effects of migration on the family extensive in terms of the numbers affected, but there are also indications that they are long-term effects influencing a family's life for many years. McDowall (1974) found that the average miner spends 35 per cent of his working life on the mines, which means that he spends a total of approximately 15 years away from home; and that migration tends to occur when a man is in his twenties, thirties and forties. These findings point to the migrant's being mostly absent during the critical years of his marriage and during the years when his children are growing up.

The nature of labour migration in Lesotho and its extent, in terms of both the numbers involved and the length of time that migrants are away from home, mean that migration plays a critical role in shaping the lives of Basotho families. Migrant labour can be seen as defining the very structure of family life in Lesotho, determining what it has come to mean for the people of the country. Inter-action between family members follows the cyclical careers of its migrants. Members live apart for much of the time, coming together on the migrants' leaves and visits home, during the periods between contracts when they may remain at home and (if it occurs) upon the migrants' retirement. The erosion of family relationships under such conditions may be substantial.

Even if it is aware of the possible consequences, the family has very little choice but to send some of its members off to work in South Africa. The decision is made reluctantly, with an understanding of the risk to the family's well-being that it implies. To put it simply, the lack of job opportunities in Lesotho means that potential breadwinners must work in South Africa if they are to have any chance of supporting their families, whether the family members like it or not, and no matter how well or badly they manage in the migrants' absence.

THE MIGRANT FAMILY'S INSECURE FINANCIAL BASE

Under the present system of labour migration in Lesotho, the family sends its most valuable resource—its able-bodied men—to the industries, particularly the mines, of South Africa. Because of the shortage of wage-earning opportunities for those left behind, these families depend almost totally for their livelihood on the earnings of their migrants. A full 90 per cent of the households of the wives interviewed in the survey reported such a complete reliance on migrant remittances.

This lack of alternative resources and total dependence on migrant earnings give rise to a situation that is perhaps unique in the Basotho family's involvement in labour migration: as the money so earned is the family's lifeblood, any threat to its supply could, if it became reality, totally undermine the family's basic functioning.[2]

The families who invest what is often their sole financial resource and who are fully dependent for their subsistence on a return on this investment have struck a very shaky bargain. Any return is very uncertain and almost completely out of the families' control. It is the migrant himself who must make provision for the family he has left behind. Depending on the circumstances in which he finds himself, and on his personal motivations, he does this to a greater or lesser degree. The family has no guarantees. It must hope that the migrant's good intentions will prevail, and that he will not spend his money on the often tempting alternatives that are available where he works but will keep his family's needs foremost in his mind and attempt to maintain them at least at a minimal level during all the years he is away.

Providing sufficiently for his family's needs also depends upon the migrant's full understanding of their extent. When deciding how much to send, he must accurately perceive what the family requires. That family and migrant may not always agree on the amount of money necessary is indicated by a finding in our study. In a set of attitude questions relating to migration and the family, the sample of wives and the separate sample of married male migrants were found to have strikingly similar answers. Eight out of the 12 questions were answered almost identically, with no significant differences apparent. However, one of the items on which the two groups differed referred to satisfaction with the amount of money sent home by migrants. At a very significant level ($P < 0.01$) the wives were less satisfied with the amount they received than the husbands were with the amount they sent.

At best, the migrant may keep his family's interests at heart, know how much is required at home, not fall prey to temptation, and so send his family regular, adequate amounts for as long as he is away. At worst, he may use his crossing the border as a way effectively to abandon his family, sending no money at all, or less and less as the years go by.

The majority of cases probably fall between these extremes. Many men presumably try to provide for their families to some extent and manage to send money home on an irregular basis, but do not remit enough for real support. An indication of this is the finding that 66 per cent of the households of the wives interviewed considered their incomes to be inadequate, a factor that correlated very highly with strain ($P < 0.0005$).

When money is received at irregular intervals, family members never know how much they will receive, nor when it will arrive. Each month brings with it the question of whether they will have anything to live on. Having little or no control over the amount, frequency or continuity of the migrant's remittances, whilst at the same time being dependent on them, is the family's difficult and stressful lot. The rational apportionment of resources, budgeting in terms of expected income, planning for the future and taking advantage of purchasing opportunities are all beyond the reach of such families.

The present system by which money is remitted home, which is described in detail in the next section, will be seen as one that exacerbates the family's uncertainty and the tenuousness of its support. Rather than making it easier for the migrant to exercise responsible financial management and to provide regular support for his family, the present conditions discourage his providing them with a regular, dependable income. At present, considerable planning and self-denial, which are beyond the reach of most of the men, are required if a migrant is to ensure a predictable cash inflow for his family. In the light of what that family has invested and in view of its lack of alternatives, this is especially unfortunate.

The following sections investigate the present system by which the family obtains its income, and make proposals to change the system so as to facilitate its receipt. If larger amounts of money can be regularly received, a big step will have been taken towards improving the physical and mental well-being of the families left behind.

THE PRESENT SYSTEM OF REMITTANCES

We must first distinguish between the men working in the mines and those in other industries. Miners, comprising about four-fifths of the migrants, are subject to the deferred pay system discussed below. The migrants employed in other sectors do not fall under the deferred pay scheme. They presumably receive a monthly wage, which they apportion as they wish. They may, or may not, send some money home to their families. There are, at present, no regulations in this regard.

The miner's pay

The wages that a miner earns are immediately divided into two portions. During much of his usual six-month contract (i.e. excluding only the first and the last months) 60 per cent is sent by his employer direct to the Lesotho Bank as deferred pay. The miner receives the remaining 40 per cent as a monthly wage, to spend as he wishes. He may or may not send some of it home to his family. Depending upon the mining company,

117

he may be able to arrange for family remittances to be sent through the recruiting agency. This can be done regularly, through deductions made from this part of his pay by the mine office. It can also be done sporadically, when he reports to the office with cash in hand, requesting that it be sent home. The remittances are then distributed to the families by the recruiting agencies in Lesotho. As there are no regulations concerning such remittances, the mining companies that provide this service do so, in a sense, as a favour to their workers. Some of the smaller companies are reported to have declined to accept this responsibility.

The miner, of course, can send money home through other channels, either in addition to, or instead of, money sent through the employer. He can send it through the post or with a friend, or can bring it himself on a visit home.

The miner normally draws his deferred pay earnings on the completion of his contract, i.e. after his return to Lesotho. He applies to the recruiting agency with a voucher from the mine office that indicates the amount to his credit. If he works for one of the larger companies, he receives his deferred pay at the agency itself. For smaller agencies, for which the holding of large sums of cash poses a problem, the miner applies to the Lesotho Bank for his money. In either case, the interest on the deferred pay earnings must be obtained through separate application to the Bank.

Family's access to deferred pay earnings

The legislation in force in Lesotho includes provisions by which the family can receive payment from the miner's deferred pay earnings during the course of his contract. A clear understanding of the actual operation of these provisions, and the conditions under which they are applied, was felt to be critical in determining the role of such payments in the support of the family. Because the law does not clearly specify this, relevant agencies were contacted in the hope of gaining an understanding of the mechanisms involved. The agencies were found to interpret the provisions differently, with each having its own viewpoint according to its interests. This subsection is based on interviews with various officials.

The relevant provisions appear in the Deferred Pay Regulations[3] and are as follows:

5(1) An employee may authorise his employer or his employer's agent to pay from his deferred pay to a dependant a family remittance not exceeding 50 per cent of his deferred pay.

5(2) The payment of family remittances shall be subject to the terms agreed upon by the employer and the employee.

5(3) An employee may authorise his employer or his agent to pay from his deferred pay a specified amount to a dependant in case of emergency after specifying the nature of the emergency. In such a case Regulation 5(1) shall be waived to cater for such an emergency.

It was found that the critical term "deferred pay" in these provisions was being interpreted as money that the miner had accumulated to his credit in the Lesotho Bank, and not as half of that portion of a current month's wage earmarked as deferred pay. The procedure involves a miner going to the mining office with a request that his dependant be paid half the balance of his accrued deferred pay.

To enable a family withdrawal of this nature to be made, three copies of the relevant form are filled out at the mine office. One is kept at the mine office, one is sent to the recruiting office in Lesotho and one is sent to the dependant specified. The dependant then presents his copy to the recruiting agency, where it is compared with the agency's copy, and he may be asked additional questions to establish his identity. The money is paid either at the agency itself or at the Lesotho Bank. Interest on the deferred pay obtained is not, however, payable at this time but only at the end of the miner's contract.

The Lesotho Bank asserts that flexibility is applied to miners' requests to permit their families access to deferred pay earnings. Take the example of a man in the second month of his contract who has no deferred pay accrued to his credit at the bank: should he need to transfer additional money to his family, he would, according to the Bank, be permitted to have his current month's deferred pay sent home, rather than to the Bank. Also, the "emergency" clause of the Regulations (clause 5(3)) allows a miner to specify an amount greater than half the balance of his account to be made available to his family. A man can thus be permitted to withdraw the entire amount of deferred pay that stands to his credit, should he so wish.

However, in understanding what such deferred pay withdrawals mean in terms of the actual support made available to miners' families, it should be pointed out that, according to a former labour commissioner, they can be easily discouraged by the mine office. These types of payment require a fair amount of book-keeping, including a change in the computerised system by which the amount of deferred pay to be sent to the Lesotho Bank is determined each month. Such requests are therefore not welcomed.

It appears that a man is expected to have exhausted the 40 per cent of his wages received as cash in hand before applying to let his family have access to his deferred pay. He may be asked what he did with his cash that makes it necessary for him to arrange such a withdrawal. He may be told to make regular remittances from his monthly wages or to send extra cash, rather than to bother the office with the more complex procedure. It can be made clear to the miners that requests of this nature will not be tolerated more than once or twice a contract; after more frequent requests he may be viewed as a trouble-maker. This is not a useful reputation to have when a man applies for re-employment. Access to deferred pay by the family during the course of the miner's contract is thus restricted by such considerations.

Withdrawals of this nature appear to be made infrequently, perhaps once during the course of the contract, by those miners who use the system at all. They tend to be used to meet specific expenses that occur at home, such as for the payment of school fees, or for a funeral, or for a feast in honour of ancestors. They are not seen as providing regular support for the family. The deferred pay portion of the miner's wages appears never to have been used for a family remittance sent on a regular basis.

Number of remittances

Even in those companies that do send family remittances, the percentage of miners remitting money home through them is small. The largest employer of Basotho miners, TEBA, is considered to be quite liberal in this respect, with an extensive payment network throughout Lesotho. TEBA figures for the 12 months between 1 February 1977 and 31 January 1978 indicate that only 10 per cent of the miners sent money to their families through the main recruitment body every month.

Separate figures are not kept for the different types of payment to families. Both regular and occasional remittances, as well as those paid out of the cash portion of salary and those arranged as withdrawals from deferred pay, are included in this figure. Only 10 per cent of TEBA miners thus made any kind of payment to their families through their employer.

As arrangements for family withdrawals of deferred pay can be made only through the mine office, it is clear that fewer than 10 per cent of the miners took advantage of this provision. Looking at this figure from another viewpoint leads one to a similar conclusion as regards regular family remittances. As the only way possible to arrange a regular family remittance is through the mine office, 10 per cent of the miners at most appear to have done so during the year. There may, of course, have been other men who regularly sent money to their families through other channels. However, those payments involving a predetermined deduction from monthly wages and some certainty that money is regularly received at home were made by only a small minority of men: 90 per cent of the miners do not arrange such a predictable income for their families.

Getting the deferred pay balance home

In most cases, the 60 per cent of the miner's pay that is deferred is largely untouched by the miner and his family until his contract ends and he returns to Lesotho. Upon applying for his deferred pay, the miner is thus presented with what may be a fairly substantial amount of cash to carry on his person. What happens to this money depends on him. It is clear that there are institutions in Maseru, the capital, that prey upon the newly monied return migrant, attempting to ensure that little of his pay leaves its environs. If he can avoid the prostitutes, drinking halls, gambling games and thieves,[4] he may take some home to his family.

The present system can thus be seen as one in which it may be difficult, and sometimes hazardous as well, for him to do so. It certainly is not a system that makes it easy to take the maximum amount home. By being able to arrange regular remittances only from the 40 per cent of his salary left to him each month, the miner is scarcely encouraged to make such provision for his family. By receiving the bulk of his deferred pay as a lump sum upon the completion of his contract, the migrant has to do battle with a number of forces, both internal and external, in order to retain a respectable amount to take home.

The present system gives the miner little encouragement to act on any good intentions he may originally have had to provide for his family. There are few supports to help him to act responsibly and to avoid the casual spending of the cash he does receive. The prevailing arrangements help to perpetuate the present situation as regards the money that reaches the family. It is received on an irregular basis and can stop at any time.

A REGULAR REMITTANCE FOR THE FAMILY?

Are there any ways to modify the existing system so as to make it easier for the family to receive a regular, dependable remittance? A predictable income would to some extent make it possible to plan the family finances and would, it might be hoped, reduce the uncertainty and anxiety currently experienced by families waiting for a usually irregular, sometimes small and often unforthcoming sum.

Our discussion will concentrate first on changes that would better enable the well meaning migrant to earmark a portion of his monthly wage for his family's use. Second, ways to assist the family of a less well intentioned migrant to obtain a share of his income will be described. Third, a system whereby all migrant families would be assured of an income, regardless of the actions and motivations of their migrant members, will be proposed.

Assisting the well intentioned migrant

Regular remittances through deferred pay

Sending regular remittances home would be a more attractive proposition for most men if they did not have to pay for them out of their own pocket, from their cash earnings. If the remittances were deductable, at least in part, from the deferred pay portion of the miner's monthly salary, they would be more likely to be arranged. Since in any case miners do not have regular access, while under contract, to the 60 per cent of their salary that is sent to the deferred pay fund, they might choose to remit a portion directly to their families if they were given this option.

This would be especially true if permission regularly to send part of the deferred pay home as a family remittance did not depend upon the miner's having to prove that the 40 per cent of salary not deferred was insufficient for this purpose. A man might choose to keep all his cash pay for himself and yet be encouraged to make remittances from the deferred pay portion if he could. Such an option would be more likely to encourage a miner to support his family than the system currently in effect. Furthermore, putting more deferred pay money into the family's hands would serve one of the major purposes for which the deferred pay scheme was adopted, since by being dispersed throughout the rural areas of the country the money would more probably be spent within Lesotho.

Minimising the role of the mining companies

If the idea of deducting remittances from the deferred pay portion of wages is to be successfully put into effect, the role of the mining companies in the operation should be carefully evaluated. At present, remittances from miners to their families are arranged by the companies as a favour to their employees. Some employers are said to refuse to become involved in such arrangements. For those who are involved, the discouragement of withdrawals from deferred pay to the family's credit has been noted. Accordingly, to avoid their being discouraged, deferred pay remittances should not involve the companies in complicated procedures. Ideally, they should not involve the companies at all, so that any miner would be free to arrange such family payments regardless of his employer.

At present, the reluctance to allow the family access to deferred pay appears to stem from the complicated book-keeping which it entails. This, however, would occur only when, as at present, such payments are made sporadically, with a change in the instructions to the computer being necessary each time. If it were possible to deduct family remittances from deferred pay regularly, this problem could be solved.

Under such a system the maximum percentage of the deferred pay portion of salary that could be remitted would be set by regulation. At the beginning of his contract a miner would specify the total amount he wished his family to receive from his earnings every month. He would also indicate how this was to be deducted from his salary—from the deferred pay portion (within the determined limits), from the non-deferred portion or partially from each. The amount to be deducted from the miner's deferred pay each month would thus remain constant.

A fixed amount would therefore be sent to the Lesotho Bank each month. The computer would be programmed accordingly and no frequent changes in instructions would be necessary. The procedures for payment and distribution in Lesotho would be the same as those currently used for payments to families from non-deferred pay. As remittances from deferred pay would not involve arrangements greatly different from those at present in force, those employers who are currently sending remittances would probably incorporate them into the existing system without much objection.

However, current company policy could change, as a result perhaps of an increased volume of family remittances or of political considerations, and less willingness to assist the miners might be apparent in the future. Moreover, those employers who are unwilling to deal with remittances at present would probably continue to show no interest in doing so. To ensure that every miner has access to a remittance system, therefore, this responsibility should be taken out of the hands of the mining companies. If the deferred pay portion of the wages were available for remittances, this would be possible. Arrangements could be made entirely within Lesotho. Before he left the country, a miner would apply to the Lesotho Bank for a monthly payment to a dependant to come from his deferred pay earnings. The employer would have no role in this but would simply follow regulations and send the entire amount of the migrant's pay as deferred pay to the Lesotho Bank. A miner would therefore be free to make such arrangements independently of the agreement, or even the knowledge, of the company he works for.

Unambiguous regulations needed

Some thought should be given to clearly stating the regulations that pertain to migrants' remittances to their families. At present, the only regulations are those referring to the deferred pay portion of earnings described above. These provisions appear to need further clarification. The terms "deferred pay", "50 per cent", "emergency", and so on, are not clearly defined (for example, does Regulation 5(1) refer to 50 per cent of the deferred pay that stands to a miner's credit in the Bank, an amount that changes as deposits and withdrawals are made? Or to 50 per cent of the deferred pay portion of his salary, a constant 30 per cent of wages each month?). Again, Regulation 5(2), with its phrase "subject to the terms agreed upon by the employer and the employee", leaves the door open for the employer to specify any terms he may choose as to amount, frequency and other conditions of payment.

The present ambiguity in the regulations means that differing interpretations may be applied by different institutions, by different individuals within the same institution and selectively to different migrants. Too much discretion appears to have been left to the mining companies, without their having been given enough guidelines. A man contemplating sending money home should be clear about the conditions under which he is permitted to do so, and the mining company should be clear about its obligations in this respect.

The formulation of new provisions pertaining to remittances made from other sources of money should also be considered. At present, the only way in which a miner can arrange for his family to receive a regular remittance deducted from his wages is to take it from his non-deferred pay. No provisions apply to this procedure. By leaving this scheme entirely up to the initiative of the mining houses, no assurances are provided as to its future. Should the company so decide, it could be curtailed or stopped entirely. Ideally, regulations should be drawn up that clearly outline the mandatory role of the mining houses regarding family remittances. Terms, conditions, methods and procedures should be clearly stated. In order to ensure support for the families, the best solution would be to draft regulations that made their involvement in family remittances an obligation for all employers. All Basotho miners would thereby have guaranteed access to a remittance system.

The actual provisions to be adopted would have to be carefully considered. It has to be recognised that making too many demands on the mining houses, in this period of increased South African labour supply, could lead to a reluctance to hire Basotho workers, and this has to be taken into account in deciding whether all companies should be required by law to develop remittance programmes. Whatever the content of the actual provisions, they should not be as open to different interpretations as are the existing ones. All terms and conditions should be clearly defined and explained, making the intent of the law as unambiguous as possible.

Coaxing the reluctant provider

Such changes in the system, however, would not help those families whose men are not interested in making monthly deductions in their favour, whatever the conditions. Some of these men might arrange to support their families in other ways, for example by sending money directly from wages received; however, it is clear that there are men who have little or no interest in supporting their family through any channels. Such men may send no money home at all, or in such small amounts as to be negligible in terms of real support. The family thus abandoned, totally or partially, by its breadwinner has little choice at present but to get used to living without funds.

The present system

Under the present system there is little a family can do to get a greater share of its migrant's income. A wife may attempt to convince her husband of the advantages of sending money home, and beg him, or command him, to send more; but her pleas may fall on deaf ears.

Miners who do not want to deal with pressing family matters have the advantage of being far away from home, and so can easily put them out of their mind. That this is the case is borne out by the researchers of *Another blanket* (Agency for Industrial Mission, 1976, p. 2), who found that some migrants, suspecting letters from home to be about money, would simply burn them without having read them.

In the past, some recruiting agencies were apparently interested in helping wives who were not receiving sufficient funds and would write letters on their behalf, appealing to the husbands to increase the amount they sent home. These letters would stress that, even if the husband had had a difference of opinion with his wife, or did not trust her completely, any money he sent would be bound to be spent, at least in part, on the needs of the home and children. They would also point out that if a man wanted a good relationship with his children in the future and did not want to be resented by them, he had best provide for their support. These letters, which apparently were quite effective, were stopped with the introduction of compulsory deferred pay.

The legal position

It must be realised that the abandonment of dependants in this way constitutes a criminal offence in Lesotho. Under the Deserted Wives and Children (Protection) Proclamation, (No. 60 of 1959, as amended by Order No. 29 of 1971 and Act No. 1 of 1977): "Any person legally liable to maintain any other person who, while able to do so, fails to provide the person to be maintained with adequate food, clothing, lodging and medical aid, shall be guilty of an offence." A magistrate's court can fine or imprison a person convicted of this offence and may also "make an order in writing against that person to pay at such intervals, in such manner, and to such person as the Court may think fit, a reasonable sum for the use of the person to be maintained by such a convicted person".

Those migrant husbands who are earning a regular wage and so have the ability to maintain their families and yet are not doing so are contravening this statute. Wives who can be proved to have committed adultery which has not been condoned by their husbands are not, however, entitled to such maintenance, and their husbands are not committing any offence in failing to maintain them. This, however, does not apply to any children of these marriages.

While there appear to be substantial numbers of such abandoned and semi-abandoned wives of migrants, few husbands seem to have been charged under the statute. Having this law on the books, while perhaps a first step in getting payments to non-supported dependants, has not proved to be an effective way to ensure their support. This type of law is notoriously ineffective in other countries as well. Husbands can be very resourceful in avoiding the payment of awarded maintenance, and each time payment would be so defaulted the wife would bear the onus of initiating proceedings to attempt its recovery.

Perhaps more important in explaining its current ineffectiveness is that the statute and its implications are largely unknown, and its application and procedures would in any case be incomprehensible to the women concerned. Most women in such a situation have never heard of the statute, and of those who have, few would seriously consider the law in terms of its usefulness to them, or be prompted to take action; and so the families, in spite of the existence of a law aimed at assisting them to obtain support, continue to struggle on unaided, possibly in circumstances of dire need and destitution.

Assisting the non-supported families

Any attempt to assist the non-supported family should aim at obtaining for it a share of the errant provider's income, first by encouraging him to accept his responsibilities voluntarily and, failing that, to force him to do so under the existing legislation. Eekelaar (1971) discusses guidelines to be followed when proposals to assist unsupported individuals to gain financial support are considered. His reference is to unmarried mothers seeking maintenance from the fathers. He points out that "a man is far more likely to honour an agreement which he has entered into voluntarily than an order obtained against him in court" (p. 211). The goal of an attempt is "to bring the couple to amicable agreement about finances" (p. 211). One should therefore "try to avoid court proceedings altogether, and . . . remove the onus for their initiation from the mother" (p. 210).

With these objectives in mind, provisions for gaining support in the present situation could be worked out. A framework is needed within which cases of non-support could be investigated. The first goal would then be a voluntary arrangement for financial support. If it proved necessary, court proceedings against the breadwinner could be initiated by someone other than his wife. Such a framework could go a long way towards providing a resource to which the deserted families could resort.

Details would have to be carefully worked out, but it might be well to look at the law to assist unmarried mothers, since this might suggest possible and profitable solutions to the present problem. Under the Maintenance and Recovery Act of Alberta (Canada) (as described in Eekelaar, 1971, p. 211), a director of maintenance and recovery was appointed whose function it was to give these mothers aid and advice. He was empowered to enter into agreements with the fathers relating to support payments. If such a course of action failed, the director and the mother had the power to take legal proceedings against him. In the case of default, the director was responsible for taking steps to enforce the order. The director can thus be seen as an intermediary between the parties who has the force of law behind him and who can take the responsibility for legal action out of the mother's hands.

A law to deal with the present situation in Lesotho, drawn up along similar lines, could create a post of director of family maintenance to fulfil the same role for unsupported migrants' families. A migrant's wife or possibly other dependants could discuss her situation with the director, who would investigate it. Should it be warranted, he would attempt to persuade the husband to provide sufficient support through, perhaps, regular remittances from his wages. If unsuccessful in all his attempts to persuade the husband voluntarily to support his family, the director would then exercise his responsibility to institute legal proceedings, with the wife's agreement. Should maintenance be thereby awarded, the director would monitor the situation to ensure that the wife actually received regular payment. In the case of default, he would again have the responsibility of acting against the husband.

It might be noted that default could, with a degree of co-operation between the institutions concerned, be made very difficult for miners. Arrangements could be made for payments to be made direct to the wife from the husband's deferred pay earnings in the Bank or by the recruiting agency, who would deduct them from wages due.

Such a director would seek out cases and discuss them with unsupported dependants, who might be unaware of his role, or might hesitate to contact him. Proper publicity and explanation, coupled with an understanding approach on his part, could make the office accessible. Emphasis would be given to his being a source of help in a difficult, otherwise unapproachable, situation.

A state allowance for migrant workers' wives

The proposals outlined above have a serious drawback in that, in all of them, support for the family remains dependent on the actions of particular migrants. Those directed towards encouraging regular family remittances depend upon the miner's choosing to take such action. The family still does not know whether he will do so and, if he does, how much the payments will be or for how long they will continue. Obtaining support for the family of the less well intentioned migrant involves manipulating and monitoring its breadwinner, and this requires the expenditure of a considerable amount of time and effort in which success is, even then, not guaranteed. Such provisions can therefore only go so far. Even if they were implemented, there would still be families who were left without sufficient income.

A more comprehensive scheme to meet the needs of these families necessitates separating the provision of support from the actions of particular migrants. This implies introducing a system in which the family would be assured of, and could rely on, a regular, predictable income independent of the specific inputs of its migrant members. By having an income that was rightfully theirs, family members would begin to experience a degree of control over their lives, a lessening of the passive dependency that so often characterises them at present.

The adoption of a system of state allowances for migrant wives would meet these objectives. Under such a programme, wives would receive a monthly allowance from the Lesotho Government for as long as their husbands were working in South Africa. The amount of this allowance would be determined by regulation and would preferably be graduated, with different amounts for families in different circumstances—thus, those with more children would receive more money.[5] Payments would be made on a fixed date every month, as are government salaries at present, and could be sent through the post or by any other agency having easily accessible branches throughout Lesotho.

At present, because deferred pay pertains only to miners, the kind of allowance proposed could most easily be provided for miners' wives. However, it could later be extended to include workers in other industries, especially those in which workers sign contracts before they leave Lesotho. Also, if desired, the scheme could be expanded to cover family members other than wives, upon their producing proof of their status as dependants of migrant workers.

Finance for this programme could come mainly from deductions taken from miners' salaries and earmarked for this purpose. These deductions could be made by the employer or, if they were to be taken from deferred pay, by the Lesotho Bank, after the pay had been received from the mining houses. The money would be pooled in a fund set up to finance the programme.

The level of the allowances and of the deductions would have to be carefully considered so as to arrive at an equitable balance. The payments to wives would have to be made worth while, at least to some degree, while the deductions could not be so large as to burden the migrant unduly. With this in mind, the deduction could be made from the portion of pay deferred compulsorily, especially if that portion remained at its present 60 per cent level.

Supplementary payments into the fund from other revenue sources could also be considered. Such investment in the well-being of the families of Lesotho could be a worth-while use of the deferred pay fund monies, for example, or of other government revenues. In addition, the participation of the mining houses themselves (who have so far been able to avoid providing for the needs of dependants) should not be ruled out.

The large sums of money and number of people that would be involved in an allowance programme mean that an agency would have to be made responsible for its administration and distribution. This could be the present Ministry of Health and Social Welfare, the Labour Department, the Lesotho Bank or, perhaps most appropriately, a future Ministry of Labour and Social Welfare (cf. Wallis, 1977, p. 28). Safeguards would have to be introduced to ensure that funds were properly channelled and that payment was received by the legitimate recipients. The co-operation of relevant institutions would have to be secured, including that of the mining companies. A procedure would have to be developed whereby the responsible agency was informed of a wife's initial eligibility for benefits and of the duration of eligibility.

The proposal to establish a system of wives' allowances is clearly an ambitious one, involving significant changes in the existing framework. It is, however, one that would effectively tackle the problem of creating a dependable income for all migrant families. Though the level of the allowances might at first have to be set at a low level because of the outlay involved, the system would at least ensure a predictable cash inflow to every eligible household. These families, having some money income of their own to which they were entitled without question rather than on someone's else's sufferance, would gain support in achieving at least some degree of initiative, which is difficult to attain under current conditions.

USING THE DEFERRED PAY FUND FOR THE MIGRANTS
AND THEIR FAMILIES

An additional recommendation could be made regarding the uses of the deferred pay fund. It is urged that the considerable sums so accumulated be, as Wallis has suggested, "used in ways which genuinely benefit the migrants and their families" (Wallis, 1977, p. 21). If the basic commitment were made to direct these funds towards enhancing the lives of those who are most directly concerned, a range of possible projects would become apparent.

Careful consideration would have to be given to selecting the approach that would benefit the families the most. Areas of need would have to be identified, target problems singled out and examined in terms of their urgency and responsiveness to change, and workable programmes developed. A review of past and present projects should be an integral part of the development process, so that new programmes could profit from past experience and effectively mesh with existing ones.

A suggestion was made in the previous section that deferred pay monies be considered for financing the proposed allowance for migrants' wives. If this were implemented, it could serve as a foundation on which to build additional social welfare programmes, funded from the same source. Projects designed to mitigate difficulties identified by the families themselves could be considered as a priority. The wives told the present writer that their most pressing problems were those related to agriculture, health and medical care. Specialised projects, aimed at improving conditions in these areas, could be considered.

Exploring the alternative uses of the fund, and choosing between them, could most effectively be done through an expansion of the body responsible for the fund's administration. The present deferred pay board is composed of two representatives from the Lesotho Bank and one from the Ministry of Finance. If other qualified individuals were added, as consultants or full board members, the board would be better qualified effectively to invest the money for the good of the migrants and their families. Representatives of the relevant ministries and the Labour Department, a social welfare planning expert and a spokesman for the migrants themselves could all usefully be considered for inclusion in the planning and decision-making process.

Notes

[1] This rate was found to be accurate for migrants in our survey as well as in the research conducted by van der Wiel (1977, p. 34) and McDowall (1974).

[2] This may be contrasted with the situation in Swaziland where migrant earnings are more of a supplementary source of income, with families being less dependent on them. See Böhning (1977, p. 46) and Chapter 3 of this book.

[3] Employment (Deferred Pay) Regulations, 1974 (Legal Notice No. 57 of 1974), as amended by the Employment (Deferred Pay) (Amendment No. 2) Regulations, 1975 (Legal Notice No. 15 of 1975).

[4] Cases have been reported of robbery within the Bank itself immediately after a migrant has received his money. These have involved an unsophisticated but effective "snatch and run" or a more genteel "con". The con-man tells the migrant he will help him to obtain his interest; he leads him to an obscure corner of the building, telling the migrant to give him his money and wait until he returns with the interest.

[5] Increased support for large families would be extremely desirable. Our research has shown that strain is closely correlated with number of children. Women with four, five or more children experience significantly greater strain than do women with smaller families. If there were insufficient funds to allow increments for each child, increments starting with the fourth child could be considered or, alternatively, a flat payment for large families would be added to the general allowance.

COMPUTER SIMULATION AND MIGRATION PLANNING

6

W. Woods, in collaboration with M. H. Doran
and A. R. C. Low

Since Botswana, Lesotho and Swaziland can expect the number of their migrants working in South Africa to represent a diminishing percentage of their labour forces, it is important that migration planning and policies tackle the effects of declining migration. Three general effects can be expected: *(a)* an increase in the size of the resident labour force; *(b)* a decrease in income (at least in the short term); and *(c)* an increase in the number of people to be provided for, as returning migrants add to the population. However, the consideration of various policy alternatives requires a more detailed picture of what can be expected as migration declines. This will require more empirical information, as well as the most effective use of the information to hand. Computer simulation models can assist planners in both respects. A computer simulation model is an exact (in mathematical terms) statement of relationships thought to be relevant for future developments in a particular area. A computer can then be used to calculate the future consequences of such a statement of relationships. Models which focus on Swaziland and Botswana are presented below in order to illustrate how computer models may be useful in migration planning.

The first models to be presented deal with the rural and urban sectors in Swaziland. Doran's model enlarges the Todaro migration model in order to analyse relationships between rural income in Swaziland and domestic as well as external migration. Low's model looks at the importance of cropping patterns in relation to migration. Analysis with these models by Doran and Low suggests that in Swaziland increased migration to domestic urban areas may be a result of declining migration to South Africa. Doran and Low suggest that declining migration can be expected to have a beneficial effect on overgrazing in Swaziland by increasing the need for the sale of cattle. Rural development with due consideration to certain cropping patterns is suggested as a counter-measure against the detrimental effects of declining migration.

Following a summary of Doran and Low's work, a preliminary simulation model dealing with Botswana is presented. It focuses on long-term household income levels and reactions to declining migration. It can be said that in terms of scope the two analyses complement each other, because Doran and Low concentrate on the sector level while Woods' Botswana model looks at income groups within the rural sector. Woods looks at the various sources of rural income for particular households in order to analyse the effect of declining migration on the satisfaction of basic needs.[1]

It is interesting to note that there appears to be some difference of opinion regarding the conclusions obtained from each model with respect to the problem of overgrazing. Doran and Low see the problem of overgrazing in Swaziland being mitigated by declining migration, while Woods notes that in Botswana such a mitigation is likely to be accompanied by too drastic a fall in the satisfaction of basic needs. This illustrates the fact that models should not be expected to deliver the future on a silver platter. They contribute in important ways to the knowledge-creating process and discussion which is necessary to provide planners with the information they need to face the challenge—and opportunity—of declining migration.

The contributions that can be expected from models are threefold: (a) modelling requires a precise statement of assumptions and policies, including the environment within which policy is thought to function; (b) models offer the ability to deal with complex interactions and to calculate exactly their consequences on the basis of various sets of assumptions; and (c) through points (a) and (b) the most important areas for empirical research can be identified. Thus, simulation models offer unique opportunities to make the most of current knowledge (both theoretical and empirical), even if there are important gaps in information. It is worth noting that both Doran and Low, as well as Woods, have relied on sensitivity analysis of their models. Sensitivity analysis means that a model is run with various sets of assumptions (or estimates) and the results compared in order to determine the effect of altered assumptions on conclusions.

It is also worth noting that Doran and Low differ from Woods concerning the emphasis they place on the distinction between "push" and "pull" migrants. Woods feels the distinction should be emphasised less, while Doran and Low feel it is an important one for Swaziland planners. Those who are interested in the differences between the two models are urged to consult the more detailed model descriptions cited below in the brief summaries of each model written by the model authors.

SOME MACRO IMPLICATIONS OF WITHDRAWAL:
THE SWAZILAND CASE

Recent simulation and regression studies of trends in Swaziland's mine labour migration over the past decade have indicated that the key determinant in the decision to migrate to the South African mines is the differential between real incomes in rural Swaziland and on the South African mines (see Doran, 1977; Low and Doran, 1977). Furthermore, regression analysis suggests that movements in real mine wage rates have provided the explanation for approximately 70 per cent of the variation in the annual number recruited, as opposed to variations in real rural income which explain only 25 per cent.

It would thus appear that it is not so much the absolute level of poverty at home that forces migrants to seek employment on the South African mines, but rather the high income-earning potential of mine employment that attracts them. The implication is that the withdrawal of Swazi labour from the South African mines might not, in the very short term, create or substantially add to the problem of rural poverty in Swaziland. This contrasts with the conclusions of other writers who have postulated that migration from Swaziland and other Labour Reserve countries is caused by the lack of satisfaction of basic needs in the rural areas from where most migrants are drawn (see Böhning, 1977; Clarke, 1977b; Szal and van der Hoeven, 1976).

The question of the effects of possible withdrawal should not therefore merely be confined to or concentrate upon the rural poverty aspect. In the Swaziland case, the following related but broader issues warrant careful consideration if the full implications of withdrawal are to be understood: *(a)* urban growth and unemployment; *(b)* rural expenditure patterns and income opportunities; *(c)* rural labour absorption capacity; and *(d)* rural income distribution.

Urban growth and unemployment

It is frequently argued that external labour migration has acted in the past to dampen Swazi urban growth and prevent the development of the excessive urban growth and unemployment problems noted elsewhere in Africa. Simulation tests (Doran, 1977) demonstrate that a total restriction on external migration would have a negligible effect on the *net* rate of internal rural-urban migration.[2] However, the effect would be more marked under circumstances of widening rural-urban income differentials, where the inducement for a *permanent* urban migration amongst those males prevented from migrating to the South African mines would be greatest. It is nevertheless likely that restricted external migration would have a significant effect on the *gross* rate of rural-urban migration, particularly in that period of the year in which most external migration takes place at present (January to April).

We can make a rough estimate of the probable magnitude of the incremental gross inflow to the urban areas in Swaziland if we make the reasonable assumption that migrants who were prevented from going to South Africa would consider *temporary* urban migration as an alternative possibility, and that their elasticity of response to wage differentials would be the same as that estimated for gross external migration. On the basis of these assumptions Doran's model indicates that there would be an immediate large inflow of migrants to the urban areas, resulting in a substantial increase in the size of the informal sector. The resulting involuntary absorption of labour into the informal sector would probably result in serious short-term urban unemployment problems. However, this increase in the size of the informal sector would also reduce the attractiveness of urban migration, as employment prospects declined, so that *temporary* urban migration resulting from withdrawal could in time be expected to diminish.

For example, given a situation in which rural income per head remained static and urban income and modern sector job creation grew at 3 per cent per annum, the probable effect of total withdrawal on Swaziland's urban informal sector is presented in table 17. It is evident that the magnitude of the effect on the urban informal sector would depend on the average length of stay of the *temporary* migrant. Even if one assumes that a relatively short period is spent in the urban sector, the immediate effect of total withdrawal on urban unemployment would be substantial. Both the magnitude of the effect on the informal sector and the rate at which it declined would be determined by the real rural-urban income differential. Clearly, widening rural-urban differentials would accentuate both the short-term and the longer-term problems. The conclusion must therefore be that, under circumstances of withdrawal, the need to reduce rural-urban income differentials (through rural development programmes, urban wage restraint and astute modern-sector job-creation policy) would become that much more critical (see also Chapter 3 above).

Rural expenditure patterns and income opportunities

Given the large amount of remittances and deferred payments currently received in Swaziland from mine employment (see Chapter 3), a withdrawal of Swazi labour from the South African mines would inevitably result in a substantial reduction of cash inflow to the rural

Table 17. The impact of withdrawal on the percentage increase in size of the Swazi urban informal sector[1]

Average length of time during which informally employed[2]	Years after withdrawal				
	First	Second	Third	Fourth	Fifth
Six months	119	77	50	34	23
Four months	79	51	34	23	15
Two months	40	26	17	11	8

[1] Assuming that rural income per head is static, while urban income and urban modern sector job creation grow at 3 per cent per annum. [2] It is assumed that most of the temporary migrants will seek urban employment in the first six months of the year in order to retain their rural homestead ties. This being the case, a six-month informal employment period implies that the informal sector will increase in size for that period by the total number of additional workers caused by withdrawals.

Source: Doran, 1977.

areas. However, it cannot be automatically assumed that such a reduction would have an adverse effect on rural development. The impact would depend on expenditure patterns with respect to mine earnings. It is possible, and in Swaziland it is indeed probable, that the reduced cash inflow would have beneficial effects.

For example, Swaziland currently suffers from a severe overgrazing problem. Recent empirical analyses indicate that cattle sales for slaughter from traditional grazing lands are inversely related to price (Doran et al., 1979), and that this inverse price response obtains because cattle are held as a store of wealth (Low et al., 1980). It is therefore argued that: *(a)* Swazi farmers have a perceived cash requirement to meet certain needs such as school fees, clothing and transport; *(b)* cattle may be sold to meet such specific cash requirements, particularly when alternative sources of cash are not available; and *(c)* if cattle must be sold to meet specific cash needs, the minimum number will be disposed of.

Earnings surplus to immediate cash needs are therefore often invested in cattle. Mine income is no exception in this regard, as demonstrated by migration surveys which indicate that a high proportion of miners intend to, and actually do, purchase cattle with part of their earnings (see table 16, p. 64).

Clearly, if mine income is used to purchase cattle from outside the traditional grazing areas, withdrawal would alleviate the overgrazing situation by reducing the numbers of animals introduced into the traditional farm sector. It can be expected, nevertheless, that withdrawal would still have another beneficial effect even if miners purchased cattle from within the traditional grazing areas. This is because the purchase of cattle with mine earnings would tend to expand the non-slaughter market, where cattle are purchased and retained within the traditional grazing areas, at the expense of the conventional slaughter market. Conversely, the decline of the non-slaughter market as a result of withdrawal would tend to increase numbers of cattle sold through the slaughter market. Moreover, since, apart from cattle, remittances and deferred pay tend to be used for consumption purposes such as school fees and household goods, withdrawal could be expected to result in an increase in the total number of cattle sold to meet these expenses.

It may therefore be expected that withdrawal would alleviate the serious overgrazing problem in Swaziland through one or all of the following effects: *(a)* introduction of fewer cattle from outside the traditional grazing areas; *(b)* a reduction in the cash sale of cattle in the non-slaughter market and a related increase in cash sales on the slaughter market; and *(c)* an increased cash sale of cattle in both the slaughter and non-slaughter markets to meet consumption expenses otherwise provided for by mine income.

Rural labour absorption capacity

Although it would appear that a large proportion of adult male labour on Swazi farms has a zero opportunity cost (Low, 1976), there is at the same time considerable potential for labour absorption in rural areas through the introduction of labour-intensive cropping patterns and intensive livestock production such as dairying.

For example, farm survey results indicate that cotton and tobacco require, respectively, two and five times more labour per hectare than maize (Low, 1977). With the projected increase in cotton and tobacco hectarage under the expanded Rural Development Areas Programme being about 4,000 and 3,500 hectares respectively, it can be seen that the effective implementation of the Programme would offer considerable scope for coping with the increased rural workforce that withdrawal would imply. This absorption capacity would, however, depend on the relative earnings differentials obtainable in the Swazi farm and non-farm sectors. Relatively more attractive off-farm earning opportunities within Swaziland might in fact result in a diminished uptake of cash crops such that the absorption capacity forecasted in the project document relating to the Programme might be unrealistic. The importance of a genuine commitment to rural development and a reduction in the rural-urban income differential would therefore be increased under conditions of withdrawal.

Rural income distribution

Withdrawal might have an impact on rural income distribution both within and between ecological zones in Swaziland. Low's marginal cost analysis suggests, for instance, that the incentive to migrate would be greater for farmers growing purely subsistence crops than for those growing, say, cotton or tobacco (Low, 1977). Withdrawal would therefore probably result in a redistribution of income biased towards the higher-income farmers. It is possible, however, that the removal of the migration option might induce subsistence farmers more readily to consider cash cropping alternatives, if such alternatives provided a remuneration to labour at least equivalent to that obtainable in off-farm employment within Swaziland.

Furthermore, the indications are that migration from the Lowveld ecological region of Swaziland has increased in recent years. Crop potential in this region is lowest and climatic variability greatest, so that a restriction on mine migration might result in a redistribution of income which further favoured the higher potential, less climatically variable Highveld and Middleveld ecological zones. These, in addition, would receive the initial thrust of the Rural Development Areas Programme.

Summary

The Swaziland computer simulation study has attempted to highlight the impact of withdrawal of Swazi labour from the South African mines at the national as opposed to the household level. It is clear that withdrawal could be expected to have both positive and negative effects on the economy: urban and rural unemployment problems would probably increase substantially, and rural income distribution might be adversely affected whilst, on the other hand, the overgrazing situation would, in all probability, be alleviated. It is likely that withdrawal would be involuntary; but if this were not the case, there would be obvious policy conflicts to be considered. For instance, short-term problems of urban growth and unemployment would have to be weighed against the longer-term problem of overgrazing and its effect on the rural resource base. In any event, it may be concluded that the need for effective rural development programmes which expand rural employment opportunities and increase rural incomes would be more critical in the presence of than in the absence of withdrawal.

HOUSEHOLD REACTIONS AND THE SATISFACTION OF
BASIC NEEDS: THE BOTSWANA CASE

If we use basic needs as a relevant yardstick for government policy,[3] our analysis must concentrate on small units rather than a whole sector (the rural sector, for example). Much the same point is made in the National Development Plan for 1976–81, which states that "'The rural population' includes very disparate groups with different means of livelihood and different living standards. A rural development strategy that is to benefit all these groups must contain measures that are specifically tailored to each of them and reach out beyond the large villages" (Botswana, 1977, p. 67). For this reason the model developed to analyse the effects of declining migration in Botswana on the satisfaction of basic needs focuses on sets of households with similar characteristics.[4] Many such sets could each represent a target group for certain government policies.[5] How the satisfaction of basic needs would be influenced by declining migration would depend on a number of interactions, some reinforcing certain trends and others tending to stabilise some trends for the group under consideration. Even with limited information the model development process can contribute significantly to the creation of an improved knowledge base for policy decisions.

The model development process

The twin assumptions upon which modelling builds in order to improve planning in conditions of declining migration are: *(a)* planning is best when based upon the most objective method possible;[6] and *(b)* the relevancy and correctness of relationships tend to improve as the amount of knowledge about them increases.[7] Not only does knowledge have a better chance of increasing when supposed relationships are stated as precisely as possible (as in computer programmes), but computer simulation offers a unique opportunity to analyse the consequences of a variety of relationships that would otherwise have to be more or less guessed at.[8]

Owing to the present lack of information, migration planning must rely to a significant extent on subjective expectations. The path toward improved planning requires that these subjective expectations be objectified and tested. The benefits of modelling can be achieved earlier in the process of objectification than many people realise. Critics tend to overlook the diagnostic function of modelling when simulation is applied in a situation where there are important gaps in information.[9] Of course, the modelling approach that is most suitable will depend upon the type of information available, the research questions that are posed and the resources that are available for the modelling exercise.

In the case of the Botswana model the question of the satisfaction of basic needs in the face of declining migration has guided model development. The amount of available information (or the lack of information compared with what is available in many developed countries) means that there are limits on the conclusions that can be drawn from sensitivity analysis. Conclusions can point out to planners the possibility that the distinction between "push" and "pull" migrants is meaningless. A mòre firmly stated conclusion requires better information. The model cannot say whether a particular policy would be able to combat the undesirable effects of declining migration, for this requires that more precise information be available concerning migration and migrant transfer income, weather conditions, the effects of particular government policies, the marginal productivity of returning labourers, and so on.

However, the probable usefulness of various policies can be evaluated according to their ability to increase the satisfaction of basic needs under a variety of assumptions about uncertain variables, such as rainfall, developments in crop income or various patterns of migration decline. If the success of a policy is found to vary according to another variable, such as the tendency of households to invest in cattle, the need for better information concerning that variable (for instance, household investment behaviour) has been underlined and research activities should be directed accordingly. On the other hand, a particular government policy may be found to lessen the reduction in the satisfaction of basic needs under declining migration, no matter what reasonable assumptions are used for uncertain variables. With limited government resources for both planning and implementation, it would then seem wise to consider the immediate implementation of such a policy rather than wait for further empirical research. Obviously, the usefulness of a model in this manner depends on the degree to which the model's structure is felt to be a reasonable abstraction of reality.

The amount of confidence that a model enjoys depends upon the outcome of several different types of test of the model's credibility. First, the model's structure can be evaluated on the same terms as any verbally expressed description of conditions affecting migrant households. Does common sense say that the various relationships contained in the model are reasonable and in agreement with available empirical evidence? Second, a more objective test can be carried out: a model can be run on a computer to determine whether the relationships it contains react as a whole in a way that is reasonable. If they do not, answering the question "Why not?" often leads to new insights—especially if the model has passed the first test.

When a model is available that has passed these two tests, it can be used to help to identify the most promising areas for empirical research. Better empirical data, more model runs, analysis and model revisions, analysis, research, and so forth, will all contribute to improvements that increase the model's trustworthiness. More precise tests of the model will thus be possible as more and better data are accumulated.

In short, the information available at present is insufficient for precise forecasts concerning the effects of declining migration, but the model presented briefly below can lead to improvements in precision and indicate general trends, as well as contribute to sorting out relevant variables and relationships. Further development can result in a model which will yield forecasts that can be tested empirically. Such a model could be used directly in policy-making. The path to such a model will be easier and quicker if models are used today because of their advantages over verbal expositions of relevant relationships affecting migrant households.

Description of the Botswana model

The Botswana model aims at providing a summary in mathematical form of theoretical and empirical information. It should be considered more as an opening presentation for debate than as a final statement. It draws on the work of experts in a number of diverse fields and represents an important step towards objectification because the consequences of much diverse information can be precisely calculated, given model assumptions. The calculations can be independently replicated and therefore altered to test the consequences of different opinions regarding model assumptions. The model presented below has been through twelve sets of major revisions as a part of this dialogue process.

The model seeks to reflect the options open to a predefined set of households as external migration declines. Ecological conditions (including rainfall, range condition and soil depletion) and income from a number of sources interact to provide an indication of the degree to which basic needs are being met. The level of income necessary for minimum subsistence increases with the passage of time, but only if income is large enough to allow for sustained discretionary consumption which, as the years go by, can come to be viewed as necessary rather than discretionary.

The best way to get a quick impression of the model is to look at the model's sectors one by one. The most important for an understanding of the model are the following: *(a)* the rainfall generator; *(b)* the crop-farming sector; *(c)* the demographic sector; *(d)* the income allocation sector; and *(e)* the livestock sector.

Rainfall generator. Since a knowledge of rainfall variations is vital in assessing the satisfaction of basic needs, various possibilities allowing for rainfall in the model are necessary. What is needed is a facility that can deliver adequate data on variations in rainfall so that a sufficient spectrum of rainfall possibilities can be included in the analysis of the satisfaction of basic needs. To do this a rainfall generator combining two basic patterns has been used. The two patterns depend upon random number generators to produce rainfall according to its likelihood *(a)* from month to month in the course of a year, and *(b)* from year to year, i.e. depending on the probability of the year as a whole being relatively wet or dry. Thus both inter- and intra-yearly variations are included. A third possibility is also available: stipulated rainfall. Drought years, for example, can be imposed on the year-to-year random pattern. This is an important facility for testing the model.

Crop-farming sector. Crop income is generated here on the basis of rainfall and labour availability and assumptions involving the terms of trade for crop production and soil fertility, as well as differing assumptions concerning the marginal productivity of labour employed in crop agriculture.

Demographic sector. This sector includes calculations for population growth and migration. The extent of migration is determined outside the model, i.e. in South Africa. In this sector the income accruing to Botswana households from migration is calculated.

Income allocation sector. In this sector total income is calculated on the basis of migrant remittances, livestock income, crop income and income from all other sources. On the basis of income per head, the inclination to invest (defined before each run) and what households consider necessary for minimum subsistence, resources are allocated to subsistence consumption, discretionary consumption or investment in livestock. The accepted subsistence income level rises as income per head increases.

Livestock sector. Because of its size this sector has been divided into three subsectors: *(a)* pasture and grazing; *(b)* stock numbers; and *(c)* income deriving from stock. In the first subsector cattle numbers and rainfall determine the extent of overgrazing. Stock numbers are influenced by the availability of fodder as well as by purchase and sale. Cattle are sold (to someone outside the model) when income fails to cover subsistence needs. Cattle are purchased (from outside the model) with a portion of income that is above subsistence. Thus, the investment function of cattle is consistent with observations for both Swaziland (Doran et al., 1979) and Botswana (Woods, 1978). Income is derived from sales of stock, milk and whatever can be salvaged from dead animals.

An important income source should be added to the model, namely migrant remittances for those households within the income group being studied who have migrants in other areas of Botswana. Such *domestic* migration should be included in the model since it is influenced by and influences government policy. This migration could be included by following the path of Doran's model for Swaziland (Doran, 1977).

There are many other ways in which the model could be improved, even though it is more complex than this brief description may suggest (the model contains over 100 equations). There are three important sources for further improvements: *(a)* the results of tests with the model involving alterations in assumptions and estimates; *(b)* debate concerning the model's structure and results; and *(c)* new empirical information, especially from Botswana's National Migration Survey.

Tests conducted with the model

As mentioned in the sector descriptions, it has been necessary to supply reasonable estimates or assumptions concerning certain relationships about which current empirical evidence is at best sketchy. As noted, the forthcoming results of current research will provide a firmer basis for many of these relationships. The estimates of relationships still lacking in empirical information can be tested.[10]

The test method involves altering estimates—say, to a reasonable extent in the opposite direction—and observing whether the general trend in variables important for the satisfaction of basic needs is altered. Of course, a number of combinations of alterations should be included in the analysis. This is important because a particular government policy (or incorrect estimate of a relationship) may influence the satisfaction of basic needs via a circuitous chain of influences. The "system dynamics" method, which has been used to develop the Botswana model, focuses on feedback and feedback loops as the transmitters of such circuitous influences (see Woods, 1978).

Because of the indirect effects of policy as well as estimation errors, a large number of tests under various combinations of assumptions are necessary to draw conclusions on the basis of existing information. To illustrate the technique the results of 44 separate tests will be presented. The tests conducted so far can be divided into six categories.

Declining migration versus continuing migration. A declining external migration pattern was contrasted with continuing migration to isolate the effects of a migration decline. The declining pattern is admittedly drastic: recruiting falls from 25 per cent of the *de jure* workforce per year to zero in the course of five years. The decline starts three years into the run.

Relatively wet versus relatively dry weather conditions. A random rainfall pattern which turned out to be slightly above the long-term average was contrasted with a pattern below the average.

Two levels of investment. The inclination to invest a surplus in livestock has been estimated at 50 per cent. Runs have also been carried out at 20 per cent.

142

Conditions pertaining to crop agriculture. The result of soil depletion, changes in the terms of trade and the introduction of improved production methods in crop agriculture have been simulated with three assumptions about the maximum attainable gross margin for crops during the course of the 15-year model run: *(a)* no change: this was meant to simulate soil depletion and/or a deterioration in the crop terms of trade where the increase in the *de jure* workforce was required for crop labour in order that the gross margin should not decline; *(b)* a 5 per cent increase from 1981: this was meant to simulate improved technologies and/or an improvement in the crop terms of trade, which meant that if rainfall was constant the gross margin improved by 5 per cent if the *de jure* workforce laboured in crop agriculture; and *(c)* the same as *(b)*, but with a rate of increase of 8 per cent.

Constant versus declining marginal productivity of labour. Two assumptions about the tendency in the productivity of increases in crop labour have been tested: declining and constant.

Two recommendations in case of drought. If drought should occur at any time during, or near, a decline in migration, one would expect serious complications for policy-makers. In a recent report on drought submitted to the Botswana Government the recommendation was made that under drought conditions farmers should be encouraged to "sell many of their livestock, and thus to reduce pressure on the rangelands and provide a better chance for the livestock remaining to survive" (Sanford, 1977, p. 46). This was called the *sell* policy and was contrasted with a *do-nothing* policy. Because of the importance of livestock and the overgrazing problem it would be useful to see if declining migration in conjunction with a *sell* as against a *do-nothing* policy might have implications for the satisfaction of basic needs. Therefore, the tests described above were all run with a *do-nothing* policy and run again with a *sell* policy simulated by the addition to the model of equations causing animals to be sold to an extent directly proportional to the extent that animals were dying of starvation-related diseases. Thus in a severe drought many animals would be sold and in a moderate drought fewer animals would be sold (cf. Woods, 1978, pp. 17–18 and Appendices 4 and 5).

It should be clear from the foregoing that the present model represents an early stage in a process. Conclusions based upon the tests described should be treated with caution as regards their applicability to reality, even though they certainly deserve the same consideration as a verbal analysis in which the effects of a number of relationships are calculated subjectively. Further testing of the model is necessary to determine whether the conclusions stated below will stand up when the model is run with different estimates for uncertain relationships.

Some results of the model tests

In drawing conclusions about general tendencies, we used the following method. Several key variables were selected and the results for each of these key variables for each of the 44 runs were put into a table from which the results of selected runs could be drawn. Runs were then compared in which the only difference involved relationships pertinent to one of the six test categories. Thus, declining migration could be compared with continuing migration under the wet weather pattern, under the dry weather pattern, without any increase in the maximum attainable crop gross margin, with two rates of increase, and so forth. The only difference in this case is migration, and the conclusions relating to declining as against constant migration represent the observed trend under differing assumptions regarding other test categories. How this one difference affects the satisfaction of basic needs under a variety of circumstances can therefore be tested with certainty, given the model's structure. The approach was applied to each of the six test categories.

As expected, the *decline in migration* caused an improvement in the long-term carrying capacity of the range measured at the end of the model run. However, noticeable improvements in range condition were generally accompanied by unacceptable income levels seen from a basic-needs point of view and a rate of dissaving which must be considered catastrophic. Therefore, although the reasoning behind a suggestion that less attention be paid to overgrazing, given declining external migration, is correct, the conclusion is placed in doubt because success in combating overgrazing with the help of declining migration demands too high a price in terms of the satisfaction of basic needs. Thus, policy measures are required to neutralise any significant effect of declining migration on overgrazing in order to ameliorate the detrimental effects of such declining migration on the satisfaction of basic needs.

A consistent pattern, although one varying in degree, emerged from the comparisons of dry and wet *weather conditions*. The extent of overgrazing was less under the low rainfall pattern. There are two reasons for this. First, higher rainfall means higher incomes and therefore higher net livestock flow (purchases minus sales), all of which come from outside the model (cf. the Swaziland case study in Chapter 3). Second, the rate of increase of the herd is higher. Both these factors mean that the stocking rate is higher, causing greater damage during periods of low rainfall.

The importance of the *investment level* needs to be investigated further. In conjunction with the *sell* versus *do-nothing* policy, comparisons in which only the investment level was altered have indicated very significant differences in overgrazing effects (it should be remembered that all purchased cattle come from outside the model).

The variations in *crop income* are most interesting with respect to their effects through feedbacks on other variables. Even modest improvements in crop income were able to reduce to a meaningful degree the rate of over-all net dissaving occasioned by drought and declining migration.

The constant *marginal productivity of labour* in crop agriculture (as opposed to declining marginal productivity) also contributed to improvements in crop income with the same type of effect as that noted in the preceding paragraph.

The *sell policy* produced generally higher averages of income per head, but this was most pronounced under conditions of continuing migration (as there was a higher surplus to invest in livestock which was then sold during dry spells). The average and final herd size, as well as overgrazing damage, were all consistently lower under the sell policy.

Another form of analysis carried out on each of the 44 runs involved the analysis of the developments of scores of variables during the course of each of the 44 runs. Examples are presented in a more complete report on the model (Woods, 1978, pp. 20–30) showing how, under reasonable circumstances, migrants who would have been considered "pull" migrants quickly slipped into the "push" category, suggesting the need to de-emphasise this demarcation for planning purposes.

Nevertheless, there appears to be over-all agreement between the results from Swaziland and those from Botswana. Well considered and carefully implemented rural development programmes are even more necessary in the face of declining migration. It appears also that computer simulation has an important contribution to make towards better planning. Indeed, one of the most important conclusions that can be drawn from both the Swaziland and the Botswana models lies in the usefulness of modelling coupled with sensitivity analysis for migration planning and probably for planning in other contexts in developing countries as well. Care must be taken, though, to prevent models and their advantages from becoming the exclusive preserve of a small group of experts. For this reason the structure of models (and if possible all model equations) having any sort of relationship to planning should be publicised in an understandable form, so that as many people as possible can come to understand and criticise the ideas stated very precisely in model formulations.

Notes

[1] A key concept of the basic-needs approach is the preoccupation (for planning purposes) with the relationships between the micro and macro levels. The Botswana model described here can be

programmed to represent groups having different characteristics within the rural sector. An important aspect of the model is that the environment within which households function can easily be altered so that the effects of various macro policies on diverse groups can be dealt with. The reader may envisage Botswana's traditional rural sector as being characterised by the type of household detailed in Wood's work, and by this type only. In these circumstances, this sector of Botswana's economy and the typified household are identical economic agents.

[2] The net rate of migration is defined as that proportion of the total rural workforce which migrates and remains in the urban sector in any given period. The gross rate of migration is that proportion of the total rural workforce which migrates to and returns from the urban sector in any given period.

[3] The Government of Botswana clearly places a high priority on the satisfaction of basic needs (see Botswana, 1972, for general government policy). The objectives of rural development are stated more concretely in Chambers and Feldman, 1973, and Botswana, 1973.

[4] A more detailed summary of work with the Botswana model is given in Woods, 1978, which also contains a discussion of each model equation and the results of all model tests.

[5] One household group has been examined so far. Its characteristics are derived from various estimates by the author—an approach that was made necessary by the current lack of information. Various studies in progress at present should help to fill this gap, the most important of which are the National Migration Survey and the analysis of the Rural Income Distribution Survey (Botswana, 1976) on a per head basis. (See also Woods, 1978, footnotes 1–4, 1–13.) Thus this contribution describes a method that can be applied even more usefully as more information becomes available.

[6] What distinguishes objective methods from subjective methods is the explicit and precise statement of the process(es) by which conclusions are reached. Objective analysis can be independently replicated while subjective analysis yields conclusions based upon the researcher's own mental processes which cannot be independently replicated. Note that both subjective and objective analysis can draw on data that are either subjective or objective and that examples of simplicity and complexity can be found for both types of analysis.

[7] This should not be interpreted as a call for a sheer quantitative increase. The point is that by looking at one time at a larger number of relationships than can be analysed at once by human intuition, there is a better chance that the relationships thought correct will be so in reality. Knowing the consequences of a number of interactions is helpful even if it is desirable that more and better empirical information should be available concerning them. At least we shall know if several theories interact as expected, given reasonable assumptions.

[8] It is to be expected that the modelling technique used here could be useful in a variety of contexts for planning in developing countries. In Botswana the Government has clearly recognised the need for more precision in planning for special groups: "The diversity of rural needs and the constraint on government implementation capacity both point to a need for greater precision. For each project, Government must be clear precisely which group it is trying to assist, precisely what it can achieve, and precisely how it can achieve this" (Botswana, 1977, p. 67).

[9] Critics of modelling in a particular context find themselves on the horns of a dilemma. If an analysis with the help of models is abandoned because of uncertainties surrounding a number of relationships, very often the uncertainty vanishes when it comes to stating the conclusions of subjective calculations regarding the interaction of the many important relationships. Modelling and sensitivity analysis offer the best solution to this dilemma of conclusions versus relationship uncertainty.

[10] Of course, better established relationships can also be tested for an indication of the importance of possible empirical errors.

REDUCING DEPENDENCE ON MIGRATION IN SOUTHERN AFRICA

7

C. W. Stahl and W. R. Böhning

BACKGROUND

Throughout history and in all parts of the world, national and international migration has occurred in response to pressing difficulties at home or beckoning opportunities elsewhere. As a rule, it has led to an improvement in the individual migrant's personal well-being. For the social groups or countries of origin, it has eased the burden on domestic resources—especially land, the essential source of the food, shelter and clothing required to satisfy basic needs. Whether, beyond this, it has influenced positively the factors that shape economic progress is a matter for speculation. Empirical observation would seem not to confirm such a thesis, because case studies demonstrating the development of productive capacity as a consequence of out-migration are conspicuous by their absence.

The region of southern Africa has experienced large-scale migration for over a century. The White farms and mines of South Africa have always relied heavily on migrants from outside the country, who were prepared to work at the going (that is, low) rates of pay, in order to fill shortfalls in the South African labour market. Occasionally, the migration of these Africans got under way before the White colonial Powers had penetrated their settlements. More often, it was the intended result or the accepted by-product of levying taxes on the African population. Almost everywhere, the migration can be traced back to the appropriation of African lands by White settlers, to the restrictions on the acquisition of new land or on educational and occupational advancement, and to the confinement of African producers to unprofitable markets.

The burgeoning urban areas associated with mining developments provided a ready market for agricultural products. In many areas Africans produced agricultural surpluses and marketed cattle to satisfy not only the tax collector but also the growing cash component of their rising conventional subsistence standards that stemmed from exposure to

147

the money economy and its diverse range of non-traditional goods. However, subsidies to White producers and transport impediments for African producers placed Black agriculture in a more and more uncompetitive position. In addition, population growth reduced the amount of arable land per head. Stagnation, even dislocation, ensued.

With fewer possibilities for obtaining cash, and yet an ever growing need for it, large numbers of Africans migrated to wage employment in the modern sector. Their large numbers, and the common front presented by the employers, ensured that wages would remain low (Stahl, 1974; Bardill et al., 1977). On top of this—sometimes by design, at other times by accident, but always with the same result—the wages were inadequate to meet the needs of the migrant's family during his employment or either his own needs or those of the family after his return. Having thus been forced in the past by economic circumstances to keep his family living and working in the rural hinterland and to return thereto, and being forced today by the laws of apartheid to do the same, the migrant has become the unwitting mechanism by which a burden is placed on the area from which he comes that should rightfully be borne by the people who employ him. The rural labour-supplying areas are not only drained of their most productive manpower but also have to carry what in economic jargon would be called the infrastructural costs of supplying labour. Hence it can be argued that the economically poor home countries are forced to subsidise the economy of South Africa, thereby perpetuating apartheid. In this way migration has been one of the factors contributing to the ever widening gap between the booming White core economy and the impoverished Black periphery.

There are other features of the southern African migration system which warrant investigation. First, to what extent have the supplying areas benefited from the collective relief function of emigration? The answer is, at best, very little and, at worst, only temporarily, because South Africa has sought to prevent the permanent settlement of Africans in White areas. This has suffocated, in particular, those areas whose present borders enclose a territory where there is an inherently unviable or precarious relationship of people to land (especially Lesotho and Botswana, respectively). Second, through legislative measures, South Africa has denied migrant workers a wide range of basic human rights, such as the reunification of families and the formation of proper trade unions. The tearing apart of families has undermined family and social life, while the repression of the right to organise has hampered migrant workers in their struggle against exploitation.

The main result of the above has been to leave the labour-supplying countries both severely underdeveloped and with a high degree of dependence on South Africa. (Dependence in this context means that one country can inflict grave damage on another without incurring comparable harm sufficient to deter it from doing so.) In other words, a century of migration has left the supplying countries with an unprotected flank on the economic front. In the conditions in which they find themselves today they cannot break away from the migrant labour system; they are not the masters of their own fate since their welfare in the short term depends on the country that employs them; and they lack full control of domestic investment and accumulation. It is exactly this economic vulnerability that South Africa has been threatening to exploit since the chief employer of migrant labour from other countries—the gold-mining industry—started to implement plans that implied the recruitment of fewer migrant workers.

OPTIONS

What can be done about the undesirable features of international labour migration in southern Africa?

First, despite the unsatisfactory population/land relationships and the poor prospects for industrialisation in the supplier States, the option of permanent migration into South Africa must be discarded on both moral and political grounds. Indeed, the migrant-sending countries show no wish for such an option.

Second, the fight against the denial of human rights, against discrimination and for the improvement of the working conditions of present-day migrants must continue. However, the scope for action by the governments of the home countries is relatively limited (the main burden will fall on the shoulders of the migrants themselves). Any major success presupposes the dismantling of apartheid. Even if some minor successes were achieved, they would be insufficient for those countries which, on economic grounds, need permanent emigration opportunities or some other means of satisfying the basic needs of their population. Therefore, the battle for elementary rights must be supplemented by effective measures to enable each country to attain certain minimum standards of living. The alternative is to wait for a miracle (or, more likely, a holocaust) to provide a sounder ratio of people to resources—and to do so may well, in the meantime, demand unbearable sacrifices from present and future generations.

The debilitating effect of migration could theoretically be mitigated by pressing for fair wages. However, this would bring into the open the problem of balancing the private gains and the social losses associated with migration. When he migrates, the individual is undoubtedly better off for a while in terms of disposable cash income, and the same may be

149

true for his family. Higher wages would make this still truer and would make migration still more attractive. Yet, in the end, to do this would make the labour-supplying countries even more dependent and thus make more problematical any measures of self-reliant development.[1]

Third, therefore, the only valid option would seem to be to reduce dependence on migration by withdrawing from the migrant labour system. (To strive for interdependence would draw countries ever deeper into the morass of apartheid.) Only in this way would it be possible to stop the undermining of the economies in the countries of origin and to bolster their vulnerable defences against apartheid. Of course, such withdrawal could not be total and immediate, in the present circumstances, without risking great and lasting suffering, starvation and even death among the poorest sections of the labour-supplying areas. Withdrawal could become a practical reality only if circumstances were different.[2] Later in this chapter we shall put forward a proposal that seeks to change the circumstances by setting up a United Nations fund to facilitate the withdrawal of migrant labour from South Africa over a defined period of time.

We would give the reduction in dependence on migration priority over the reduction in dependence on trade or investment. The migration link involves human beings directly in the evils of apartheid; and it is crucial in the sense that it is the major debilitating link in the international division of labour in southern Africa. Moreover, because our proposals would resolve the migration question without even temporarily diverting financial resources from the home countries' general development efforts, there would be no danger of the reduction in dependence on migration *per se* leading to an increase in dependence on trade or investment vis-à-vis South Africa.

It should be noted that the emergence of a non-apartheid political economy would invalidate our reasoning; however, for working purposes we have had to rule this prospect out for, say, the next 15 years. We believe, however, that the collapse of apartheid would in no small measure be speeded up by the disengagement of the labour-supplying States from the migrant labour system. Not only would this lead to a greater degree of economic independence but their political independence from South Africa would thereby be reinforced; it would also strengthen the hand of South African Blacks in dealing with apartheid.

THE WITHDRAWAL OPTION

The moral, social, economic and political liabilities of the migrant labour system make an unanswerable case for withdrawal. Indeed, the victims of the system are in full agreement with "the desirability of eliminating the migratory labour system and of hastening the withdrawal of migrant labourers from South Africa".[3]

Secondary but none the less persuasive reasons are the known tendencies in South Africa to phase out migrant labour (Clarke, 1977a) and the likely decline in the demand for labour in the gold-mines (Bromberger, 1979). Gold-mines employ almost two-thirds of the migrant labour force. Compared with an average number of 450,000 African gold-miners today, of whom the proportion from outside South Africa has deliberately been pushed below 50 per cent, it seems probable that by the end of the century fewer than 150,000 Africans will be employed in the gold-mines. If an unchanged 50 per cent of these were migrants from other lands, the labour-supplying countries would by then have undergone a process of exclusion or "forced withdrawal" involving a net reduction to about one-third of the number of miners today. Evidence also indicates that commercial agriculture, once a major employer of African labour from outside South Africa, reached its employment peak at the end of the 1960s. As a result of mechanisation and other changes, employment in that industry will decline. It is possible, but not likely, that opportunities for migrants would spring up elsewhere in the meantime. Without a strategy of withdrawal, such opportunities would inevitably trap the supplying countries once more in the vicious circle from which they are trying to escape.

To go helplessly through the foreseeable period of "forced withdrawal" would be to drink to the bottom the bitter cup of migration sorrow. It would be both humiliating and disastrous. In retrospect, today's circumstances would be seen as having offered the last opportunity to disengage from the migrant labour system on one's own terms and in a planned manner. Nothing could be more far-sighted than to give the highest priority to bringing about the change from a migration-dependent economy that involves both economic exploitation and subjugation to apartheid. And nothing could be more promising than to do this in the changed circumstances provided by a United Nations back-up fund which would be given the double function of (a) disarming South Africa's threat of dumping migrants on their own doorstep, and (b) making effective planning for development possible after the return of the migrants.

One point is so obvious that we have not stated it so far. This is that the countries supplying labour to South Africa would have to plan jointly and act in concert. In principle, unilateral withdrawal is perfectly possible with the kind of United Nations back-up we have in mind. In practice, there appears to be a psychological block in the labour-supplying countries which forestalls any withdrawal move until each and every one of them agrees to share in the resulting dislocation. This is understandable. There are also fears that South Africa will play off one country against another as soon as any one country moves, and here the danger is clear. At the minimum, therefore, the case for getting together rests on the psychological need to see that every country puts up with the consequences at the same time. (Whether, beyond this, it might be possible to minimise the disruption through co-operative measures in the field of economic relations need not detain us here.) At the maximum, it is a political reinsurance policy.

To give it a name, we shall call the suggested common front for withdrawal the "Association of Home Countries of Migrants" (AHCM). Its immediate purpose would be to drain off the potential dissension on the withdrawal question, to hammer out a jointly agreed timetable for gradually pulling out of the migrant labour system and to present a joint case for the necessary support to the United Nations and other bodies that might assist the countries during the transition. It might be organised as an intergovernmental body. To get it off the ground would doubtless require agreement at presidential and prime ministerial level. To function effectively, it would seem to require a permanent secretariat of representatives (which could build upon the experience gained by the already existing intergovernmental ministerial consultative committee).

The longer-term implications, other than effecting the withdrawal, would ideally be to create a habit of acting together on regional and international questions and to pave the way for broader forms of national or collective self-reliance. A possibly automatic by-product (which would not have to be an integral part of the scheme necessitating consensus at the outset) might be the simultaneous and thorough diagnosis and remedying of the substantive economic and social problems in each labour-supplying country.

AHCM CONTROL OVER LABOUR SUPPLY

The members of the AHCM ought to assume effective control over their national supplies of migrants (numbers of workers, duration of migration and distribution over sectors of employment); they ought also to be able sufficiently to control illegal movements to South Africa; and they ought to dissuade other African countries and South Africa from moves that would substitute their labour for AHCM labour.

As regards the number of migrant workers from the five countries which we envisage would initially form part of the AHCM, we estimate that 61,000 Batswana, 200,000 Basotho, 25,000 Malawians, 55,000 Mozambicans and 26,000 Swazis are currently recruited each year, giving a total of 367,000 *recruits*.[4] The existing migration agreements between the home countries and South Africa provide a perfectly legitimate basis for controlling the number of workers any South African employer may engage.[5] To be able to recruit from an Association member, employers or their recruiting agents or runners would need a licence. Candidates would be introduced to them under the auspices of the government department which administered the migration agreement.[6] If demand and supply were matched successfully, the workers would need a valid passport to cross the border. This, then, should make it possible to issue only such numbers of passports to candidates for employment in South Africa as tallied with the withdrawal schedule.

One cannot reasonably invoke the Universal Declaration of Human Rights against this kind of passport control. The right of everyone "to leave any country, including his own" (article 13 (2)) is not infringed where a home country refuses to fill offered vacancies or where it excludes certain categories of people from waiting lists. Exclusion from schemes of public assistance to international migration for employment leaves the individual free to move to immigration countries outside the framework of publicly organised schemes. (For an elaboration of this argument, see Böhning, 1975.)

Where migrant workers stayed abroad for differing periods of employment, one would need to control not only the number of moves but also the duration of migration, i.e. the length of contracts entered into and their possible extensions. Otherwise one might be faced with a situation where the total number of *man-years* supplied by the AHCM increased even though the number of *recruits* decreased.[7] We assume that the average length of contract is nine months for Batswana, 12 months for both Basotho and Malawians, about 11 months for Mozambicans and six months for Swazis. Relating these to our earlier figures of recruits gives the following numbers of *man-years* supplied: Botswana 46,000, Lesotho 200,000, Malawi 25,000 (the latter two being equal to the number of recruits because each recruit works, on average, for 12 months), Mozambique 50,000 and Swaziland 13,000, totalling 334,000 man-years.

To control length of contract and unauthorised extensions of contract, AHCM members would have to restrict the validity of passports to a renewable period of (at least) six months or (at most) 12 months. Individuals wanting to work longer could have their passports extended through the labour representatives stationed in South Africa or while on home leave. The man-years being supplied could be monitored for each month or quarter. If the calculated number of man-years (number of recruits × number of months contracted ÷ 12) exceeded any limit foreseen in the withdrawal schedule, the introduction of candidates for migration

153

Table 18.   Average length of contract of African workers by country of origin, 1973, 1977 and 1979[1] (in months)

Country of origin	1973	1977	1979
South Africa	10.2	7.0	12.5
Botswana, Lesotho and Swaziland	12.6	12.0	15.6
Malawi	19.3	.	13.0
Mozambique	16.0	13.6	18.0

[1] Calculated by dividing number employed at 31 December by total intake in the preceding 12 months for each country and multiplying by 12.
Sources: Mine Labour Organisation: *Annual reports,* 1973 and 1977; TEBA: *Annual report, 1979.*

to employers and the extension of contracts could be suspended until the figure had fallen by an acceptable margin.

The sectoral distribution of workers in South Africa is important. Migrants from abroad are concentrated in the profitable mining sector in general (see table 7, p. 28) and in gold-mining in particular.[8] The fact that the Chamber of Mines remains the largest single recruiting agent, absorbing about 60 per cent of all Africans coming from outside South Africa, provides *(a)* some leverage for extracting an employment levy and *(b)* a framework for planning an orderly, phased withdrawal. As regards the latter, it is envisaged that the Chamber of Mines would be asked to employ annually a *(declining) minimum* number of Association workers. Assuming that 200,000 recruits would be supplied and that the length of contracts continued to be; on average, very close to 12 months (today's situation, although there are variations among nationalities: see table 18), under a withdrawal schedule stretching over 15 years the number of recruits withdrawn from the Chamber of Mines would be 13,333 each year.

If the Chamber of Mines were free to displace as many workers from abroad as it wanted and when it wanted, this would create difficulties in planning and implementing an alternative employment programme. We shall show later that the AHCM would seem to have sufficient bargaining powers to force the Chamber of Mines to adhere to a specified decreasing number of recruits annually. However, the AHCM's powers might be insufficient to force employers other than the Chamber of Mines to adhere to the suggested withdrawal schedule (and to pay for their portion of the Association's alternative employment programme). There is a risk that employers other than the Chamber of Mines would not ask for enough workers to bridge the gap between the (declining) minimum quota for the Chamber of Mines and the (declining) maximum quota for all migrant employment. In these circumstances there would be several alternatives. First, the size of the employment levy to be paid by the

Chamber of Mines could be made to reflect the financial requirements of the total withdrawal and re-employment programme (rather than merely a proportionate 60 per cent, or the 95 per cent according to the optimal solution we illustrate below under the heading "Sources of negotiating power" and in table 23). As will be seen later, there is no doubt of its ability to pay. Second, the Chamber of Mines could not only be enabled to compete with other employers for the number of recruits available above its own quota (on the basis of "first come, first served" or on the basis of highest wage offered) but could also be asked to employ such numbers as would be unlikely to be taken up by other employers. However, this could be pushed only to a certain degree. In the improbable case that the displacement of AHCM labour from non-Chamber employers proceeded at a rate significantly faster than foreseen, a portion of the proposed United Nations back-up fund could be used to employ within their own country, or to support, that number of migrants scheduled to be supplied but who could not find employment abroad.

It ought to be possible to prevent illegal migration for employment and the unauthorised extension of contracts by the kind of passport control discussed above. Circumvention of the official channels for introducing candidates to South African employers could be made a punishable offence both for the worker and for the employer. The worker could be excluded from schemes of public introduction to South African employment, and the recruiter or employer could have his licence withdrawn. Public opprobrium should be thrown on the offence, and elected or civil service authorities could be asked to assess the situation regularly, if necessary with the aid of random spot visits.

The power of the AHCM to prevent the faster-than-foreseen replacement of its supply by South African labour is discussed in a later section. We are convinced that the AHCM could control this crucial variable. The displacement of Association labour by Africans from other countries would be a much lesser threat. On becoming independent both Tanzania and Zambia voluntarily cut their migration links. They seem sufficiently set against apartheid not to be tempted by South African offers in this field. An independent Namibia would appear immunised against the migrant labour system and in any case needs all its workers in the course of development. Angola, which was but a marginal labour supplier under the Portuguese colonial administration, seems similarly to need no moral persuasion to abstain, though the same does not necessarily hold for the insurgents located in its southern areas. Towards the end of 1980 the Zimbabwean Minister for Mines declared that Zimbabwe would not renew the WNLA agency's contract to recruit migrant labourers for the South African mines.

155

SUGGESTED WITHDRAWAL SCHEDULES

In our view, withdrawal should be spread in an orderly manner over, say, 15 years. The reason for this lies in the limited short-term employment-creating capacity of the labour-exporting economies. This, in turn, is largely due to their distorted economic structure, which indicates their deep involvement in the migrant labour system. The problem is one of designing and implementing projects to create jobs for former migrants which would contribute to a higher degree of self-sufficiency. This would take time. As emphasised in a recent World Bank report on the possibility of quickly re-employing migrants in Lesotho: "Labour-intensive methods should not be attempted without careful advance planning, organisation and training, particularly in regions where these methods have not been commonly practised" (IBRD, 1975, p. 9).

There would be many ways to spread the withdrawal over countries and over time. The simplest method would be for each country to withdraw a fixed number of recruits or man-years annually, so that all would be withdrawn by the end of the predetermined period. The annual number to be withdrawn would be each country's total migrant supply at present, divided by 15. Table 19 shows the suggested withdrawal schedule for each AHCM member.

It is a fact that some of the labour-exporting countries would be better able than others to absorb former migrants, and it is also true that some countries have many more migrants in South Africa. In Lesotho there are just over 20,000 persons in wage employment, while the average number of Basotho contract workers in South Africa is approximately 200,000. Swaziland, by comparison, has over 70,000 persons in wage employment while roughly 26,000 recruits supply 13,000 man-years to South Africa. Also, Swaziland's workforce is about one-half the size of Lesotho's. There are therefore differing degrees of dependence on labour migration among the labour-exporting countries (cf. Böhning, 1977). Conversely, these differing degrees of dependence may be said to reflect differing capacities to create new employment opportunities to absorb withdrawn migrant workers even where the necessary funds are available. One might therefore take these differing capacities into account when calculating the numbers of each country's migrants to be withdrawn annually.

A number of methods could be adopted to account for the differing absorptive capacities of the labour-supplying countries, such as GDP/population, non-agricultural output/population, number of migrants/population or total domestic formal sector employment/population (whereby the denominator should be *de jure* population). We believe that the last-mentioned is the most satisfactory weighting factor.

Table 19. Annual withdrawal of migrant labour (by number of recruits or man-years) on a proportionate basis, by country of origin

Year	Botswana[1]		Lesotho[2]	Malawi[2]	Mozambique[3]		Swaziland[4]		Total	
	Recruits	Man-years	Recruits = man-years	Recruits = man-years	Recruits	Man-years	Recruits	Man-years	Recruits	Man-years
1	4 067	3 067	13 333	1 667	3 667	3 333	1 733	867	24 467	22 267
2	4 066	3 066	13 334	1 666	3 666	3 334	1 734	866	24 466	22 266
3	4 067	3 067	13 333	1 667	3 667	3 333	1 733	867	24 467	22 267
4	4 066	3 066	13 334	1 666	3 666	3 334	1 734	866	24 466	22 266
5	4 067	3 067	13 333	1 667	3 667	3 333	1 733	867	24 467	22 267
6	4 066	3 066	13 334	1 666	3 666	3 334	1 734	866	24 466	22 266
7	4 067	3 067	13 333	1 667	3 667	3 333	1 733	867	24 467	22 267
8	4 066	3 066	13 334	1 666	3 666	3 334	1 734	866	24 466	22 266
9	4 067	3 067	13 333	1 667	3 667	3 333	1 733	867	24 467	22 267
10	4 066	3 066	13 334	1 666	3 666	3 334	1 734	866	24 466	22 266
11	4 067	3 067	13 333	1 667	3 667	3 333	1 733	867	24 467	22 267
12	4 066	3 066	13 334	1 666	3 666	3 334	1 734	866	24 466	22 266
13	4 067	3 067	13 333	1 667	3 667	3 333	1 733	867	24 467	22 267
14	4 067	3 067	13 333	1 667	3 667	3 333	1 733	867	24 467	22 267
15	4 067	3 067	13 333	1 667	3 667	3 333	1 733	867	24 467	22 267
Total	61 000	46 000	200 000	25 000	55 000	50 000	26 000	13 000	367 000	334 000

Assumed average contract length (Chamber of Mines plus other sectors for): [1] Botswana, 9 months; [2] Lesotho and Malawi, 12 months; [3] Mozambique, 11 months; [4] Swaziland, 6 months.

It is readily available and is subject to the fewest conceptual or practical measurement problems.

By way of illustration we present in table 20 a suggested withdrawal schedule using this weighting factor. On the basis of the most recent data we estimate the formal employment/population ratios for the five countries as follows: Botswana 0.0906, Lesotho 0.0175, Malawi 0.052, Mozambique 0.012 and Swaziland 0.135. Each country's share of the annual target of 24,467 recruits to be withdrawn corresponds to its share of the employment/population ratio in the sum total of ratios. In the first year Botswana would be responsible for 29.5 per cent, Lesotho for 5.7 per cent, Malawi for 16.93 per cent, Mozambique for 3.91 per cent and Swaziland for 43.96 per cent.[9] In the second year these shares do not change; but they do so in the third year because Swaziland, in pulling out all its remaining 4,490 recruits, withdraws a lower percentage of workers than it was previously entitled to; and so on.[10] To establish the weighted withdrawal schedule for man-years, one needs only to adjust the results obtained for recruits in the case of Botswana, Mozambique and Swaziland, owing to the fact that the average length of contract for Basotho and Malawians in South Africa is 12 months. The adjustment factor can be calculated by dividing each country's total of man-years to be withdrawn by the total number of recruits (e.g. in the case of Botswana, $46,000 \div 61,000 = 0.7541$). Multiplying the "Recruits" columns of table 20 with this adjustment factor gives the weighted withdrawal schedule in terms of man-years.

Swaziland, by virtue of its small numbers of migrants and relatively high level of formal-sector wage employment, would be the first to complete its withdrawal in this example. Malawi would complete its withdrawal at the end of five years; Botswana at the end of six years; Mozambique at the end of 11 years; and Lesotho, if it were thought necessary, could spread its withdrawal over the whole 15 years.

It should be clearly emphasised that rapid disengagement, such as would occur in the Swazi case, would not put that country at a disadvantage vis-à-vis the other members of the Association. As will be discussed in detail below, each country would receive compensation from the employment fund in accordance with the number of migrants it had withdrawn. Thus, for example, although Swaziland would withdraw completely in three years, it would receive the same compensation per withdrawn man-year as would the other countries, as long as revenues were paid out of the common pool. The reason for differing withdrawal schedules among the members of the Association is, again, a reflection of the estimated relative abilities of the countries to absorb labour productively with the funds made available from the revenue pool.

Table 20. Annual withdrawal of migrant labour (by number of recruits or man-years) on a weighted basis, by country of origin

Year	Botswana		Lesotho	Malawi	Mozambique		Swaziland		Total	
	Recruits	Man-years	Recruits = man-years	Recruits = man-years	Recruits	Man-years	Recruits	Man-years	Recruits	Man-years
1	7 218	5 443	1 395	4 142	957	870	10 755	5 377	24 467	17 227
2	7 218	5 443	1 395	4 142	957	870	10 755	5 378	24 467	17 228
3	10 516	7 930	2 032	6 035	1 394	1 267	4 490	2 245	24 467	19 509
4	12 879	9 712	2 488	7 392	1 708	1 553	complete		24 467	21 145
5	15 974	12 046	3 086	3 289	2 118	1 925		0	24 467	20 346
6	7 195	5 426	10 245	complete	7 026	6 387		0	24 467	22 058
7		complete	14 514	0	9 953	9 048		0	24 467	23 562
8		0	14 514	0	9 953	9 048		0	24 467	23 562
9		0	14 514	0	9 953	9 048		0	24 467	23 562
10		0	14 514	0	9 953	9 048		0	24 467	23 562
11		0	23 439	0	1 028	936		0	24 467	24 375
12		0	24 467	0	complete	0		0	24 467	24 467
13		0	24 467	0		0		0	24 467	24 467
14		0	24 467	0		0		0	24 467	24 467
15		0	24 467	0		0		0	24 467	24 467
Total	61 000	46 000	200 000	25 000	55 000	50 000	26 000	13 000	367 000	334 000

Note: For contract length, see notes to table 19. For basis of calculation, see text.

Table 21. Cumulative employment distribution and annual cost of alternative employment programme (based on the total number of man-years specified for each year in the last column of table 20)

Year	Private-sector employment	State enterprises		Government infrastructure	
		Employment	Annual cost (R '000)[1]	Employment	Annual cost[2] (R '000)
(1)	(2)	(3)	(4)	(5)	(6)
1	5 000	5 000	1 700	7 227	10 501
2	5 500	6 000	2 040	22 955	28 859
3	6 050	7 200	2 448	40 714	43 897
4	6 655	8 640	2 938	59 814	58 464
5	7 321	10 368	3 525	77 766	70 252
6	8 053	12 442	3 173	97 018	84 462
7	8 858	14 930	3 807	117 287	99 496
8	9 744	17 916	4 569	136 982	112 889
9	10 718	21 500	5 483	155 986	137 426
10	11 790	25 799	4 386	174 177	149 743
11	12 969	30 959	5 263	192 213	160 728
12	14 266	37 150	6 316	209 192	170 373
13	15 692	44 580	7 579	224 803	179 099
14	17 261	53 497	9 095	238 784	185 338
15[3]	18 987	64 196	10 913	250 817	165 714
16	20 886	77 035	6 548	236 079	151 927
17	22 975	92 442	7 858	218 583	137 471
18	25 272	110 931	9 429	197 797	120 305
19	27 800	133 117	11 315	173 083	99 872
20	30 580	159 740	13 578	143 680	79 487
21	33 638	191 688	0	108 674	75 526
22	37 002	230 026	0	66 972	44 546
23	40 702	276 031	0	17 267	12 001
24	44 772	331 238	0	0	0

Cost subtotals: (4) R 121,963,000; (6) R 2,378,376,000.
Total costs: (4) + (6) = R 2,500,339,000.

[1] Assumes that 20 per cent of workers are semi-skilled and receive an average annual wage of R 500 and that 80 per cent are unskilled and earning R 300 on average. [2] Cumulative total of last column of table 20 minus columns (1) and (2) of this table. [3] Withdrawal completed at end of year 15.

MIGRANT RE-EMPLOYMENT: SECTORS AND COSTS

The constant cost of an orderly alternative employment programme for all the Association's migrants is estimated in table 21. It amounts to US$2,500 million (dollars and rands are assumed to be approximately equal over the period foreseen).

Our particular illustration relates to the total of 334,000 man-years to be aimed at rather than the 367,000 recruits to be withdrawn (though the calculation can just as easily be based on the number of people involved). There are a number of reasons for this. First, not all ex-migrants would necessarily want to be employed full time. Second, not all ex-migrants should necessarily be drawn out of agriculture. For example, one could expect that among those ex-miners who had been on particularly short contracts there would be many who might be on the threshold of profitable farming. It would be unwise to induce them to leave the rural areas. They might nevertheless want to obtain occasional employment in government-sponsored or private-sector employment.

With regard to the sectoral distribution of employment of withdrawn migrants, we start with the expectation that in the first year the private sector and the state enterprises—taking all AHCM members as a whole—could each provide 5,000 man-years of employment.[11] For the subsequent years we anticipate that the ability of the Association's private sectors collectively to absorb further ex-migrant man-years would increase at 10 per cent per year (column (2)). Similarly, the growth in employment opportunities in the state enterprises, measured in man-years, is assumed to be 20 per cent per year (column (3)). Each year's residual number of man-years would have to be accommodated through infrastructural development projects (column (5)).

With regard to the cost of providing man-years of employment in the state enterprises (column (4)), it is assumed that for the first five years of the withdrawal programme the governments would have to subsidise their state enterprises to the extent of covering their entire wage bill. Thus the profits of these enterprises (in years 1 to 5) are assumed to be sufficient only to cover capital charges and operating costs (exclusive of labour costs). It is further assumed that 20 per cent of the workers in this sector would be semi-skilled and receive R 500 per year while the remainder would be unskilled and receive R 300 per year. In years 6 to 10 of the suggested withdrawal programme it is assumed that efficiency would have increased to the extent that the government would need to subsidise the state enterprise sector to the extent of only 75 per cent of its wage bill. This would decrease to 50 per cent in years 11–15, to 25 per cent in years 16–20 and would no longer be necessary afterwards. The monies for these subsidies would come from the Association's receipts of employment levies.

The infrastructural projects would have to be supported for 23 years. Here, too, wages have been put at R 300 per year for unskilled workers and R 500 per year for semi-skilled workers. A detailed account of capital costs, labour and other operating costs can be found in Appendix B at the end of this chapter. It should be made clear that, for simplicity's sake, we have taken one recent cost-accounting scheme for one country (Lesotho) and assumed that other schemes in the same or in other countries would result in similar costs.

As can be seen from table 21, we expect that the need for government funding of employment creation for former migrants would be essential up to year 23, although steadily less so after year 14. In the end, it would be the cumulative growth of employment in increasingly efficient state enterprises and private-sector employment that would remove the need for further government funding of migrant re-employment.

On the basis of our calculations we estimate that the average annual cost of re-employing migrants would be a little over R 100 million per year during the 23 years which we believe would be a sufficient period of time to absorb all former migrants productively.

NEGOTIATING A COMPENSATED WITHDRAWAL

The justification for compensation

To date, the supplier countries have not pressed the South African Government or the major employers of labour from abroad for any form of compensation for *(a)* the negative effects of migration on the sending countries and *(b)* the immense benefits which have accrued to South African industry and to the State through their having a ready reserve of cheap labour. (Only the Portuguese have obtained a number of very profitable concessions from South Africa, for the use of Mozambican labour.) Yet the justification for compensation is overwhelming.

Although the sending countries benefit from the migrants' higher incomes, through remitted earnings, their own capacity to generate income has been seriously eroded by their protracted involvement in the migrant labour system, with a consequent polarisation of development in the subcontinent. Skilled as well as unskilled labour is attracted to South Africa by both necessity and a greater earnings potential. The cost of the upbringing, education and health of this labour is assumed by the sending countries, and the fruits of its work go to South Africa. Once the labour is no longer productive, as a result of injury, sickness, old age or even an economic downswing in South Africa, it is sent back to the supplying country.[12]

From the viewpoint of South African industry, African labour from other countries has been of immense benefit. Profits have been higher and growth more rapid. The growth and profitability of the gold-mining industry can be attributed in no small measure to collusion in the African labour market and the concomitant exploitation of African labour from abroad (Stahl, 1974). By collectively expanding its labour recruitment area into other countries, the South African gold-mining industry was saved from costly wage competition with other sectors. The result was an economy-wide depression of African wage levels in South Africa and higher rates of profit.

Looking at the benefits of larger supplies of cheap labour from other countries to the gold-mining industry in particular and the South African economy in general, the Lansdown Commission reported in 1943:

The gold-mining industry of the Witwatersrand has indeed been fortunate in having secured, for its unskilled labour, native peasants who have been prepared to come to the Witwatersrand for periods of labour at comparatively low wages. But for this fortunate circumstance the industry could never have reached its present stage of development—some mines would never have opened up; many low-grade mines would have been unable to work with any prospect of profit; and, in the case of the richer mines, large bodies of ore, the milling of which has been brought within the limit of payability, could never have been worked, with the result that the lives of the mines would have been considerably curtailed. . . . That the results accruing from this cheap native labour supply have had a profoundly beneficial influence upon the general economic development of the Union is a matter which needs no demonstration (Lansdown Commission, 1943, pp. 5–6).

Since the time of the Lansdown Commission the Chamber of Mines has relied more and more on African labour from abroad as a means of circumventing wage pressure. From 1946 to 1973 the number of Africans from outside South Africa employed in the gold-mining industry nearly doubled (from 179,000 to 336,000), while the number of South African Blacks employed by the industry declined from 126,000 to 86,000. If the Chamber of Mines had had to compete with other sectors of the economy for a limited supply of domestic Blacks, the negative implications for gold-mining profitability and for economic activity in general would have been profound. The lack of competition by the Chamber of Mines in the domestic labour market has thus indirectly increased profit rates in other industries.

It is undeniable that migrants and their home countries have not derived enough benefit from the "social dividend" they have helped to generate. Such a social dividend accrues through the taxation of profits, dividend income and wages. South Africa has used this social dividend to finance its education, transport, sanitation and health facilities, and many other infrastructural elements as well. Without labour from abroad the social dividend would have been considerably smaller. A portion of it is directly attributable to migrant labour but has nevertheless accrued only to South Africans within South Africa—which means predominantly to White South Africans.

Sources of negotiating power

The evidence in support of the case for paying compensation to the labour-supplying countries is overwhelming. However, it is unlikely that either the Chamber of Mines or the South African Government would be swayed by moral reasons into voluntarily paying a levy to these countries. A compensated withdrawal could take place only if the gold-mining industry in particular and South Africa in general realised they could no longer unilaterally define the rules of the game, and that it was in their economic and political self-interest to play by the new rules. What, then, would be the latent powers that the AHCM could exercise to achieve this objective?

The sources of power are manifold and the evaluation of their individual magnitude is complex. They range from the purely economic to the purely political, with much overlapping. Let us begin by focusing on what would essentially be the economic power of the AHCM.

The economic power of the AHCM

Fundamentally, the economic power of the AHCM would derive from its ability to impose short-run costs, if necessary, which would exceed the total costs of the employment levy over a defined period of time. Thus the short-run power of the Association could be used to achieve its long-run objectives.

The economic power of the AHCM would derive from its potential ability to control some 367,000 workers meeting the labour needs of South African industry, in particular the gold-mining industry. The AHCM, if it had been in operation at the time of writing, would have had approximately 200,000 of its citizens employed in the gold-mining industry. That constitutes just under one-half of the gold-mining labour input and about 60 per cent of all AHCM labour in South Africa. Other forms of mining are also fairly dependent on labour from abroad. According to the 1970 census, 47 per cent of the workers in coalmining, 53 per cent of those in non-gold metallic ore mining and 22 per cent of those in "other mining" came from outside South Africa. African workers from abroad are also found in the non-mining sectors, although they are fewer than in mining (cf. table 7, p. 28).

Of all South African industries, gold-mining relies most heavily on migrant labour. Furthermore, the gold-mining industry is the cornerstone of the South African economy. It is our opinion that the negotiating power which the AHCM could exercise by virtue of its control over gold-mining labour supplies could be used to reach agreement on the employment levy to be carried by Association workers both in gold-mining and elsewhere.

The negotiating power stemming from AHCM control over so much labour involves two factors: *(a)* the cost to South Africa of an immediate loss of migrant labour; and *(b)* the ability of the AHCM to impose that cost by a co-ordinated immediate withdrawal. In our view this latter could become reality only if a United Nations back-up fund were created, with enough resources to absorb immediately and productively as many former migrants as possible and to provide the remainder with unemployment compensation while they waited for productive employment.

In Appendix A we present a detailed analysis of the ability of the gold-mining industry to replace its African migrant labour force rapidly. This is the opposite of the economic power of the AHCM vis-à-vis the Chamber of Mines. Our analysis concludes that South African Blacks strongly prefer non-mining employment. They have recently been forced to accept mining employment because of recessionary conditions in South Africa. An upswing in the South African economy would quite probably reduce the number of South African Blacks seeking work in the gold-mines *at the wage levels offered by that industry at present.* This view has also been expressed by officials of the Chamber of Mines.

If an economic *upswing* were to occur, either during or after an immediate withdrawal of migrant workers, we believe that the Chamber would find it essential to increase wages to maintain its South African labour supply. Given the clear preference of South African Blacks for non-mining work, those wage increases would probably have to be very substantial. The reduced profitability of the industry and the concomitant threats to marginal mines would be likely to push the entire South African economy into another recession.

But what would happen in the South African labour market under *recessionary conditions* if Association labour were withdrawn completely and rapidly? Undoubtedly, the existing unemployment among South African Blacks would make it easy to substitute domestic Africans for Africans from abroad. Whether complete substitution could be affected over, say, two years without severely disrupting the South African economy remains a matter for speculation. In the case of the gold-mining industry, it would have to fill an employment gap of about 200,000 man-years. On the basis of our analysis, it would be fair to assume that a very great majority of new substitute recruits could be obtained only on six-month contracts. On the assumption that all replacement recruits were obtained on six-month contracts, the Chamber of Mines would need to find an additional 400,000 South Africans. If we were to estimate, generously, that there are at present 50,000 South Africans "waiting in the queue" for gold-mining employment and that these were employed immediately, the Chamber of Mines would still have to find 350,000 inexperienced miners.[13] We believe that this would require substantial increases in the wages offered by the industry—increases which would be not less than 50 per cent and perhaps as much as 75 per cent higher than 1977 wage levels.[14]

If the South African economy were to recover before withdrawal and if unemployment declined, the wage increases necessary to secure a wholly South African mining labour force could be double the current wage level. Thus, it could be expected that the Chamber of Mines would be unlikely to react adversely to a development levy which, though increasing its total African wage bill by arount 60 per cent in the first year, would decline steeply each year thereafter.

However, the problem is more complex than simply increasing mine wages to secure more South African labour. Such action would have profound implications for other sectors of the South African economy, particularly agriculture. For years there has been a "gentleman's agreement" between the Chamber of Mines and White agriculture to the effect that the former would not encroach upon the latter's sources of labour. However, this has already happened. In its recent attempt to replace Malawian labour and reduce its reliance on Mozambique, the Chamber of Mines drew labour heavily from White farms. The ensuing shortage of farm labour forced up agricultural wage rates as that sector attempted to halt the exodus of young Blacks to the mines. For the Chamber of Mines to attempt to drain off another 350,000 workers from agriculture, when that sector would already have lost 15,000 man-years as a result of the AHCM withdrawal, would undoubtedly lead to a severe political conflict.

Of course, it can be argued that the Chamber of Mines has other means to augment the rate of replacement of Association labour. The South African Government has on many occasions introduced legislation which, whether by design or spillover effect, has had a substantial impact on the supply of South African labour available to the gold-mining industry. For example, only recently the Government introduced to Parliament the Bantu Laws Amendment Bill which would allow the Government to remove any urban Black who had been unemployed for more than 122 days in any calendar year (ILO, 1978, p. 11). This was bound to please the Chamber of Mines, whose recent drive to recruit urban Blacks proved to be a dismal failure. None the less, whether the South African Government would enforce the existing legislation affecting labour supplies more stringently or introduce new legislation to aid the gold-mining industry to draw its labour supplies from within South Africa remains a matter for speculation. Its action would probably depend on which course of action would give the greatest net economic and political benefit. As already mentioned, from a political viewpoint the Government could run into difficulties if it let the Chamber of Mines draw large numbers of contract and regular workers away from White agriculture. On the other hand, large multinational enterprises such as Anglo American Corporation would undoubtedly be wary of being associated with the introduction or enforcement of repressive legislation seen to be directly beneficial to the gold-mining industry.

However, such an analysis begs the question whether the Chamber of Mines might even want to recruit its labour force entirely and rapidly from within the country. At present the Chamber is faced with a surplus of South African labour. Yet it is not continuing to recruit that labour at a rate consistent with the surplus. Clarke (1977a) advances a number of reasons why the Chamber might want to maintain a certain proportion of workers from abroad in the long run. There are very sound economic reasons why it might not wish rapidly to recruit from within the country in the short run also. The Chamber is aware of what a co-ordinated withdrawal of 200,000 workers would do to economic viability if alternative supplies could not be rapidly organised. It is also aware of the costs of a rapid recruitment of South African labour: decreased efficiency through a loss of experienced workers, higher training costs and higher recruitment costs per man-year associated with a shorter average length of contract.

To highlight these latter points we turn back to table 11 (page 40). As can be seen, the turnover or "net wastage" of employees remained fairly constant from 1971 to 1973, i.e. before the recruitment of South African workers began in earnest. After 1973, however, wastage increased significantly, being about 65 per cent greater in 1976 than in 1973. There is little doubt that if the recruitment of South African workers were to be greatly accelerated the wastage/employment ratio would also greatly accelerate. This is further confirmed by the Chamber of Mines, which said: "The change in the pattern of the labour force [as a result of internal recruitment] has brought many problems" (Chamber of Mines: *Annual report 1976*, p. 12).

In the end, the increased labour costs per worker associated with a wholly South African labour force (increased wages and decreased efficiency) would in our opinion be very high relative to the increase in the wage bill associated with an AHCM employment levy. Thus it would seem incredibly foolish for a "market-wise" industry to take a stance which would result in a withdrawal of its best workers, when the cost of co-operation would actually be quite low and could easily be afforded. This is not to deny that some mines would be hit harder than others, to the point of their having to rely still more on government subsidies than they do already, or to close down. But the distribution of the cost of the development levy—within the Chamber of Mines or between South African employers and the Government—is not an issue for the AHCM to solve. Moreover, there is no danger that the employers would claw back the employment levy from African wages. The forces currently pushing wages higher are strong enough to prevent this.

Other sources of AHCM negotiating power

The "market power" of the AHCM discussed above, when given reality by the proposed United Nations back-up fund to be discussed below, appears to be considerable. However, this is not the only source of potential negotiating power which could be exercised by the AHCM. First, a not insignificant amount of South African capital, both private and public, can be found in the supplier countries. Is it too much to hope, therefore, that an intransigent South Africa might be confronted with the prospect of asset confiscation? Second, assuming that the AHCM could receive backing from the major gold-holding countries of the world, might the gold market perhaps be manipulated to the detriment of South Africa? One needs only to be aware of the impact of the sales of gold by the United States and the International Monetary Fund on gold-mining profitability to realise the bargaining strength that such backing could provide. Third, might a direct appeal to the stockholders of such firms as Anglo American Corporation conceivably result in the introduction of resolutions at stockholders' meetings in support of the objectives of the AHCM? It seems to us reasonable to suppose that, in general, such companies would want to avoid the adverse international publicity that would result from a recalcitrant bargaining position. Fourth, might representations at a government-to-government level perhaps be made on behalf of the AHCM by countries such as the United Kingdom and the United States? And might it also be possible to get backing from the International Organisation of Employers?

The suggested employment levy

As already demonstrated, the alternative employment programme for migrants in their own countries might involve an expenditure of some US$2,500 million over a period of 23 years. We envisage that, by charging an employment levy for each worker still to be recruited during the phased withdrawal, the funds essential for the re-employment of migrants could be obtained from South African sources. Since the gold-mining industry employs over one-half of the Association's labour, let us begin the discussion of South Africa's "ability to pay" by focusing on that industry.

From table 10 (p. 39) we see that in recent years gold-mining profits per African worker have soared. They increased more than fourfold between 1971 and 1978. Over the same period the total working profit for the industry as a whole rose from R 352 million to at least R 1,750 million.

We have calculated that an employment levy fixed at a constant R 1,500 per man-year supplied over the withdrawal period would cost the Chamber of Mines, on average, R 160 million per year. This amounts to less than 10 per cent of the 1978 working profit. In fact, the first year's levy payments would be the largest because fewer migrants would be involved as time went by. Even so, the R 300 million which the Chamber of Mines

168

Table 22.   Revenues from employment levy by origin: Chamber of Mines R 1,500, other employers R 100 per man-year supplied (in thousands of rands)

Year	Chamber of Mines	Other employers	Total
1	300 000	13 400	313 400
2	280 000	13 010	293 010
3	260 000	12 620	272 620
4	240 000	12 000	252 000
5	220 000	11 225	231 225
6	200 000	10 520	210 520
7	180 000	9 650	189 650
8	160 000	8 625	168 625
9	140 000	7 100	147 100
10	120 000	6 580	126 580
11	100 000	5 560	105 560
12	80 000	4 450	84 450
13	60 000	3 340	63 340
14	40 000	2 225	42 225
15	20 000	1 110	21 110
Total	2 400 000	121 415	2 521 415
Annual average	160 000	8 094	168 094

would have to bear in the first year represents only 17 per cent of the working profit of its affiliates in 1978. To illustrate further how light the largest burden placed on the Chamber of Mines would be, we can deduct this charge from the 1978 profits and find that nearly R 1,500 million remains, which is between four and five times the level of profits before the rise of the gold price.

Table 22 shows the annual payments the AHCM would receive from the Chamber of Mines with the imposition of a R 1,500 employment levy per man-year supplied over the withdrawal period.[15] This amount compares favourably with what a wholly South African mining force would be likely to add to the Chamber's costs. As indicated in the discussion of the potential economic power of the AHCM, the 50 or more per cent increase in wages and the decrease in efficiency associated with a wholly South African mining labour force could increase annual operating costs by substantially more than the R 300 million of the employment levy of the first year. Moreover, the increased wage costs, unlike the employment levy, would not decline in subsequent years.

The issue of withdrawal and compensation as it affects employers other than the Chamber of Mines is somewhat more complex. One could envisage a lower employment levy being charged: R 100 does not seem unrealistic, and we suggest that it would be best to charge this amount per man-year supplied. If it were attached to the number of recruits, two problems arise. First, it would make short-term labour, such as three-month contractees in agriculture, relatively expensive and would hence run the risk of pricing Association labour out of the short-term labour market; and second, it would tend to push up the average length of contract per recruit without the AHCM receiving compensation for the increase. Ideally, annual withdrawal should be specified in terms of numbers of recruits while the employment levy should be charged on the basis of man-years supplied.

In table 22 we have also calculated the annual employment revenues to be received from employers other than the Chamber of Mines. Over the withdrawal period of 15 years it is anticipated that these other employers would contribute approximately R 121 million in employment levies.

With regard to the disbursement of funds among the AHCM members, we believe that the most equitable distribution would be on the basis of man-years withdrawn. The measure of man-years gives a much more precise estimate of the importance of migrant earnings to the economies of AHCM members than do numbers of migrants. This is simply because the average length of contract per migrant varies between the countries. For example, assume that migrants remit R 250 per one-year stay in South Africa. Comparing Malawi and Swaziland, we know that the average length of contract of a Swazi migrant is one-half that of a Malawian migrant. If 100 migrants were withdrawn from each country, Malawi would lose R 25,000 in remittances whereas Swaziland would lose one-half of that amount.

THE SUGGESTED UNITED NATIONS BACK-UP FUND:
A PREREQUISITE

The latent but significant economic power of the AHCM could become a reality only if the Association could afford to withdraw its workforce quickly and wholly. To put teeth into the withdrawal threat it would in our view be essential to have an insurance policy in the form of a commitment of funds that could be drawn upon if immediate withdrawal became imperative. For this purpose we suggest that the AHCM as a group approach the United Nations with a proposal for a special fund to be set up under United Nations auspices, in line with the resolution on accelerated economic development and international action adopted by the 1978 ECA Conference on Migratory Labour in Southern Africa.[16] The fund could be made up, for instance, of voluntary commitments from all but the least developed countries. At best, the commitments would never have to be called upon. At worst, they would provide the emergency funds needed to absorb the returning migrant workers.

If South Africa failed to accept or implement the withdrawal procedure, with the employment levy and annual supply quotas it entails, we maintain that withdrawal should be total and immediate. The cost to the South African economy of such an action would be immense; but so would the short-run cost to the AHCM members. Under such circumstances the United Nations back-up fund would be immediately activated. On an annual basis, it would cover the cost of the public programmes designed to absorb returning migrants and of the unemployment scheme devised to take care of those who could not be absorbed quickly. But it is important to note that the fund would aim at absorbing into productive employment as many former migrants as possible each year and, in this respect, would not differ from the employment levy fund. The annual payments from the back-up fund would continue until all former migrants, without displacing non-migrants, had been absorbed into jobs requiring no further state subsidy or expenditure. On the basis of our calculations, we estimate that time to be 23 years.

In table 23 we have calculated the necessary size of the suggested back-up fund. Column (2) accumulates the sum of the number of man-years which could be absorbed each year by the private sector (productive employment), state enterprises (initially non-productive but fully productive employment after 20 years) and infrastructural projects, using the preferred withdrawal schedule as a basis (weighted man-years). (A detailed breakdown of the sectoral distribution of the numbers in column (2) can be found in table 21.) The cost of this re-employment to the budgets of AHCM members as a whole is calculated in column (3). It is the sum of the support required for state enterprises and infrastructure projects. Immediate and complete withdrawal would imply that approximately 316,773 man-years could not be absorbed in the first year (334,000 minus the 17,227 which could be absorbed during the first year). Column (5) gives an estimate of the unemployment benefits which would need to be paid to those who had not been absorbed. The numbers in columns (4) and (5) decline annually, as more and more unemployed former migrants are absorbed into employment. The figures in column (6) are the sum of the annual cost of the employment programme (3) plus the annual cost of unemployment benefits (5). These, therefore, are the amounts that under our proposals would need to be committed to the United Nations back-up fund each year and that would have to be put at the disposal of the Association's members in the event of an emergency.

Although the commitments would in principle have to cover the whole of the 23-year period until the need for Association government support of the alternative employment programme ended, it should be

Table 23. Calculation of the size of the proposed United Nations back-up fund needed for emergency withdrawal of all countries (in constant rands)[1]

Year	Absorption into employment (weighted withdrawal schedule)[2] (Man-years)	Annual employment cost to AHCM members[3] (R '000)	Remaining employment problem in emergency[4] (Man-years)	Annual unemployment cost in emergency[5] (R '000)	Total annual cost of emergency (3) + (5) (R '000)
(1)	(2)	(3)	(4)	(5)	(6)
1	17 227	12 201	316 773	71 274	83 475
2	34 455	30 899	299 545	67 398	98 297
3	53 964	46 345	280 036	63 008	109 353
4	75 109	61 402	258 891	58 250	119 652
5	95 455	73 777	238 545	53 673	127 450
6	117 513	87 635	216 487	48 710	136 345
7	141 075	103 303	192 925	43 408	146 711
8	164 642	117 458	169 358	38 106	155 564
9	188 204	142 909	145 796	32 804	175 713
10	211 766	154 129	122 234	27 503	181 632
11	236 141	165 991	97 859	22 018	188 009
12	260 608	176 689	73 392	16 513	193 202
13	285 075	186 678	48 925	11 008	197 686
14	309 542	194 433	24 458	5 503	199 936
15	334 000	176 627	0	0	176 627
16	complete	158 475	0	0	158 475
17	0	145 329	0	0	145 329
18	0	129 734	0	0	129 734
19	0	111 187	0	0	111 187
20	0	93 065	0	0	93 065
21	0	75 526	0	0	75 526
22	0	44 546	0	0	44 546
23	0	12 001	0	0	12 001
24	0	0	0	0	0

Cost subtotals: (3) R 2,500,339,000 (5) R 559,176,000.
Total costs: (3) + (5) = R 3,059,515,000.

[1] Rands and US $ are assumed to be approximately equal over the period. [2] Cumulative total of last column of table 20. [3] Sum of column (4) plus column (6) of table 21. [4] 334,000 man-years minus column (2) of this table. [5] Unemployment benefits are assumed to be R 225 per unemployed man-year.

stressed that the subscribers to the back-up fund would not be called upon to make available the total sum when the scheme was set up. *Only a certain amount of money would be required each year*, and rather less to start with than during the middle years of the scheme. For example, if the Association had to withdraw all its labour during the first year (or if South Africa dumped all the migrants on the doorsteps of the AHCM members), only about $83.5 million would be required during the first year. In this most extreme case we calculate that the annual commitments to and disbursements from the back-up fund would rise to a peak of $200 million in the fourteenth year and then decline rapidly until the completion of the alternative employment programme by the end of the twenty-third year. The total cost to the back-up fund of such an immediate and complete withdrawal would be a little over $3,000 million; the average annual cost would be around $133 million. The total sum is naturally somewhat larger than the cost of the alternative employment programme under conditions of orderly, phased withdrawal duly compensated through employment levy receipts ($2,500 million). The reason is that those migrants who could not be absorbed into employment under emergency conditions would need to be supported for some time through unemployment payments. For every year that the phased withdrawal proceeded according to plan, the annual commitments made would not need to be activated and the total size of the back-up fund would decline accordingly. Unless withdrawal were forced upon the AHCM, the amounts shown in column (5) would never have to be made available.

At any time during the phased withdrawal South Africa might perhaps attempt to hasten the process by reducing its employment of Association labour by more than scheduled or to issue unauthorised contracts. With appropriate monitoring of labour supplies, this would be immediately detected by the AHCM administration. At such a time we envisage that the Association could request immediate consultations with the relevant South African authorities. If a satisfactory solution to the problem were not reached quickly, the Association could give, say, 90 days' notice of its intention to withdraw completely. Other bargaining powers could also be brought to bear. If total withdrawal became a reality, however, the back-up fund could be activated, ensuring adequate unemployment compensation and the ability of AHCM to continue with its alternative employment programme without disruption.

It is most unlikely that the fund would ever need to be activated. Yet there would be a continued need for it. It is our firm belief that without the back-up fund the AHCM could not, if future South African action made it imperative, withdraw; and if it could not withdraw wholly and immediately during any phase of the planned withdrawal schedule, its economic bargaining power would be lost.

Notes

[1] If it were desirable to reduce the attractiveness of migration, governments might consider taxing that part of the current income gain deriving from migration which is associated with the migrant, i.e. his wages.

[2] As the Botswana Commissioner of Labour put it at the 1978 ECA Conference on Migratory Labour in Southern Africa: "In our case it would be an unthinkable proposition to withdraw labour prior to any arrangements to provide facilities which would absorb migrant labourers in productive activities, thereby providing them with continued earnings and ensuring their livelihood."

[3] "Resolution on the creation of a labour committee for southern Africa", in United Nations, Economic Commission for Africa: *Report of the Conference on Migratory Labour in Southern Africa*, op. cit., p. 11.

[4] Zimbabwe gained independence between the writing and the publication of this chapter and could be expected to join the above-mentioned countries in the scheme exemplified here. However, neither the status nor the numbers of Zimbabwean miners are sufficiently fixed at the moment to permit a valid re-ordering of the calculations. Technically, a number of non-South African workers finding employment in South Africa are "not recruited". Thus, we are using the term "recruits" to mean all workers from other countries finding employment in South Africa regardless of whether or not they are recruited. With the establishment of the AHCM all Association labour employed in South Africa would have to be recruited through official channels.

[5] Moreover, withdrawal moves, whether gradual or abrupt, would not run counter to the stipulations of these agreements. See Rugege, 1978.

[6] This could be done on the basis of "first come, first served" or on the basis of seniority. In Chapter 3 de Vletter called attention to the special needs of career miners. Bardill et al. (1977) argue that the changing production methods in gold-mining will lead to a greater degree of stable employment for migrant workers with skills.

[7] To illustrate this point, assume that in the first year 367,000 recruits work an average of 12 months so that 367,000 man-years are supplied. In the second year the AHCM supplies one-fifteenth less, or 24,467 fewer recruits. If the average length of contract in the second year were to increase to 13 months, the remaining 342,533 workers would actually supply more man-years (371,077) than the previous year's larger number of workers. (See also p. 169, and especially footnote [15].)

[8] According to the 1970 South African census the numbers of African workers born abroad were: 268,040 in gold-mines, 39,020 in non-gold metallic ore mines, 31,640 in coalmines and 13,780 in other mines. Department of Statistics; *Population census, 1970*, op. cit.

[9] The ratios add up to 0.3071. Botswana's share in this figure is $0.0906 \times 100 \div 0.3071 = 29.5$ per cent. As a proportion of the 24,467 recruits to be withdrawn, this yields 7,218 workers. These percentages could be reviewed at intervals to reflect relative changes in the absorptive capacities of the countries. New percentages would give both new numbers and new time profiles of withdrawal for each country.

[10] In the third year the ratios total 0.1721 ($= 0.3071$ minus Swaziland's weight). Deducting Swaziland's 4,490 recruits from the annual target of 24,467 recruits gives 19,977. Botswana's share in this figure amounts to $0.0906 \times 100 \div 0.1721 = 52.64$ per cent, which yields 10,516 workers.

[11] This would mean that in the first year the private sector and state enterprises in the five countries would each have to provide 1,580 man-years of employment in Botswana, 405 in Lesotho, 1,200 in Malawi, 255 in Mozambique and 1,560 in Swaziland.

[12] From the sending countries' perspective there is also the problem of balancing private and social gains and losses associated with migration. The individual bases his migration decision on benefits and costs which do not necessarily coincide with society's gains and losses. Indeed, it is most likely that individual net gain will exceed social net gain, with the result that too many workers migrate for too long periods of time (Stahl, 1977).

[13] In an attempt to replace the migrant workers quickly the Chamber of Mines could possibly increase the minimum length of contracts from six to nine months or even to one year. Yet this could have the opposite of the desired effect. One of the variables that the Chamber of Mines manipulated in order to recruit South African workers was to offer shorter contracts. This implies that there is a negative relationship between the length of contracts and supplies of South African labour: increasing the length of contracts could actually reduce the total number of South African man-years supplied. It is also possible that the Chamber of Mines could raise the bonus paid to workers returning within three months of the completion of their last contract in an attempt to speed up the recycling of workers. The extent to which this would increase the supply flow remains a matter for speculation.

[14] We have calculated the elasticity of labour supply over the period 1974–77 as being roughly 1.4. We have assumed that 25,000 man-years can be filled immediately, leaving 175,000 man-years to be filled. This is 82 per cent more than the 1977 figure of 214,200 South African man-years. Given a supply elasticity of 1.4, this implies that a wage increase of approximately 60 per cent would be necessary to close the supply gap. However, with an upswing in the economy the elasticity of supply

would be surely reduced (see 1972–74 data in Appendix A) and, consequently, the necessary wage increase would have to be correspondingly larger.

[15] The question whether the employment levy should be charged per man-year or per recruit deserves discussion. If the *employment levy* is charged per *recruit*, regardless of the length of contract, the employers would have an incentive to increase the length of contracts offered to Association recruits (Stahl, 1977). This is because it would be to their advantage to spread the fixed cost (represented by the employment levy) per recruit over a greater number of working days so that the fixed cost per working day declines. Thus the *total man-years supplied* by the AHCM could possibly increase even though a specified number of *recruits* were being *withdrawn* annually. On the other hand, if *withdrawal* is specified in *man-years*, employers could possibly increase the length of contract and fill their annually specified man-year quotas with fewer Association *recruits*. Ideally, the Association should *withdraw* a specified number of *recruits* per year and charge the *employment levy* on the number of *man-years* supplied. Even if the average length of contract were to increase, the Association would receive its due compensation. If, however, it were to increase to an extent which the AHCM believed to be inconsistent with its desire to reduce its dependence on South Africa, a maximum length of contract would have to be imposed.

[16] See United Nations, Economic Commission for Africa: *Report of the Conference on Migratory Labour in Southern Africa*, op. cit., p. 7. The resolution "requests the Executive Secretary of the Economic Commission for Africa, to ask the Secretary-General of the United Nations to mobilise financial and manpower resources within the United Nations system and from donor countries to be used to assist countries affected by the migratory labour system practised in South Africa . . ." .

APPENDICES

A. The Chamber of Mines' ability to replace migrants from abroad

Recent events affecting the gold-mining industry, and the industry's reactions to those events, afford some insight into the Chamber of Mines' possible reaction to the Association's demands for an employment levy on each worker and for a minimum but decreasing number of jobs per annum for Association recruits.

In the past the Chamber has maintained a low-wage policy which was reflected in the failure of African real wages to increase for more than eight decades (Wilson, 1972a). The ability of the Chamber to maintain low wages in the face of rapidly expanding and more highly paid employment opportunities for South African Blacks elsewhere in the economy was largely a result of its increasing reliance on Africans from outside South Africa (who were denied access to the higher-paying sectors). As a consequence, by 1973, 80 per cent of the industry's African labour input was derived from sources abroad.

In spite of its large international labour recruitment network the industry was once again faced with a shortage of labour in the late 1960s. This shortage, in combination with, and to a certain extent attributable to, the decreasing number of South African Blacks, sparked off a debate in the industry over what should be done to alleviate the labour shortage. The question the debate centred on was whether the Chamber should resolve the shortage by casting its recruitment net even further afield or whether it should raise wages both to halt the exodus of South Africans from the industry and to obtain more of them by entering into wage competition with other sectors of the economy. As the debate continued, certain events took place which were to resolve it in favour of those arguing for wage increases.

In 1971 the price of gold began to rise. As can be seen from table 9 (p. 38), it rose by 11 per cent in 1971, 39 per cent in 1972 and 64 per cent in 1973; and the rise continued, despite occasional slumps, for the rest of the decade. The industry was in the almost embarrassing situation of enjoying a phenomenal growth in profits while at the same time witnessing a continued stagnation of the real wages of Africans.

Strikes by Africans over wages in Durban and the growing British concern over African wage levels in South Africa undoubtedly increased the Chamber's solicitude over its past low wage policy. Whatever the reason, in 1973 it began to increase wages. As can be seen from table 3 (p. 15), significant wage rises did not take place until that year. In fact,

175

Table A.1. Total South African labour intake (recruits and non-recruits); number of South Africans employed on 31 December, and average annual earnings, 1972–79

Year	Total intake ('000)	Employment at 31 December ('000)	(2) ÷ (3)	Average annual earnings (rands)
(1)	(2)	(3)	(4)	(5)
1972	91.3	87.2	1.05	257
1973	101.1	86.8	1.16	350
1974	112.5	87.4	1.29	565
1975	205.0	121.9	1.68	948
1976	311.2	158.5	1.96	1 103
1977	366.2	214.2	1.71	1 235
1978	311.4	250.3	1.24	1 420
1979	265.8	274.2	0.97	1 669

Sources: Mine Labour Organisation: *Annual reports, 1972–77*; TEBA: *Annual report, 1979.*

between 1969 and 1971 real wage levels showed no growth. However, from 1973 onwards we see an important rise in both money and real average annual earnings of African gold-miners. Between 1972 and 1974 average annual earnings rose by 120 per cent while real earnings increased by 80 per cent, after eight decades of stagnation.

The events of 1974 were to oblige the Chamber to look closely into the recruitment of workers from inside South Africa. The loss of their Malawian labour supplies and the high degree of uncertainty surrounding the Mozambican supplies clearly demonstrated the need to speed up greatly the process of internal recruitment. Indeed, towards the end of 1974 the Chamber undertook a detailed investigation to "assess the short-term potential for additional recruitment of South African Blacks to the gold-mines, following the cessation of supplies from Malawi in April 1974, and the uncertainty of future supplies from Mozambique" (Parsons et al., 1974, p. i). The report concluded that "the requisite number of working-age Black males is physically present in South Africa" (ibid., p. iii). The problem was how to attract them to mining. The report made three recommendations in this regard: *(a)* to increase wages, especially in the lower skill categories; *(b)* to improve the image of mining as an occupation, essentially through improving living conditions in the compounds; and *(c)* to assist White agriculture to mechanise in order to release labour from White farms.

Between 1972 and 1976 the Chamber increased wages by no less than 329 per cent. The reaction of South African Blacks to these wage increases is interesting. When one inspects the employment data, the first thing to strike one is the seeming lack of response on their part, between 1972 and 1974, to significant improvements in mine wage rates. Whereas, as stated above, between 1972 and 1974 average annual earnings increased by 120 per cent, the increase in the end-of-year employment of South African Blacks was a mere 0.2 per cent (table A.1). This lack of response is noteworthy. It may well be that before late 1974 the Chamber did not intensify its recruitment effort in South Africa. Yet it would be difficult to argue that South African Blacks were not aware of the increases in the wage rates offered by the mines. Such information is rapidly disseminated by way of the "grapevine", if not formally advertised by the employer. Also, the Chamber has a very extensive recruitment network within South Africa as well as a scheme to assist "non-recruited" workers to make their own way to the mines. Thus, with the exception of those Africans isolated both *de jure* and *de facto* on White farms, it could be argued that Blacks were voluntarily unemployed *with respect to the employment opportunities on the gold-mines.* Further, there is no evidence that "fit" South African Blacks were refused employment on the mines in those years. And, finally, the number of unemployed South Africans was quite obviously growing over this period.

There are several possible explanations for this phenomenon. First, it may be that because of South Africans' preferences for non-mining work they were voluntarily unemployed vis-à-vis mining employment opportunities, while at the same time being involuntarily unemployed vis-à-vis employment in the industrial and tertiary sectors. Second, although cash earnings plus payments in kind made earnings in mining competitive with those in other sectors, the wages in the secondary and tertiary sectors are much higher in terms of the amount of work effort per rand of remuneration. Third, comparing the social and physical environments of work, mining employment is undoubtedly considered to be much more inferior to non-mining employment and much more dangerous. Fourth, increasing wages in both mining and other sectors, reflected in growing African real income per head, may be allowing Africans to search longer for suitable non-mining employment.

In addition to increasing wages substantially in its bid to recruit its labour supplies from within the country, the Chamber also intensified its South African recruitment effort. As an important part of this effort, shorter contracts were offered to South Africans. As can be seen from table 18, the average length of a contract for a South African declined from just over ten months to seven months between 1973 and 1977. This reflects the Chamber's offer of six-month contracts to South Africans after 1974. Thus a very large proportion of the new intake of South Africans after 1974 must have been taken on under six-month contracts.

With increased wages on the mines, shorter contracts and, probably the most important point, rising unemployment among Black South Africans, one could expect that the Chamber's desires for internal recruitment would be at least partially fulfilled. From table A.1 we see that from 1974 to 1977 the total intake of South Africans (recruits plus non-recruits) increased from 112,500 to 366,200—an increase of 226 per cent. However, these figures are misleading in so far as one of the variables employed to encourage the recruitment of South Africans was the offer of shorter contracts. This is reflected in the growing difference, as the years went by, between the *intake* of South Africans and the average number employed at 31 December each year. A more accurate account of the increase in South African *manpower* in these years can be obtained from column (3) of table A.1. Using the latter figures one finds an increase in South African manpower of approximately 145 per cent between 1974 and 1977.

Using the manpower figures from column (3), one can compare the supply responses of South African Blacks over various periods. Over the period 1972–77 the supply response of South African Blacks was relatively poor, the wage elasticity of supply being 0.434—surprisingly inelastic. Yet further investigation of the supply data indicates two distinct periods with regard to supply response: 1972–74 and 1974–77. For the first period the wage elasticity of supply is, for practical purposes, zero. For the period 1974–77 the elasticity is 1.425, a relatively elastic supply function.

Things changed even more in 1978. Reports from that year indicated that the Chamber was having to turn down South African Blacks because of an over-supply (*The Star*, 18 Mar. 1978). The Chamber did not say, however, whether those it was turning down were within the segment of the labour market from which it draws its manpower (18- to 40-year-old "fit" males).

B. Cost structure of a typical labour-intensive infrastructural construction unit

Year 1			Rands
Local staff:	53	semi-skilled man-years at average R 500 per year	26 500
	285	unskilled man-years at R 300 per year	85 500
Total local staff	338	Total local wage bill	112 000
Setting up costs			168 000
Operating costs (exclusive of local labour costs)			210 980

177

			Rands
Expatriate staff		146 400	
Equipment and fuel		59 580	
Miscellaneous		5 000	
Total cost per construction unit in year 1			490 980
Total cost per local man-year			1 453

Year 2

Local staff:	63	semi-skilled man-years at average R 500 per year	31 500
	410	unskilled man-years at R 300 per year	123 000

Total local staff	473	Total local wage bill	154 500
Operating costs (exclusive of local labour costs)			238 460
Expatriate staff		146 400	
Equipment and fuel		85 060	
Miscellaneous		7 000	
Total cost per construction unit in year 2			392 960
Total cost per local man-years			830

As in our scheme there is a further inflow of new migrants in year 2 for whom new projects will have to be set up, entailing higher running-in costs, the total cost of the local man-years in year 2 is the cost of the second generation (R 830 per head) plus the cost of the first generation (R 1,453 per head).

Year 3

Local staff:	6	skilled man-years at R 4,400 per year	26 400
	63	semi-skilled man-years at R 500 per year	31 500
	410	unskilled man-years at R 300 per year	123 000

Total local staff	479	Total local wage bill	180 900
Operating costs (exclusive of local labour costs)			152 060
Expatriate staff		60 000	
Equipment and fuel		85 060	
Miscellaneous		7 000	
Total cost per construction unit in year 3			332 960
Total cost per local man-year			695

As in our scheme there remain new migrants to be absorbed into new projects, the total cost of the local man-years in year 3 is the cost of this first generation (R 1,453 per head) plus the cost of the second generation (R 830 per head) plus the cost of the third generation (R 695 per head).

Year 4 and following years

Total cost per local first-generation worker	1 453
Total cost per local second-generation worker	830
Total cost per local third-generation worker	695

Source: IBRD, 1975, Annex V.

Note: In its calculations the World Bank assumed that unskilled labour could be secured at R 264 per man-year. This amounts to approximately R 1 per day for a full-time unskilled worker. We have used a higher figure of R 300 per man-year, or approximately R 1.20 per day for a full-time worker. Further, we have used the average figure of R 500 per semi-skilled man-year rather than the figure of R 894 used by the Bank.

BIBLIOGRAPHY

Agency for Industrial Mission. 1976. *Another blanket*. Report on an investigation into the migrant situation, June 1976. Horison (South Africa).

Arrighi, G. 1970. "Labour supplies in historical perspective: A study of the proletarianization of the African peasantry in Rhodesia", in *The Journal of Development Studies* (London, Frank Cass), Apr. 1970, pp. 197–234.

Barber, W. J. 1961. *The economy of British Central Africa*. London, Oxford University Press.

Bardill, J.; Southall, R.; Perrings, C. 1977. *The State and labour migration in the South African political economy, with particular respect to gold mining*. Geneva, ILO. Mimeographed World Employment Programme research working paper; restricted.

Bevan, G.; de Vletter, F. 1977. *Wages in Swaziland*. Manzini, Federation of Swaziland Employers, Mimeographed.

Bloch, N. 1978. *The demand for African technicians*. Cape Town, Southern Africa Labour and Development Research Unit. Working paper No. 9.

Böhning, W. R. 1975. "Some thoughts on emigration from the Mediterranean basin", in *International Labour Review* (Geneva), Mar. 1975.

——. 1977. *Black migration to South Africa—What are the issues?* Geneva, ILO. Mimeographed World Employment Programme research working paper; restricted.

Botswana. 1972. *Rural development in Botswana*. Gaborone, Government Paper No. 1.

——. 1973. *National policy for rural development*. Gaborone, Government Paper No. 2.

——. 1976. *The Rural Income Distribution Survey in Botswana 1974/75*. Gaborone, Central Statistics Office, Ministry of Finance and Development Planning.

——. 1977. *National Development Plan 1976–81*. Gaborone, Ministry of Finance and Development Planning.

Breytenbach, W. J. 1972. *Migratory labour arrangements in southern Africa*. Johannesburg, Southern African Institute of Race Relations.

Bromberger, N. 1979. *Mining employment in South Africa 1946–2000*. Geneva, ILO. Mimeographed World Employment Programme research working paper; restricted.

de Bruyn, E.; Levitas, B. 1975. "Is the gold-mining industry attracting a better educated Black worker?" in *Monitoring Bulletin* (Johannesburg, Chamber of Mines, Human Resources Laboratory), No. 7–1.

Chambers, R.; Feldman, D. 1973. *Report on rural development*. Gaborone (Swaziland), Ministry of Finance and Development Planning.

Clarke, D. G. 1977a. *The South African Chamber of Mines: Policy and strategy with reference to foreign African labour supply*. Pietermaritzburg, University of Natal. Mimeographed Development Studies Research Group working paper, No. 6.

——. 1977b. *Foreign migrant labour in southern Africa: Studies on accumulation in the Labour Reserves, demand determinants and supply relationships*. Geneva, ILO. Mimeographed World Employment Programme research working paper; restricted.

——. 1978. *International labour supply trends and economic structure in Southern Rhodesia/Zimbabwe in the 1970s*. Geneva, ILO. Mimeographed World Employment Programme research working paper; restricted.

Denoon, D. 1972. *South Africa since 1800*. London, Longmans.

Desmond, C. 1971. *The discarded people: An account of African resettlement in South Africa*. Harmondsworth (Mddx.), Penguin Books.

Doran, M. H. 1977. *Swaziland labour migration—Some implications for a national development strategy*. Geneva, ILO. Mimeographed World Employment Programme research working paper; restricted.

——; Low, A. R. C.; Kemp, R. L. 1979. *Overgrazing and livestock development in Africa: lessons from Swaziland*. Mbabane, Ministry of Agriculture. Mimeographed.

Doxey, G. V. 1961. *The industrial colour bar in South Africa*. Cape Town, Oxford University Press; London, Greenwood Press.

van Drunen, L. J. M. 1978. *Lesotho village life and migrant labour: A case study of the impact of the pressures of migrant labourers and returned migrants on rural life*. Utrecht, Rijksuniversiteit. MA thesis.

Eekelaar, John. 1971. *Family security and family breakdown*. Harmondsworth (Mddx.), Penguin Books.

Frankel, S. H. 1969. *Capital investment in Africa*. London, Oxford University Press.

Funnel, D. C. 1977. *Preliminary estimates of the change in rural incomes to Swazi households 1966–75: A report for the ILO migration project*. Kwaluseni, University College of Swaziland. Mimeographed.

Gordon, E. 1978. *The women left behind: A study of the wives of the migrant workers of Lesotho*. Geneva, ILO. Mimeographed World Employment Programme research working paper; restricted.

Gordon, L. et al. 1978. *A survey of race relations in South Africa 1977* (Johannesburg, South African Institute of Race Relations), Vol. 31.

Gordon, R. J. 1977. *Mines, masters and migrants: Life in a Namibian compound*. Johannesburg, Ravan Press.

Hailey, Lord. 1957. *An African survey: A study of problems arising in Africa south of the Sahara*. London, Oxford University Press.

Hobart Houghton, D. 1960. "Men of two worlds", in *The South African Journal of Economics* (Braamfontein, Economic Society of South Africa), Sep. 1960, pp. 177–190.

——. 1967a. "Economic development, 1865–1965", in *Oxford history of South Africa*, Vol. II. London and New York, Oxford University Press.

——. 1967b. *The South African economy*. Cape Town, Oxford University Press. Second edition.

Höpfner, K. H.; Huber, M. 1978. *Regulating international migration in the interest of the developing countries, with particular reference to Mediterranean countries*. Geneva, ILO. Mimeographed World Employment Programme research working paper; restricted.

van der Horst, S. 1942. *Native labour in South Africa*. London, Frank Cass.

Hughes, A. J. B. 1964. "Incomes of rural homestead groups", in J. F. Holleman (ed.): *Experiment in Swaziland: Report of the Swaziland Sample Survey 1960*. Cape Town, Oxford University Press.

Human Resources Laboratory, Chamber of Mines. 1977. "The Black mineworker: Some of his characteristics and how he reacts to certain aspects of life on a mine", in *Monitoring Report* (Johannesburg), Vol. 1, No. 1 (restricted).

Humphreys, A. S. B.; McClelland, C. 1964. "Wage employment and labour resources", in J. F. Holleman (ed.): *Experiment in Swaziland: Report of the Swaziland Sample Survey 1960*. Cape Town, Oxford University Press.

Hutt, W. H. 1964. *The economics of the colour bar: A study of the economic origins and consequences of racial segregation in South Africa*. London, André Deutsch for the Institute of Economic Affairs.

IBRD. 1975. *Lesotho: Report of the Migrant Workers Re-employment Mission*. Washington, DC. Report no. 614a-LSO.

——. 1978. *Migration from Botswana, Lesotho and Swaziland*. Washington, DC. Report no. 1688-EA.

ILO. 1978a. *Fourteenth special report of the Director-General on the application of the Declaration concerning the Policy of Apartheid of the Republic of South Africa*, International Labour Conference, 64th Session, Geneva, 1978.

——. 1978b. *Labour conditions and discrimination in Southern Rhodesia (Zimbabwe)*. Geneva.

——. 1979. *Fifteenth special report of the Director-General on the application of the Declaration concerning the Policy of Apartheid of the Republic of South Africa*, International Labour Conference, 65th Session, Geneva, 1979.

——. 1980. *Sixteenth special report of the Director-General on the application of the Declaration concerning the Policy of Apartheid of the Republic of South Africa*, International Labour Conference, 66th Session, Geneva, 1980.

ILO/JASPA, 1977. *Reducing dependence: A strategy for productive employment and development in Swaziland*. Report to the Government of Swaziland by a JASPA Employment Advisory Mission. Addis Ababa.

Knight, J. 1976. "Labour supply in the South African economy and its implications for agriculture", in *Saldru Conference on Farm Labour*. University of Cape Town.

——; Loots, L. J. 1976. "Unemployment in South Africa: A sensitivity analysis of the 'full-time job equivalent' concept used by Simkins", in *Saldru Conference on Farm Labour*. University of Cape Town.

Knowles, L. C. A. 1936. *Economic development of the British overseas empire*, Vol. III. London, Routledge.

Kuper, H. 1947. *The uniform of colour: A study of White/Black relationships in Swaziland.* Johannesburg, Witwatersrand University Press.

Lansdown Commission. 1943. *Witwatersrand Mine Natives' Wages Commission* (UG No. 21, 1944).

Legassick, M. 1974. "Legislation, ideology and economy in post-1948 South Africa", in *Journal of Southern African Studies* (London, Oxford University Press), Oct. 1974, pp. 5–35.

Leistner, G. M. E. 1967. "Foreign Bantu workers in South Africa: Their present position in the economy", in *The South African Journal of Economics*, Mar. 1967, pp. 30–56.

——; Smit, P. 1969. *Swaziland: Resources and development.* Pretoria, Communications of the Africa Institute of South Africa, No. 8.

Lesotho. n.d. *Second Five Year Development Plan, 1975/76–1979/80.* Maseru Central Planning and Development Office.

Low, A. R. C. 1976. *Farm management survey report, No. 2.* Mbabane, Ministry of Agriculture. Mimeographed.

——. 1977. *Migration and agricultural development in Swaziland: A micro-economic analysis.* Geneva, ILO. Mimeographed World Employment Programme research working paper; restricted.

——; Doran, M. H. 1977. *Labour migration from Swaziland to South Africa—A necessity or an opportunity?* Background paper for the Informal Meeting of Principal Researchers and Experts on Planned Migration in Southern Africa, Maseru (Lesotho) Dec. 1977. Mimeographed.

——; Kemp, R. L.; Doran, M. H. 1980. "Cattle wealth and cash needs in Swaziland: Price response and rural development implications", in *Journal of Agricultural Economics* (Ashford (United Kingdom), Agricultural Economics Society), May 1980.

McDowall, M. 1974. *Basotho labour in Southern African mines: An empirical study.* Mimeographed.

Massey, D. 1980. "The changing political economy of migrant labour in Botswana", in *South African Labour Bulletin*, Jan. 1980, pp. 4–25.

Mauer, K. F. 1976. "Urbanization, education and mining", in *Monitoring Bulletin*, Mar. 1976.

Murray, C. 1976. *Keeping house in Lesotho: A study of the impact of oscillating migration.* Unpublished PhD thesis (University of Cambridge).

Native Land Commission. (UG No. 26, 1916.)

Natrass, J. 1976. "Migrant labour and South African economic development", in *The South African Journal of Economics*, Mar. 1976.

Owen, K. 1964. *Summary of the Report of the Committee on Foreign Africans (1963).* Johannesburg, South African Institute of Race Relations.

Parsons, J. A. 1977. "Novices in gold mining", in *Monitoring Bulletin*, July 1977.

—— et al. 1974. *Manpower trends in the South African mining industry: Forecasting models and some preliminary forecasts of manpower in the gold-mining industry.* Johannesburg, Human Resources Laboratory.

Report of the South African Native Affairs Commission. 1906.

Rosen-Prinz, B. D.; Prinz, F. A. 1978. *Migrant labour and rural homesteads: An investigation into the sociological dimensions of the migrant labour system in Swaziland.* Geneva, ILO. Mimeographed World Employment Programme research working paper; restricted.

Rugege, S. 1979. *Legal aspects of labour migration from Lesotho to the South African mines.* Geneva, ILO. Mimeographed World Employment Programme research working paper; restricted.

Rutman, G. 1974. "Temporary labour migration: A process of wealth formation in the indigenous economies of southern Africa", in *South African Journal of International Affairs*, 1974, No. 2, pp. 24–32.

Sanford. 1977. *Dealing with drought and livestock in Botswana.* London, Overseas Development Institute.

Schapera, I. 1947. *Migrant labour and tribal life: A study of conditions in the Bechuanaland Protectorate.* London, Oxford University Press.

Schumann, A.. W. S. 1975. "Mine labour: The fast-changing scene", in *Mining Survey*, Vol. 76, No. 2.

Sebatane, E. M. 1979. *An empirical study of the attitudes and perceptions of migrant workers: The case of Lesotho.* Geneva, ILO. Mimeographed World Employment Programme research working paper; restricted.

Simkins, C. 1976. *Employment, unemployment and growth in South Africa, 1961–1977.* Cape Town, Southern Africa Labour and Development Research Unit. Working paper No. 4.

Simons, H. J.; Simons, R. 1978. "Changing conditions of labour in South African mining." Paper presented at the ECA Conference on Migratory Labour in Southern Africa (Lusaka, 4–8 April 1978) (doc. ECA/MULPOC/LUSAKA/100, Apr. 1978).

South African Congress of Trade Unions (SACTU). 1978. "Health, accidents and workers' compensation on the South African mines." Paper presented at the ECA Conference on Migratory Labour in Southern Africa (Lusaka, 4–8 April 1978) (doc. ECA/MULPOC/LUSAKA/103, Apr. 1978; mimeographed).

Stahl, C. W. 1974. *A spatial theory of monopsonistic exploitation and its implications for a development strategy of the labor exporting countries of Southern Africa.* PhD thesis (University of California, Santa Barbara).

——. 1975. "A commercial strategy in the labour export market with reference to Botswana, Lesotho and Swaziland", in *Botswana Notes and Records*, Vol. 7.

——. 1977. *Labour export in southern Africa: Some welfare and policy implications with regard to a joint policy on recruitment fees.* Geneva, ILO. Mimeographed World Employment Programme research working paper; restricted.

——. 1979. *Southern African migrant labour supplies in the past, the present and the future, with special reference to the gold-mining industry.* Geneva, ILO. Mimeographed World Employment Programme research working paper; restricted.

——; Böhning, W. R. 1979. *Reducing migration dependence in southern Africa.* Geneva, ILO. Mimeographed World Employment Programme research working paper; restricted.

Steenkamp, W. F. J. 1962. "Bantu wages in South Africa", in *The South African Journal of Economics*, June 1962.

Swaziland. n.d. *Second National Development Plan 1973–1977*. Mbabane.

Szal, R. J.; van der Hoeven, R. 1976. *Inequality and basic needs in Swaziland*. Geneva, ILO. Mimeographed World Employment Programme research working paper; restricted.

Thompson, L. 1971. "Subjection of the African chiefdoms, 1870–1898", in *Oxford history of South Africa*, Vol. II. London and New York, Oxford University Press.

Union Corporation. 1979. "Aspiration awareness with academic backing", in *Coal, Gold and Base Minerals of Southern Africa* (Johannesburg, Pithead Press), Jan. 1979, p. 57.

de Vletter, F. 1978a. *Migrant labour in Swaziland: Characteristics, attitudes and policy implications*. Geneva, ILO. Mimeographed World Employment Programme research working paper; restricted.

——. 1980. *Migrant labour conditions in South Africa: A case study of the gold mines*. Geneva, ILO. Mimeographed World Employment Programme research working paper; restricted.

Wallis, M. 1977. *Bureaucracy and labour migration: The Lesotho case*. Geneva, ILO. Mimeographed World Employment Programme research working paper; restricted.

Wallman, S. 1972. "Conditions of non-development: The case of Lesotho", in *The Journal of Development Studies*, Jan. 1972, pp. 251–261.

van der Wiel, A. C. A. 1977. *Migratory wage labour: Its role in the economy of Lesotho*. Mazenod (Lesotho), Mazenod Book Centre.

Wilson, F. 1971. "Farming, 1866–1966", in *Oxford history of South Africa*, Vol. II. London and New York, Oxford University Press.

——. 1972a. *Labour in South African gold mines 1911–1969*. Cambridge University Press.

——. 1972b. *Migrant labour*. Johannesburg, The South African Council of Churches and SPRO-CAS.

——. 1975. *International migration in Southern Africa*. Geneva, ILO. Mimeographed World Employment Programme research working paper; restricted.

Wingfield Digby, P.; Colclough, C. 1978. *Skills for the future: Education and manpower perspectives in Swaziland*. Mbabane, Ministry of Finance and Economic Development.

Wolpe, H. 1972. "Capitalism and cheap labour-power in South Africa: From segregation to apartheid", in *Economy and Society* (Henley-on-Thames, Routledge and Kegan Paul), Dec. 1972.

Woods, W. M. 1978. *LR-12: A preliminary simulation model of the effects of declining migration to South Africa on households in Botswana*. Geneva, ILO. Mimeographed World Employment Programme research working paper; restricted.